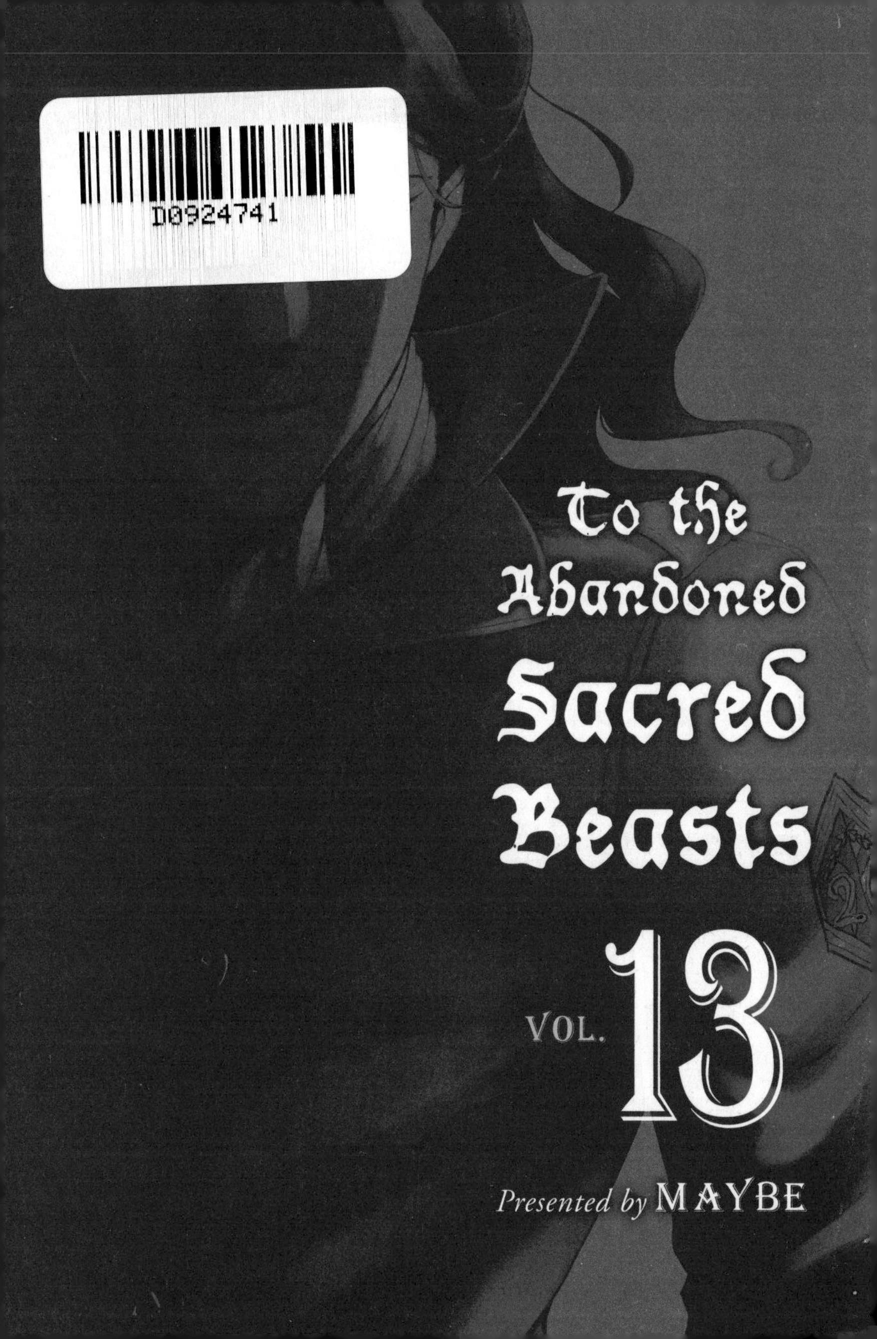

To the Abandoned Sacred Beasts

VOL. 13

Presented by MAYBE

CONTENTS

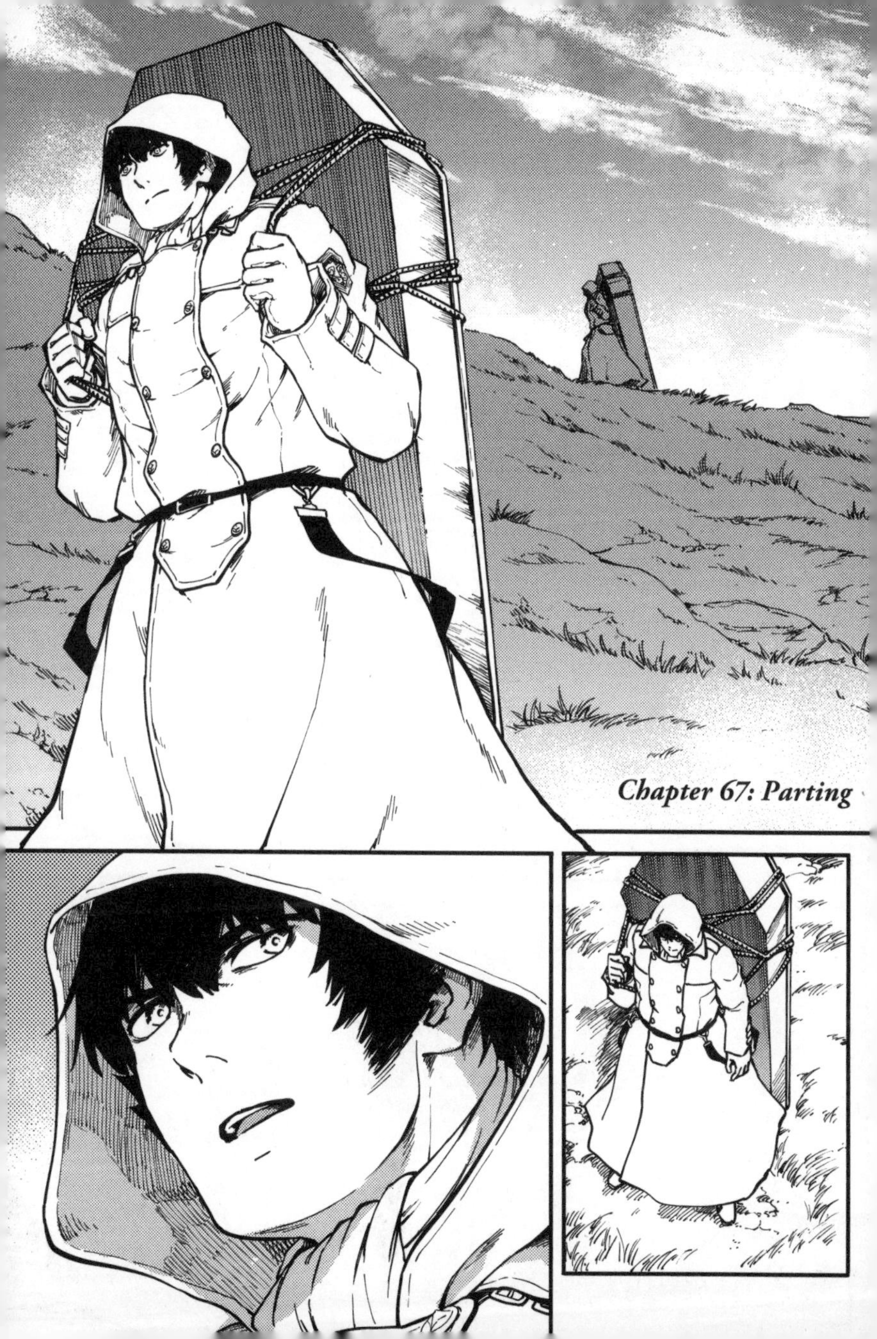
Chapter 67: Parting

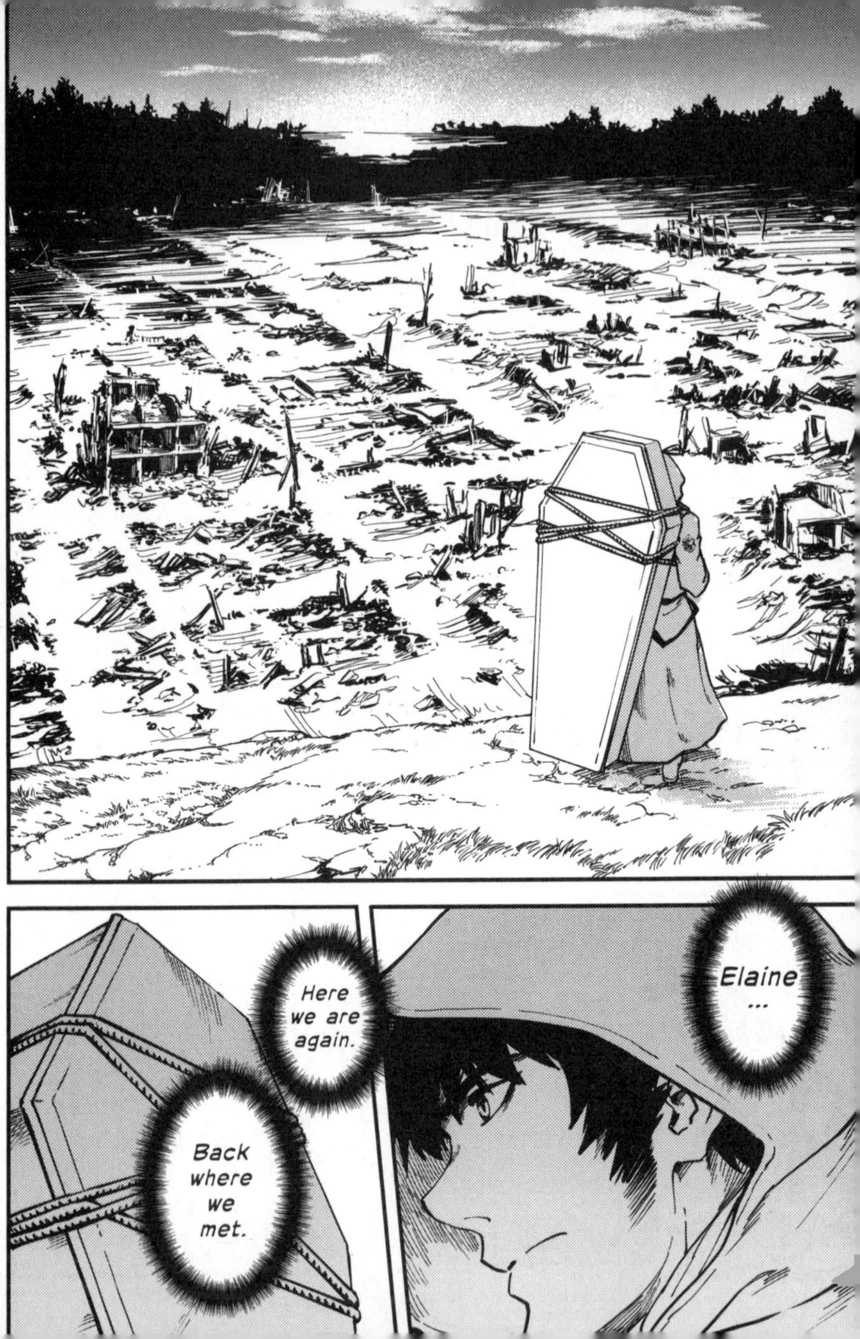
Elaine ...
Here we are again.
Back where we met.

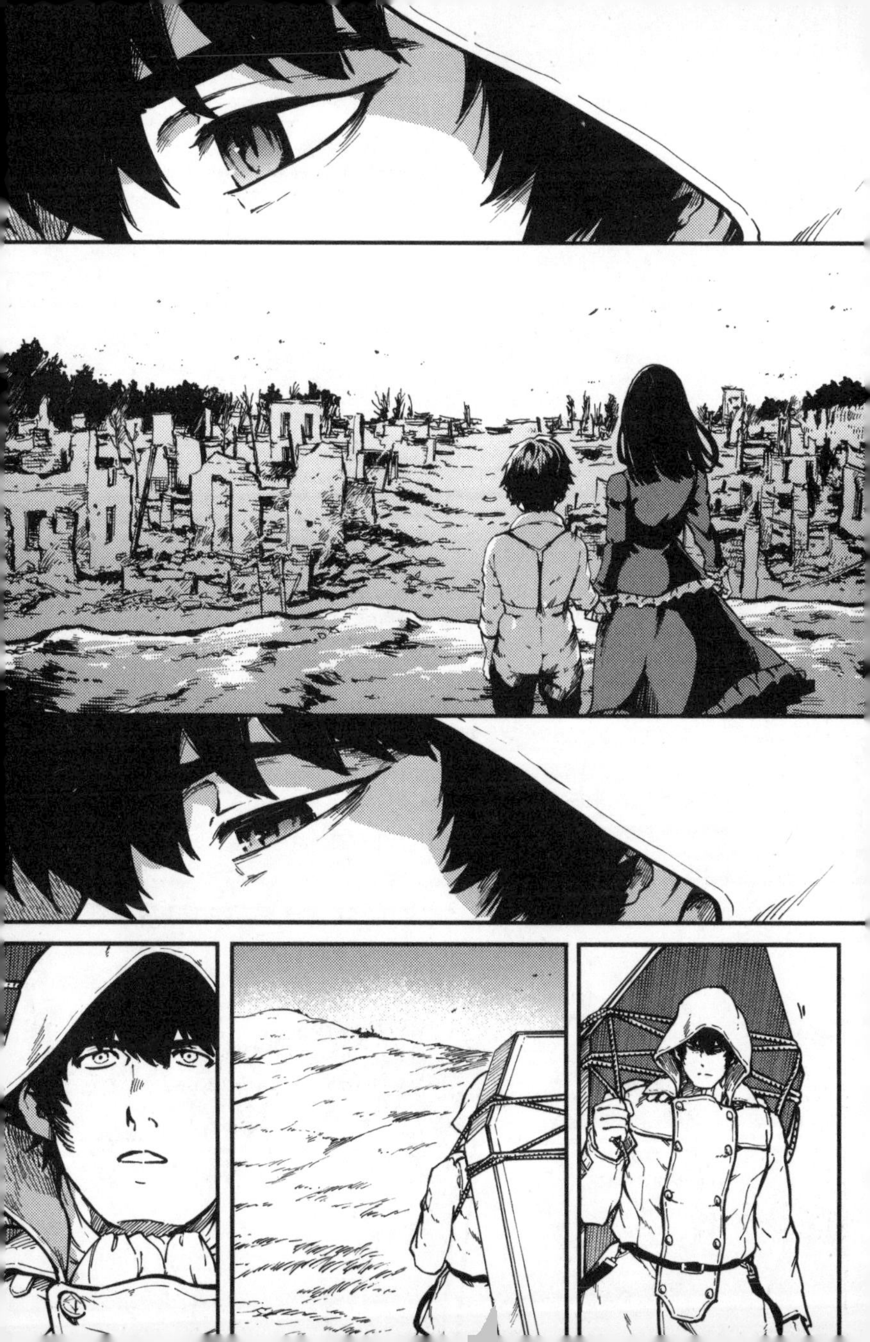

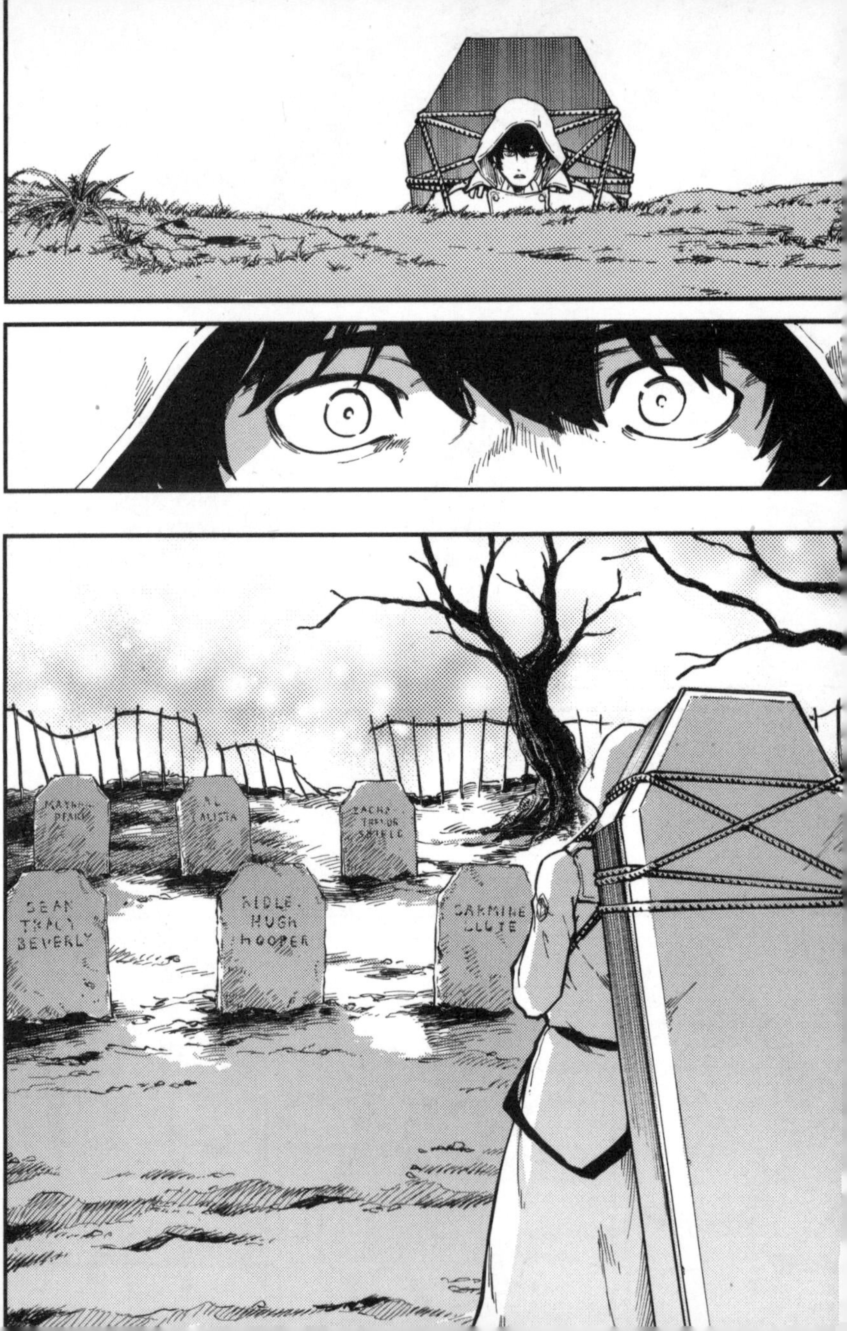
CARMINE
CLUTE
RIDLE
HUGH
HOOPER
SEAN
BEVERLY

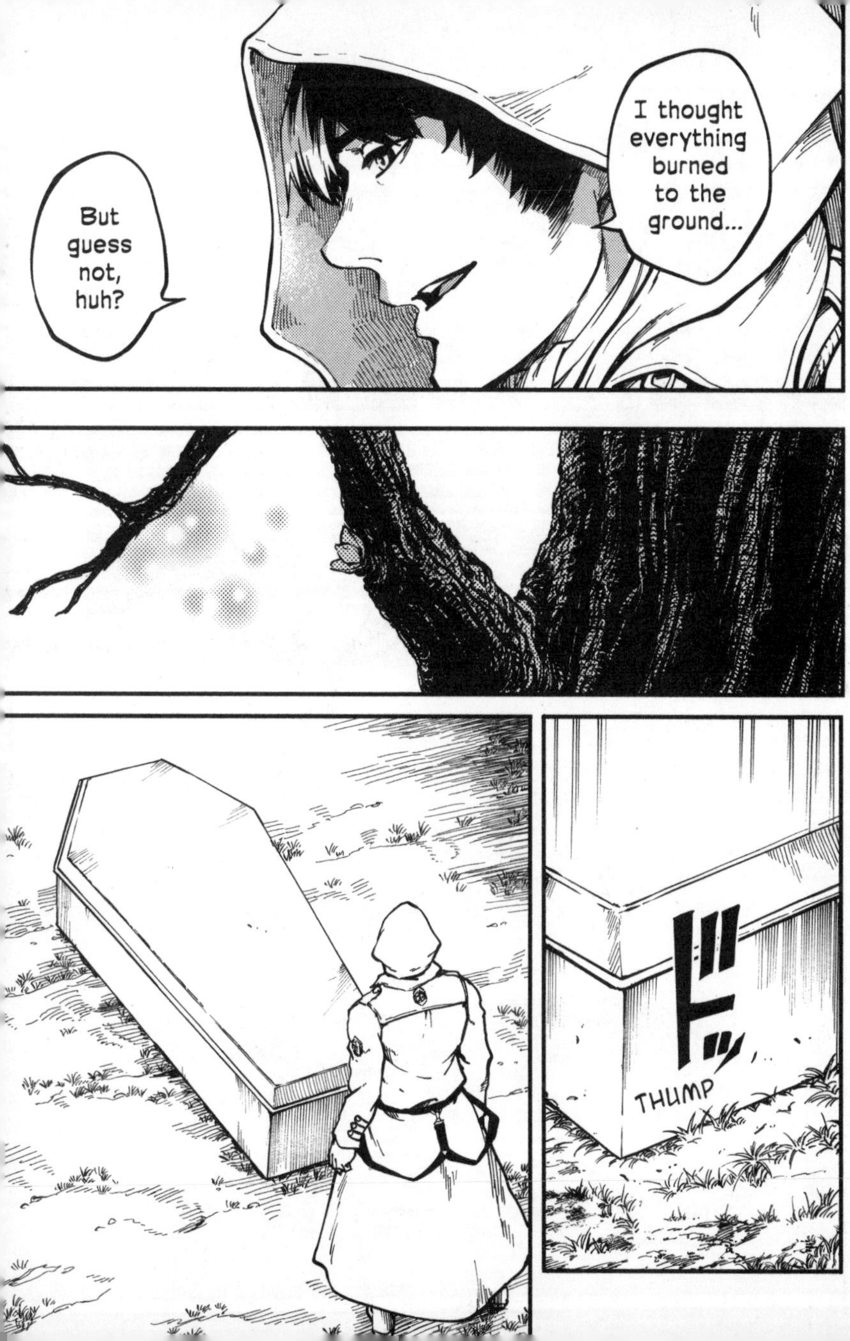

I thought everything burned to the ground...
But guess not, huh?
THUMP

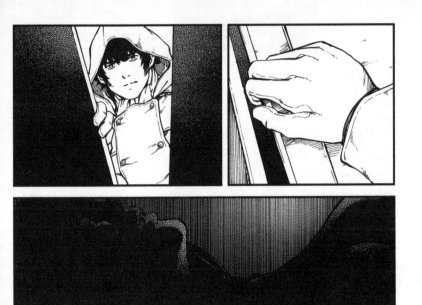

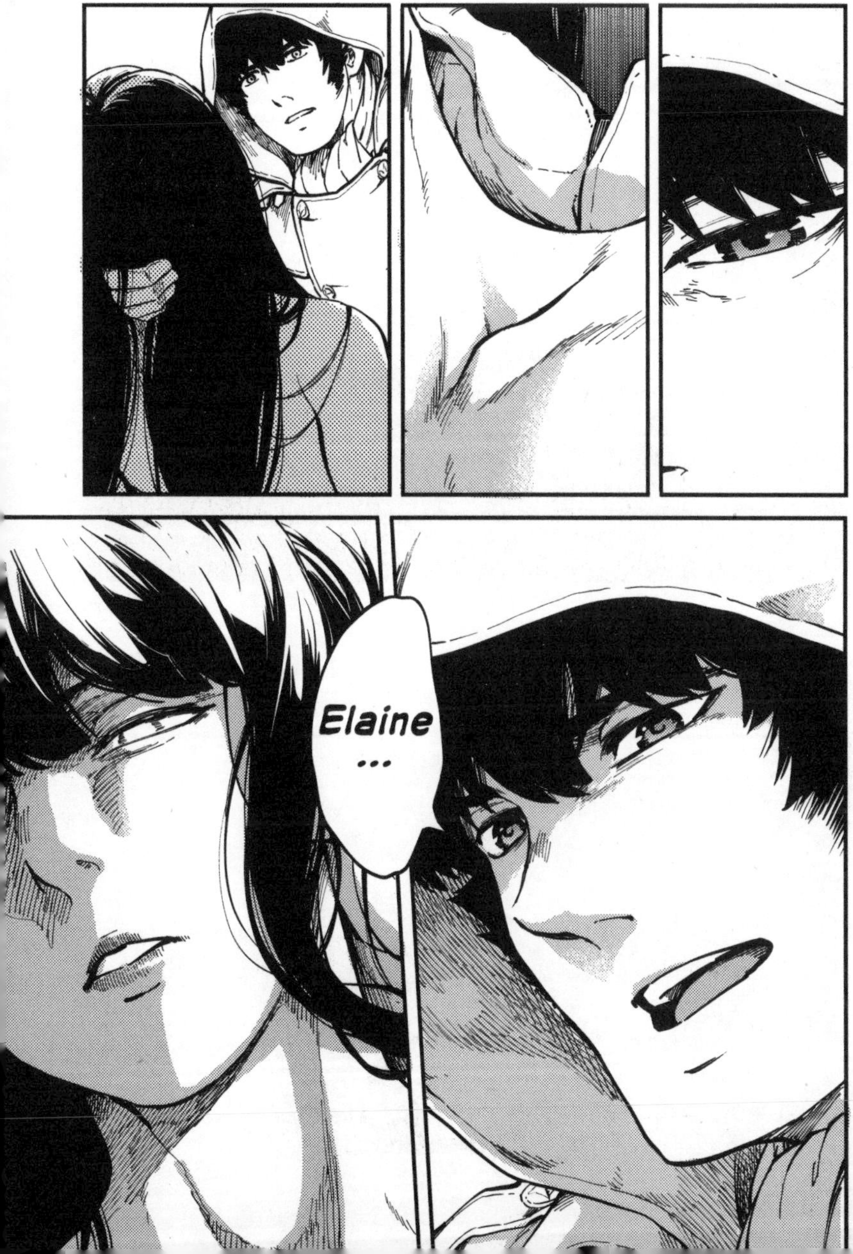
Elaine
...

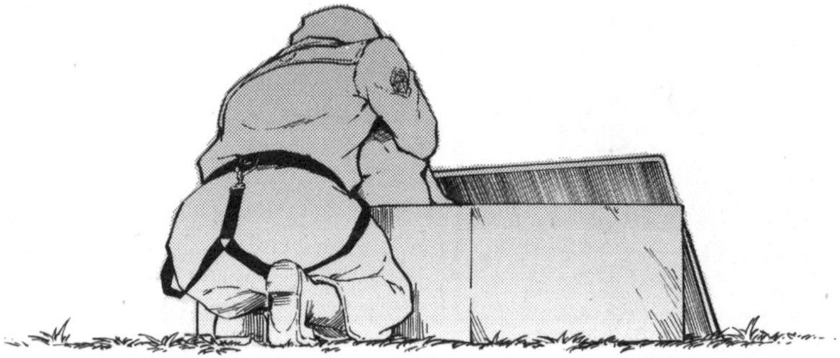
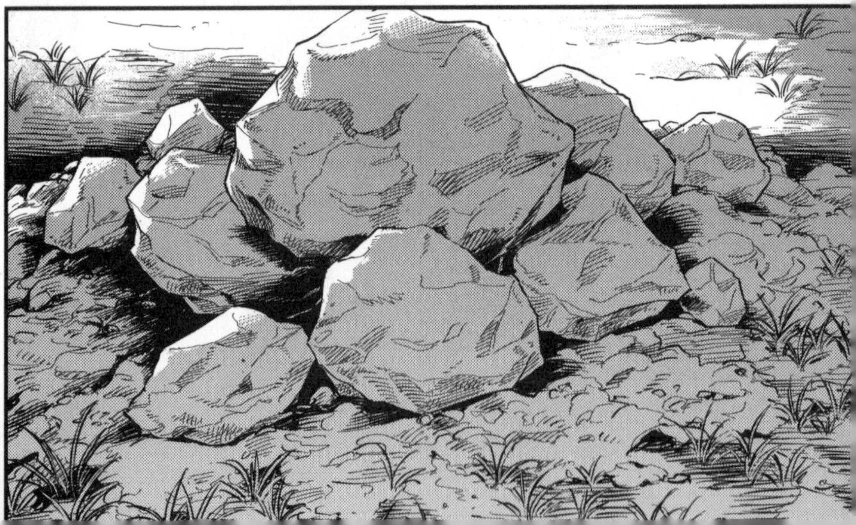

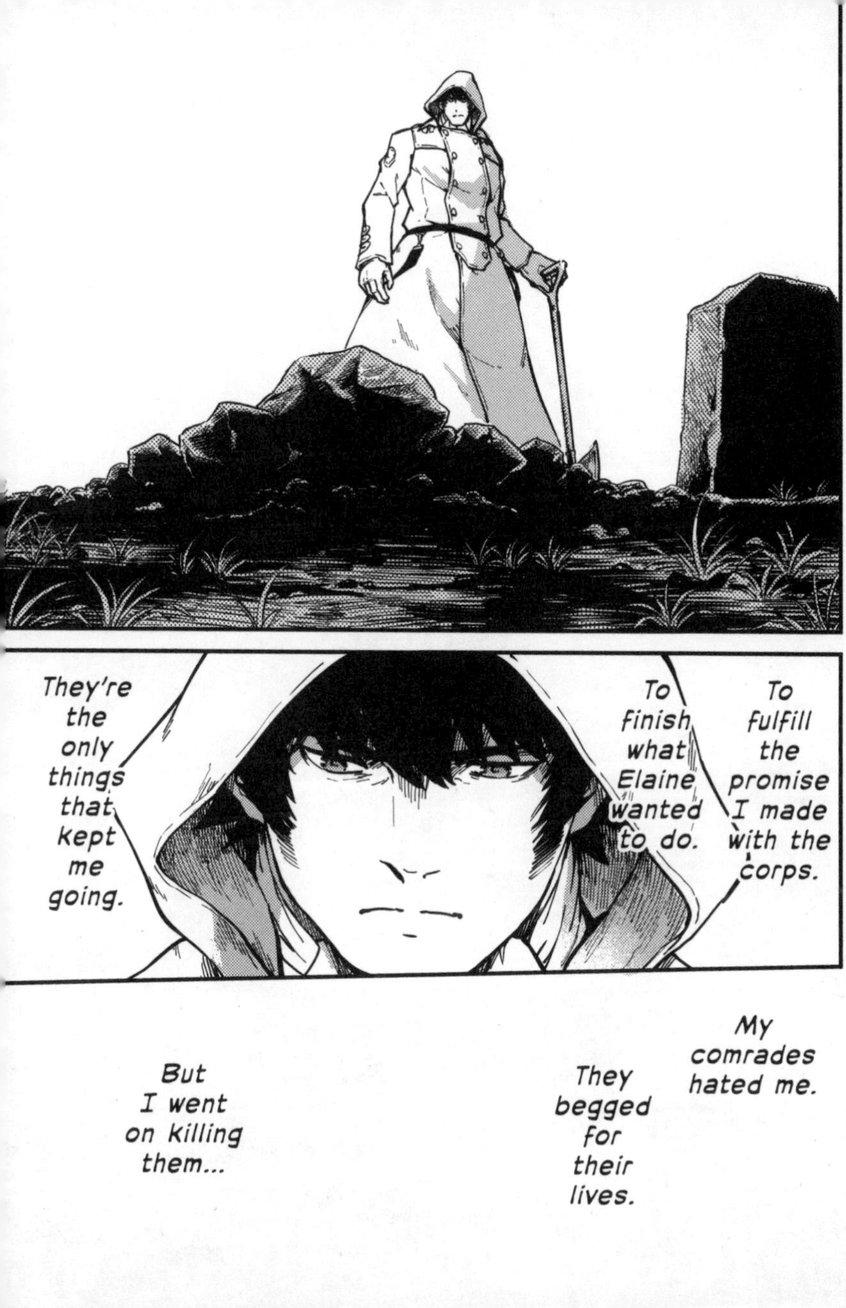
To fulfill the promise I made with the corps.
To finish what Elaine wanted to do.
They're the only things that kept me going.
My comrades hated me.
They begged for their lives.
But I went on killing them...

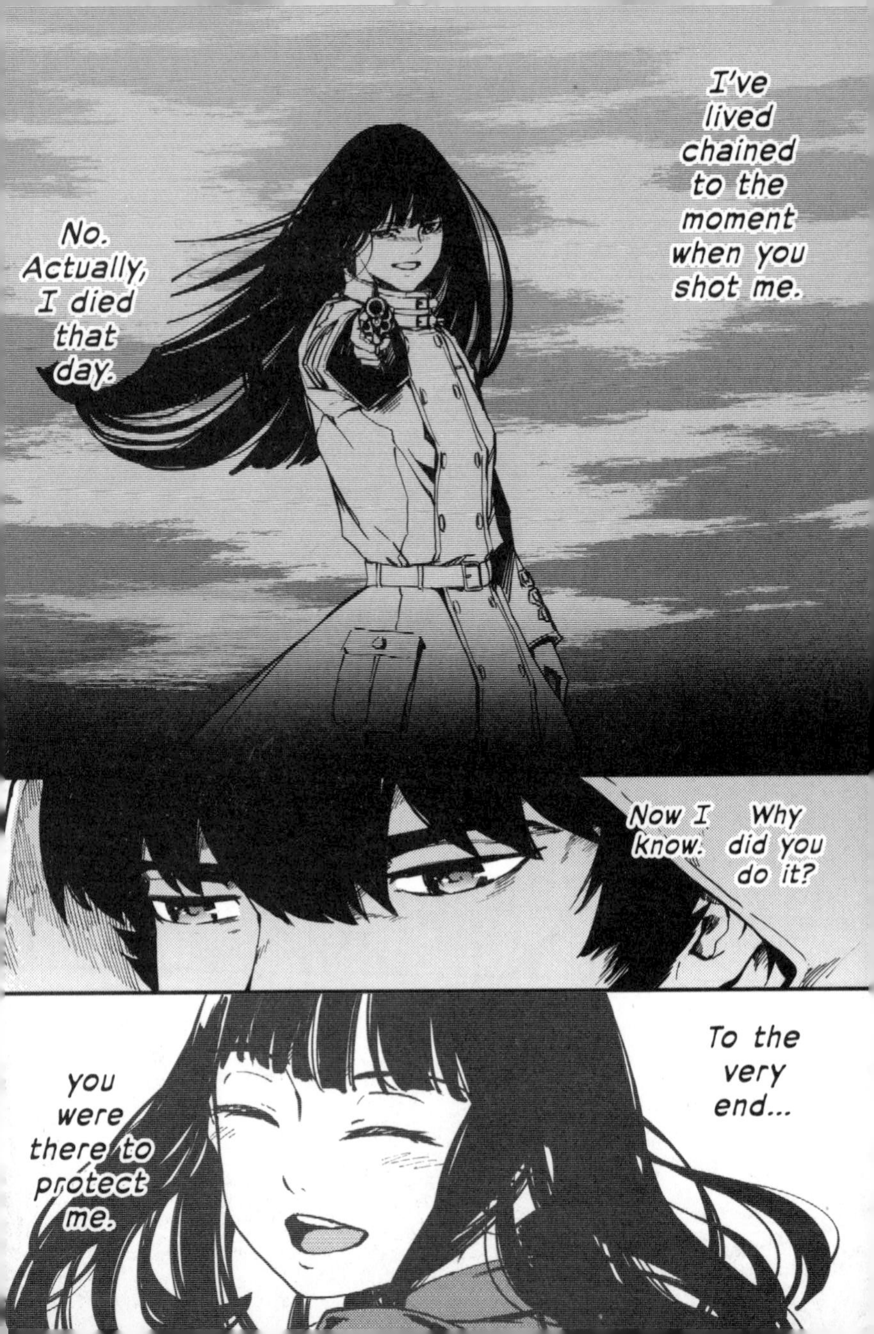
I've lived chained to the moment when you shot me.
No. Actually, I died that day.
Why did you do it?
Now I know.
To the very end...
you were there to protect me.

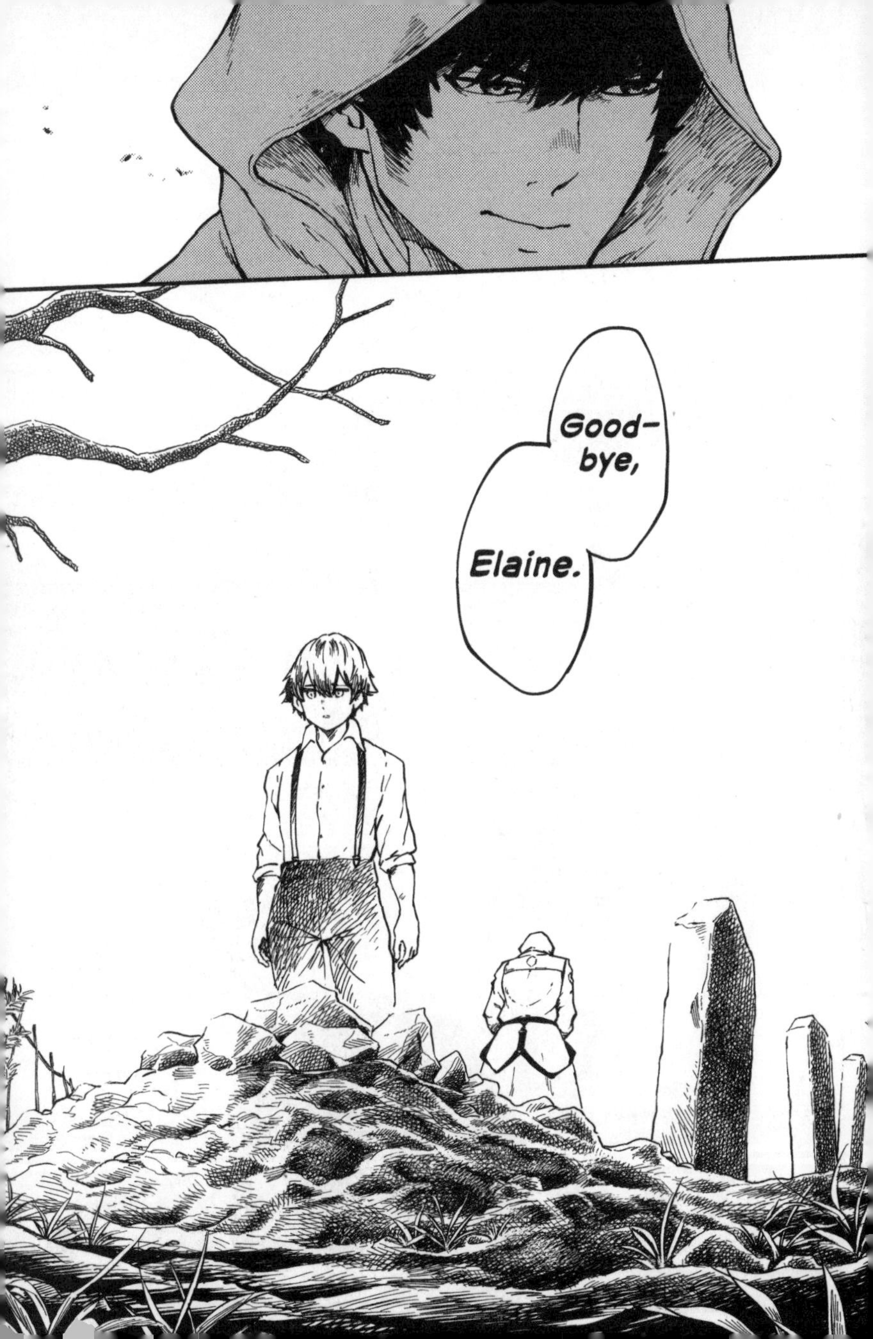
Good-bye, Elaine.

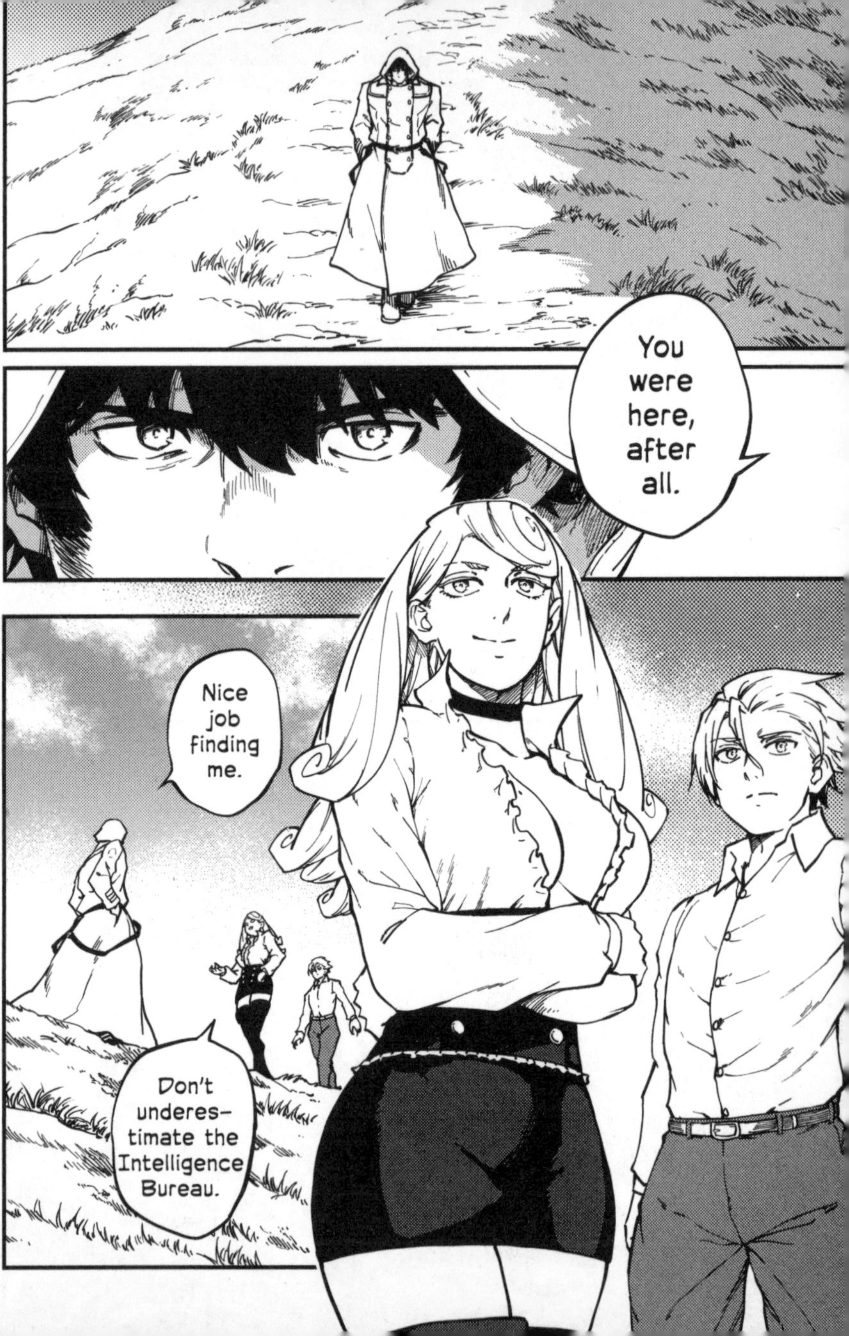
You were here, after all.
Nice job finding me.
Don't underes-timate the Intelligence Bureau.

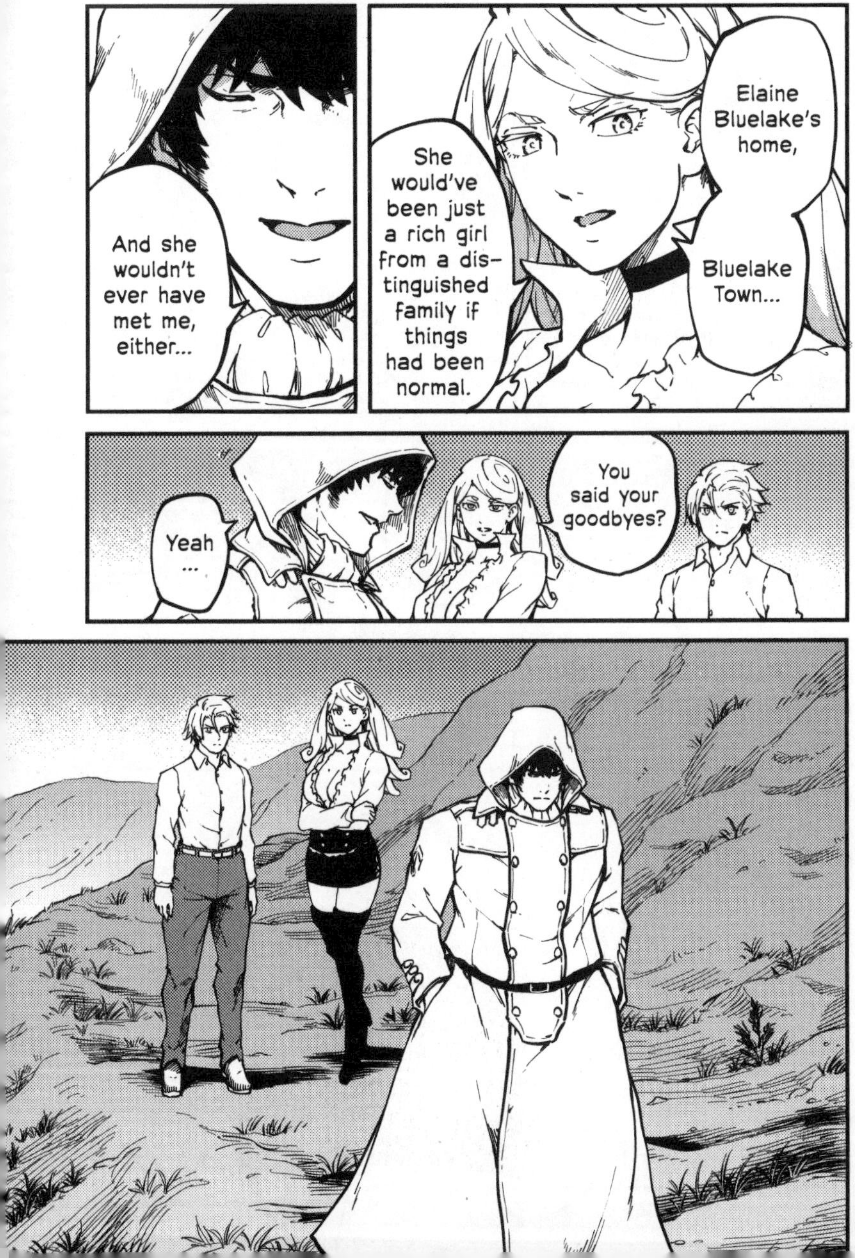
Elaine Bluelake's home,
Bluelake Town...
She would've been just a rich girl from a dis- tinguished family if things had been normal.
And she wouldn't ever have met me, either...
You said your goodbyes?
Yeah ...

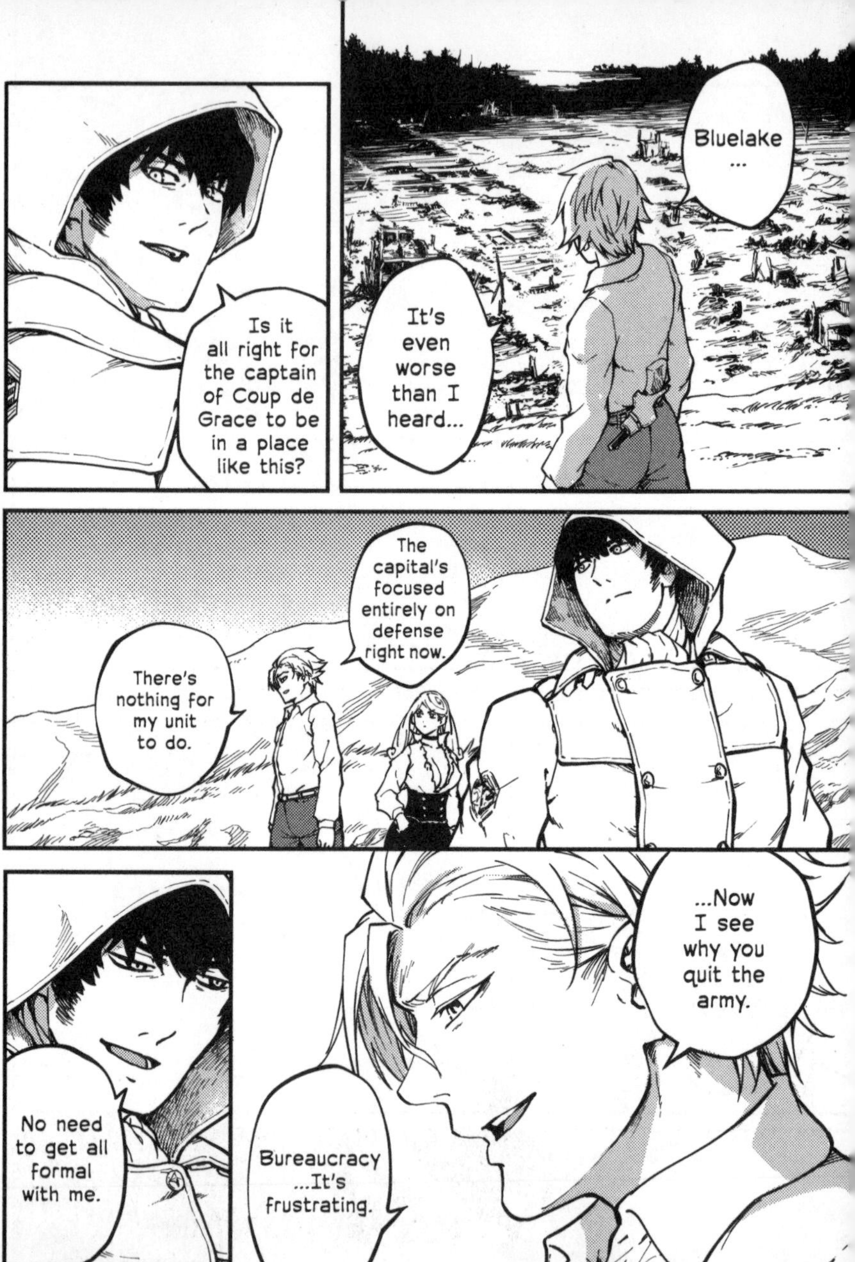
Bluelake ...
It's even worse than I heard...
Is it all right for the captain of Coup de Grace to be in a place like this?
The capital's focused entirely on defense right now.
There's nothing for my unit to do.
...Now I see why you quit the army.
Bureaucracy ...It's frustrating.
No need to get all formal with me.

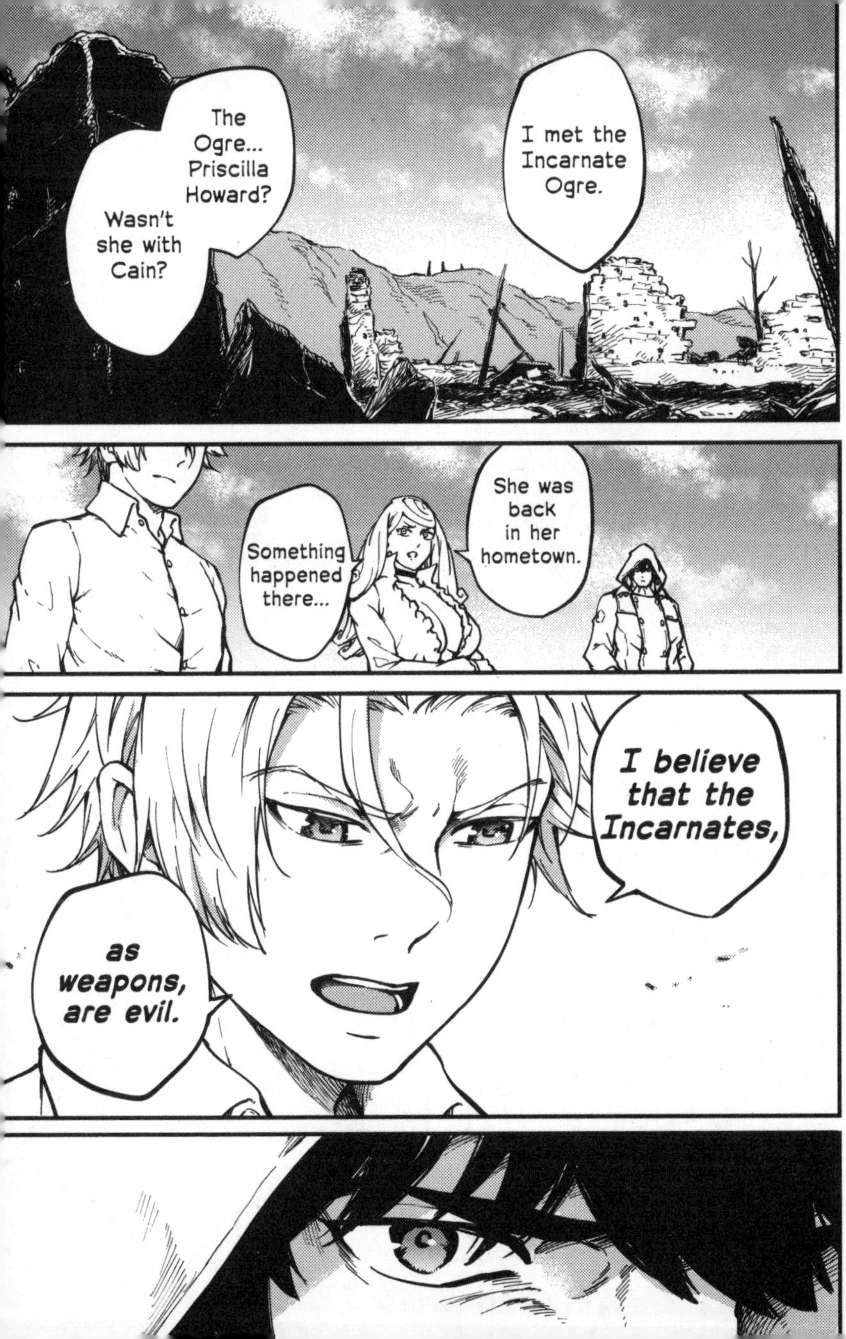
I met the Incarnate Ogre.
The Ogre... Priscilla Howard?
Wasn't she with Cain?
She was back in her hometown.
Something happened there...
I believe that the Incarnates,
as weapons, are evil.

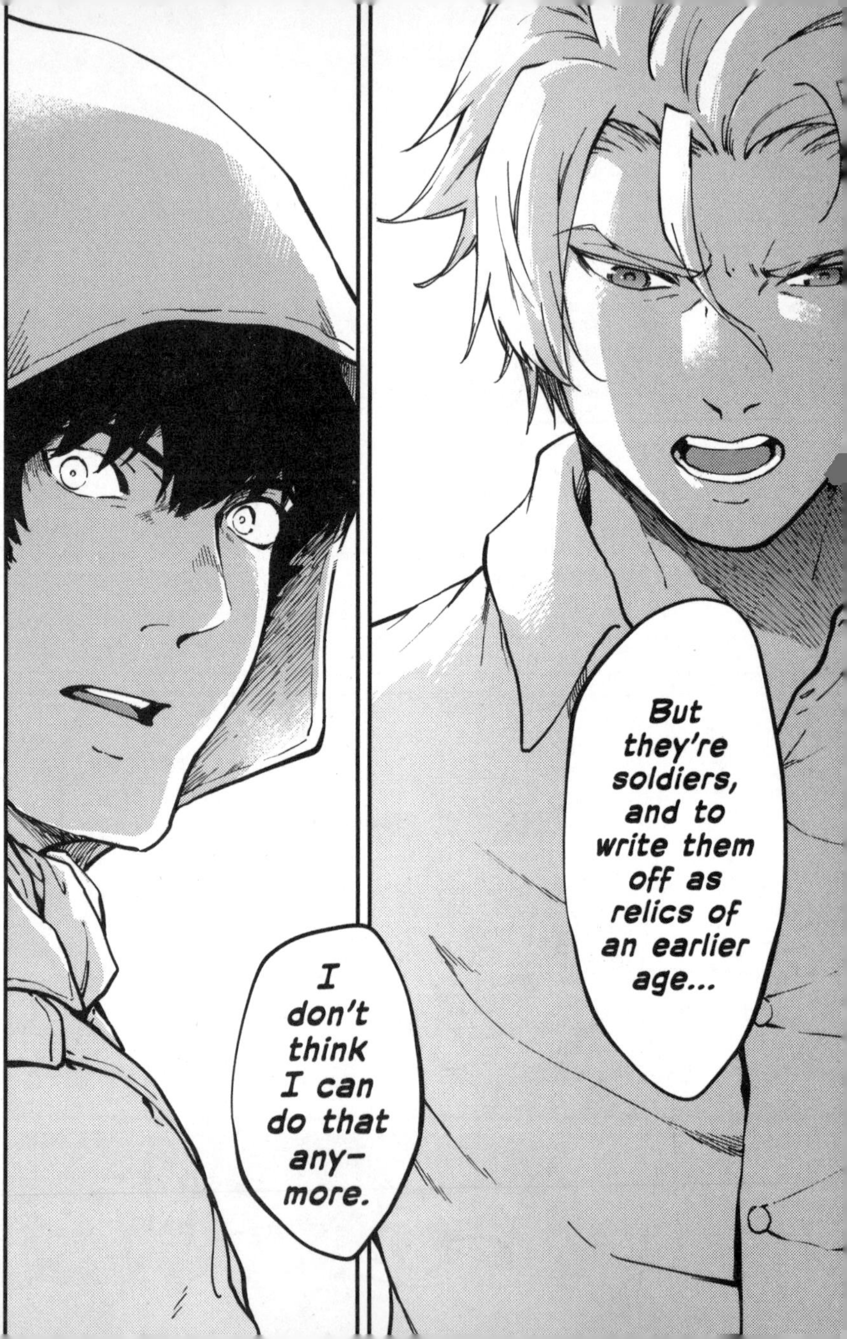
But they're soldiers, and to write them off as relics of an earlier age...
I don't think I can do that any-more.

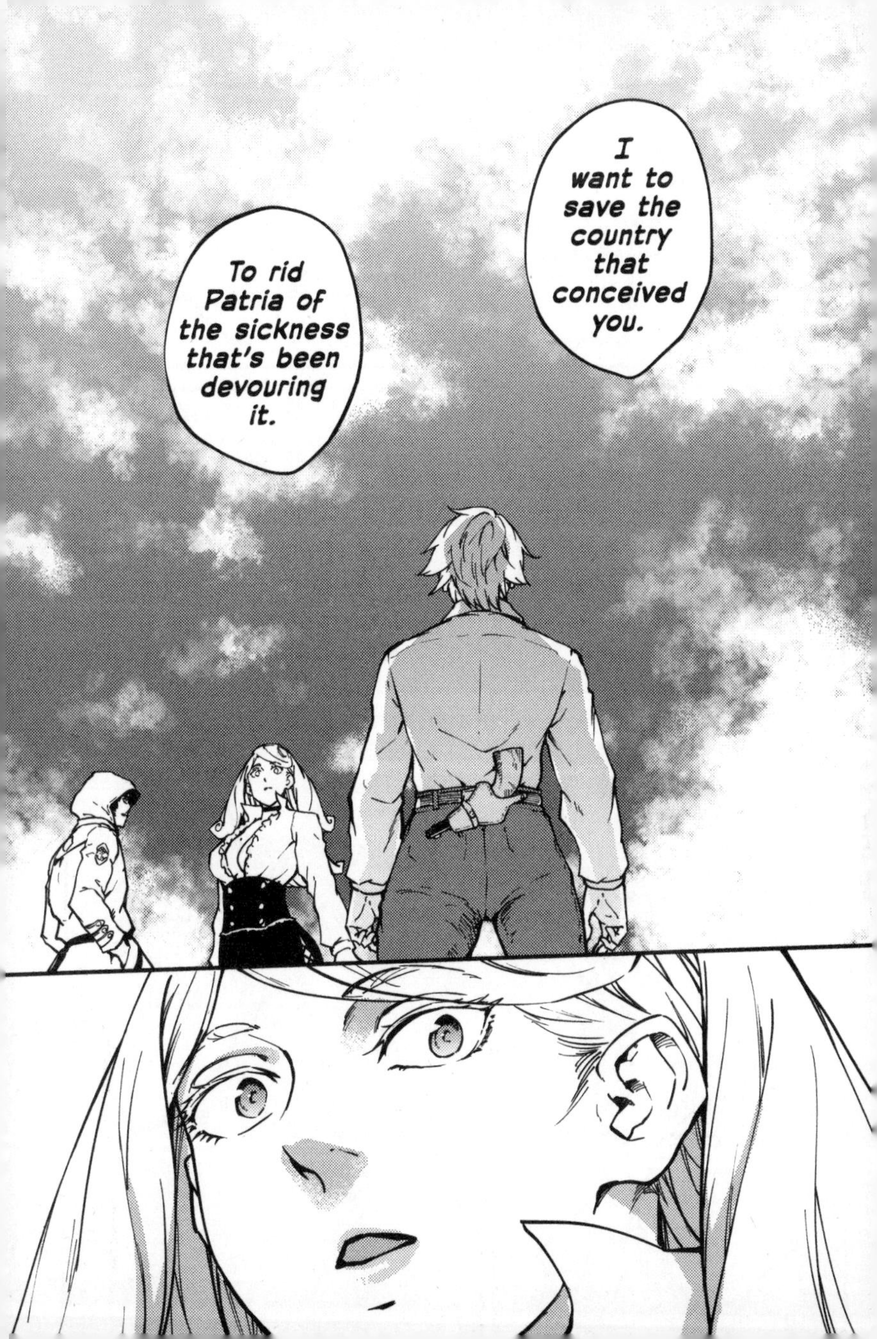
I want to save the country that conceived you.
To rid Patria of the sickness that's been devouring it.

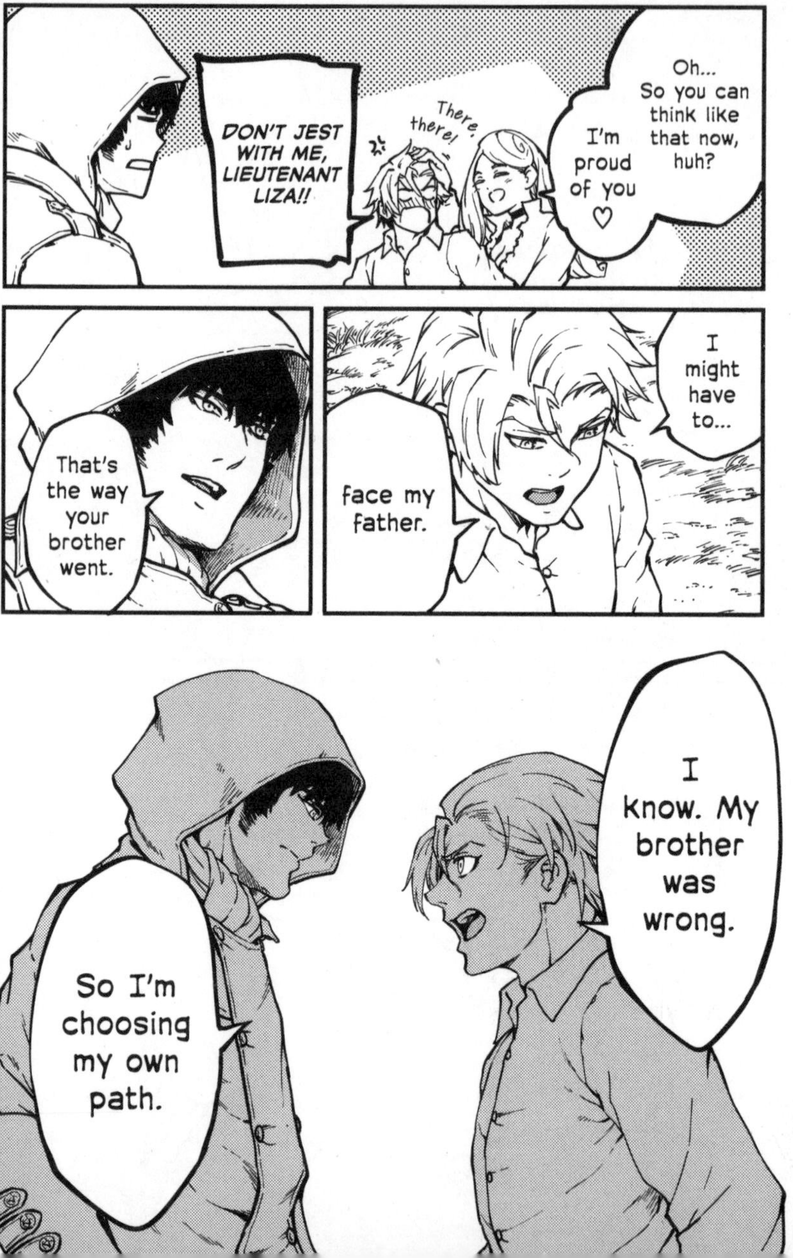
Oh... So you can think like that now, huh?
I'm proud of you ♡
There, there!
DON'T JEST WITH ME, LIEUTENANT LIZA!!
I might have to...
face my father.
That's the way your brother went.
I know. My brother was wrong.
So I'm choosing my own path.

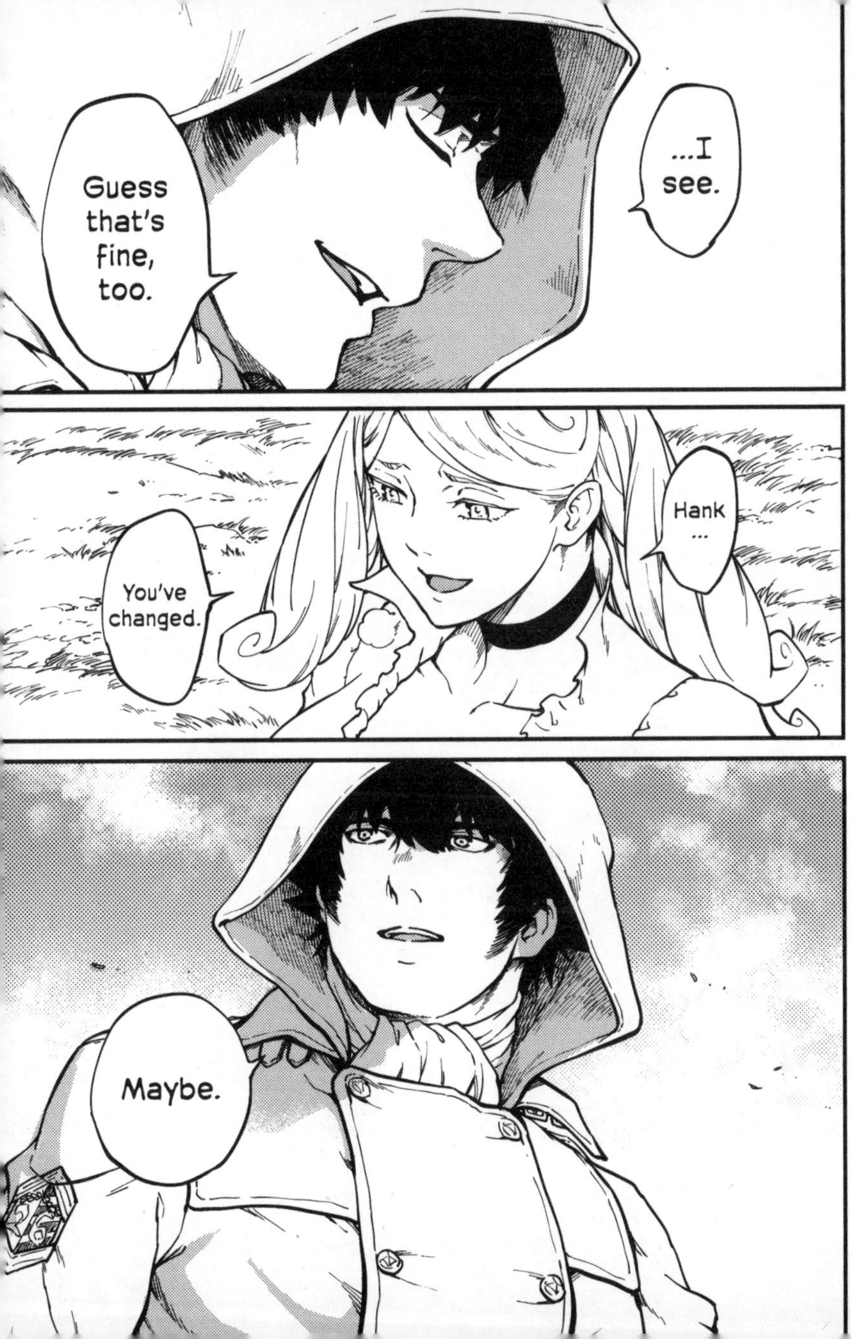
...I see.
Guess that's fine, too.
Hank ...
You've changed.
Maybe.

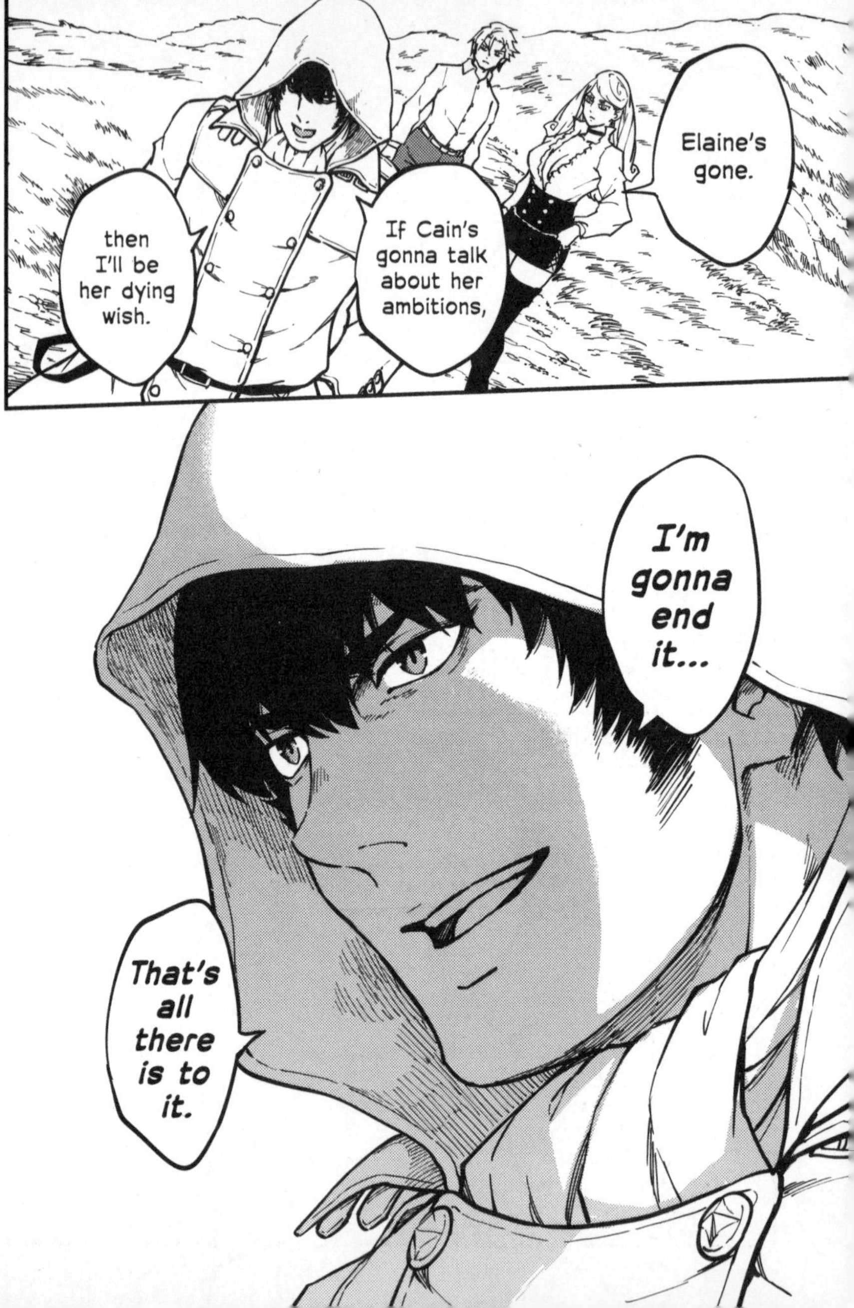
Elaine's gone.
If Cain's gonna talk about her ambitions,
then I'll be her dying wish.
I'm gonna end it...
That's all there is to it.

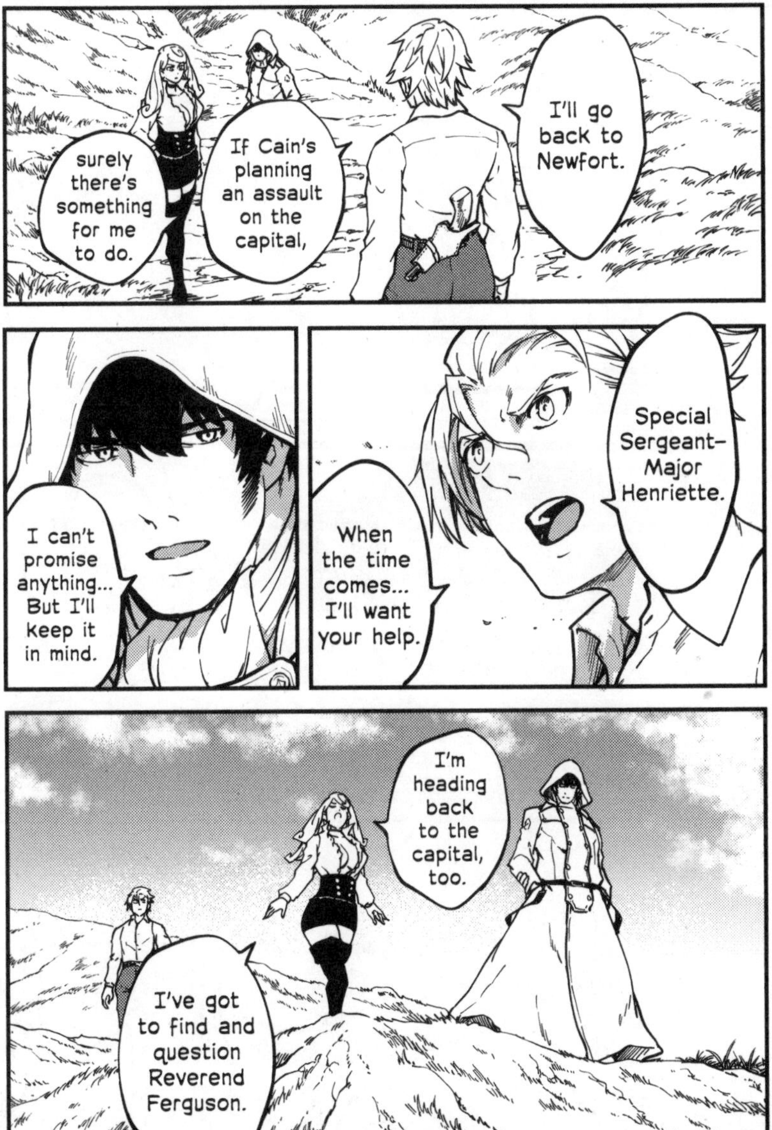
I'll go back to Newfort.
If Cain's planning an assault on the capital,
surely there's something for me to do.
Special Sergeant–Major Henriette.
When the time comes... I'll want your help.
I can't promise anything... But I'll keep it in mind.
I'm heading back to the capital, too.
I've got to find and question Reverend Ferguson.

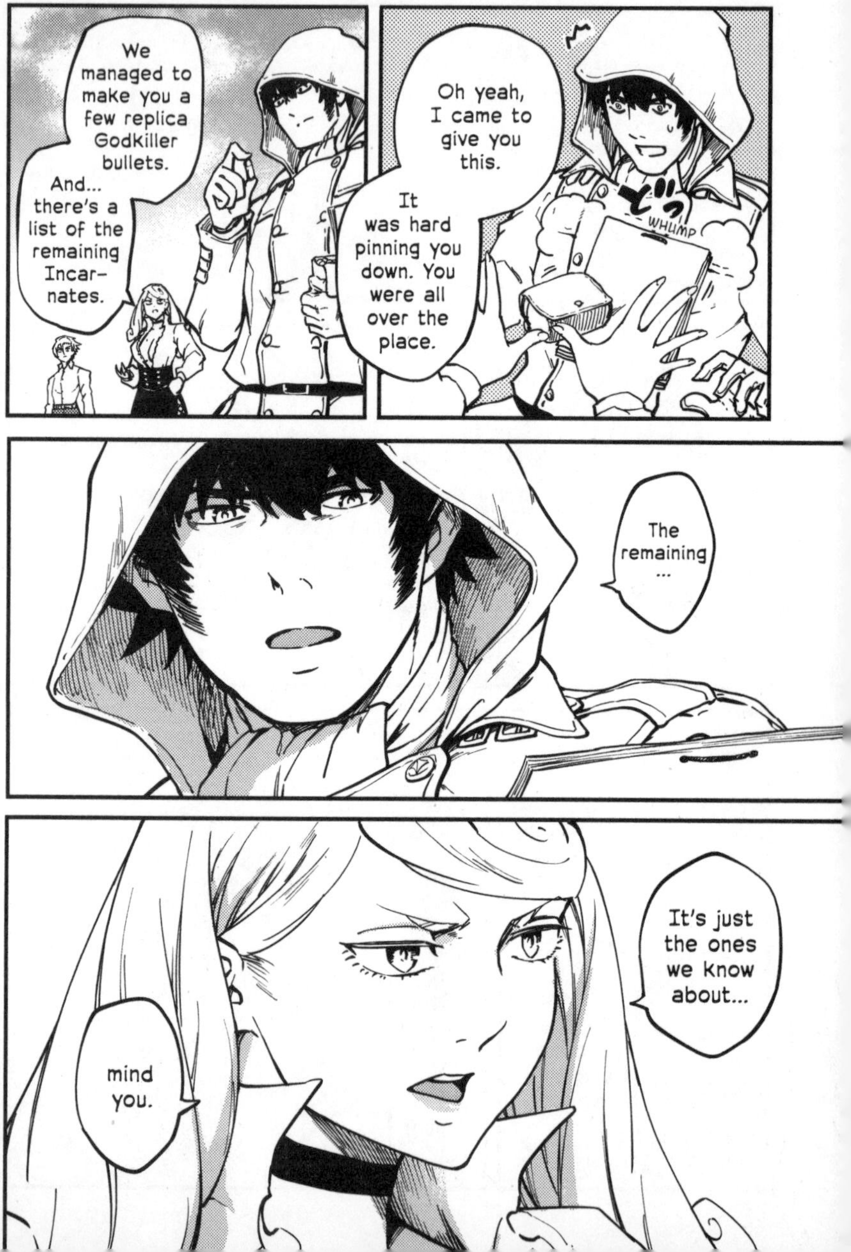
Oh yeah, I came to give you this.
It was hard pinning you down. You were all over the place.
どっ
WHUMP
We managed to make you a few replica Godkiller bullets.
And... there's a list of the remaining Incar-nates.
The remaining...
It's just the ones we know about...
mind you.

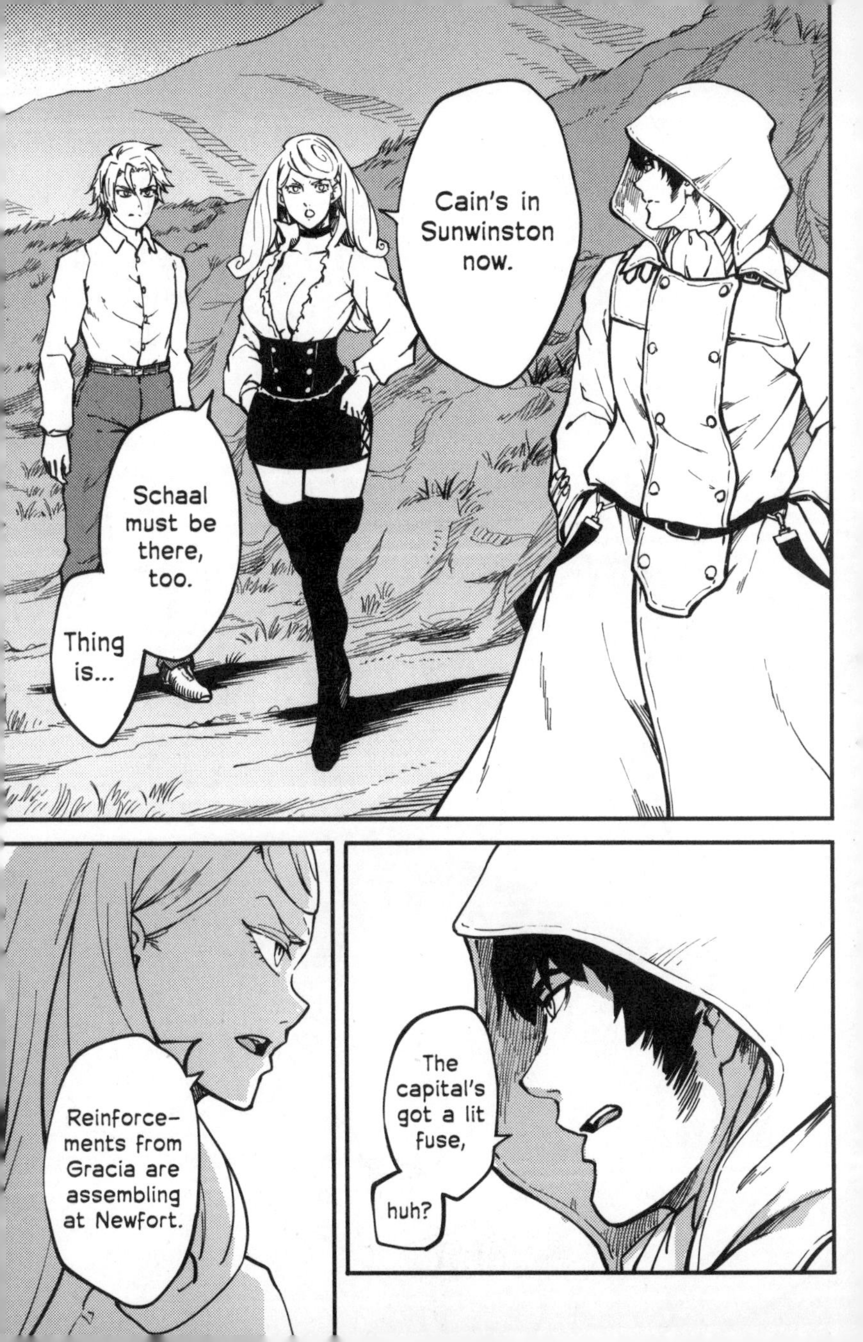
Cain's in Sunwinston now.
Schaal must be there, too.
Thing is...
The capital's got a lit fuse,
huh?
Reinforcements from Gracia are assembling at Newfort.

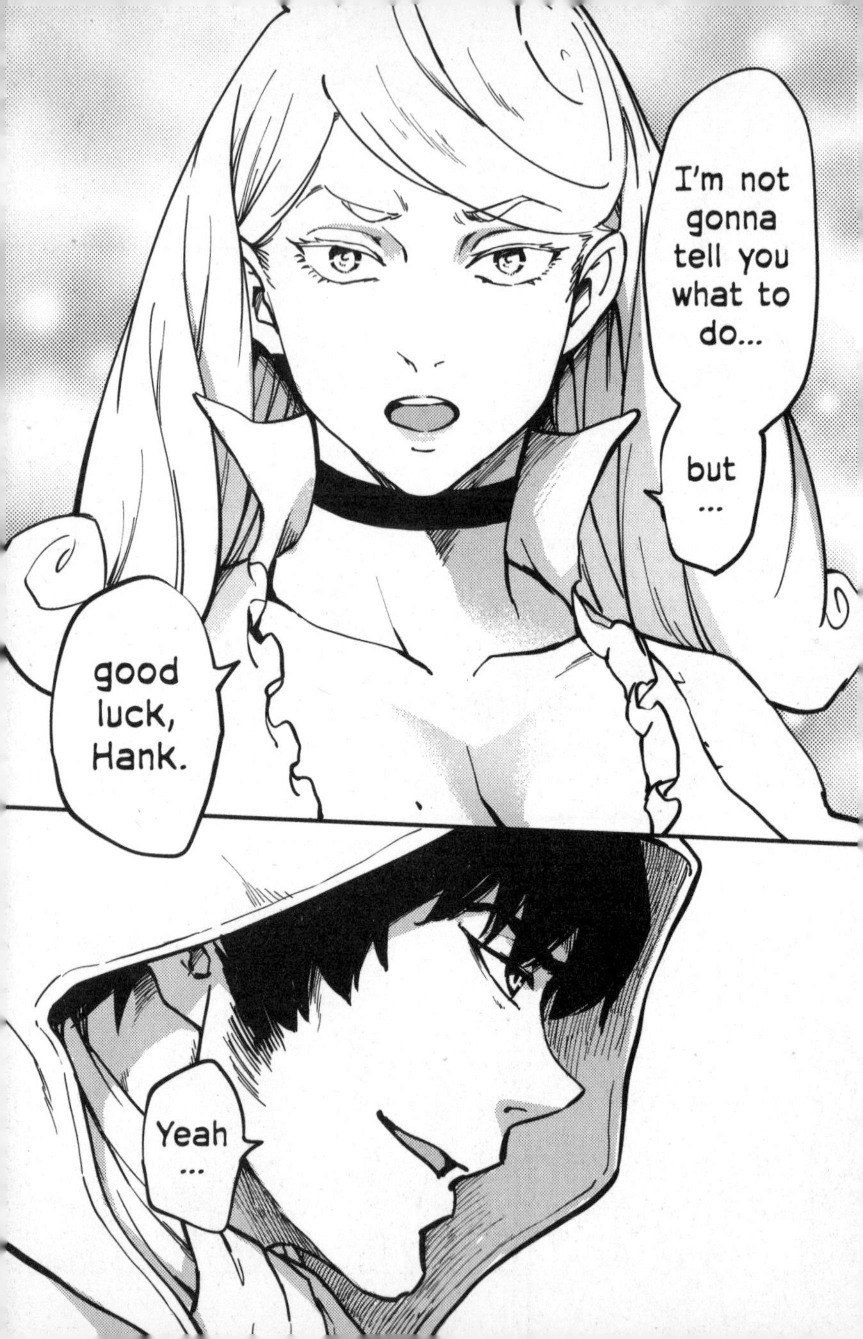
I'm not gonna tell you what to do...
but ...
good luck, Hank.
Yeah ...

To the Abandoned
Sacred Beasts

To the Abandoned
Sacred Beasts

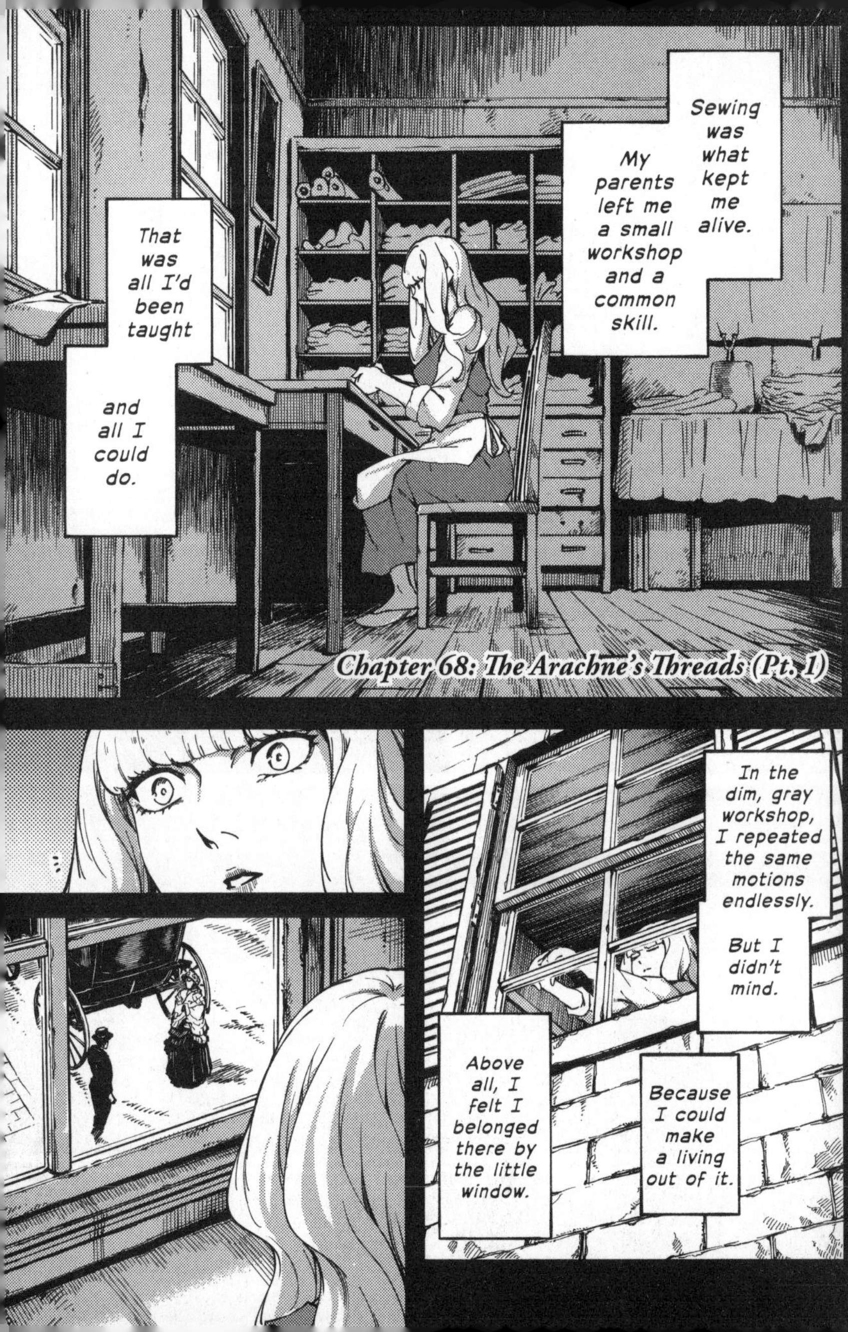
Sewing was what kept me alive.
My parents left me a small workshop and a common skill.
That was all I'd been taught
and all I could do.
Chapter 68: The Arachne's Threads (Pt. 1)
In the dim, gray workshop, I repeated the same motions endlessly.
But I didn't mind.
Because I could make a living out of it.
Above all, I felt I belonged there by the little window.

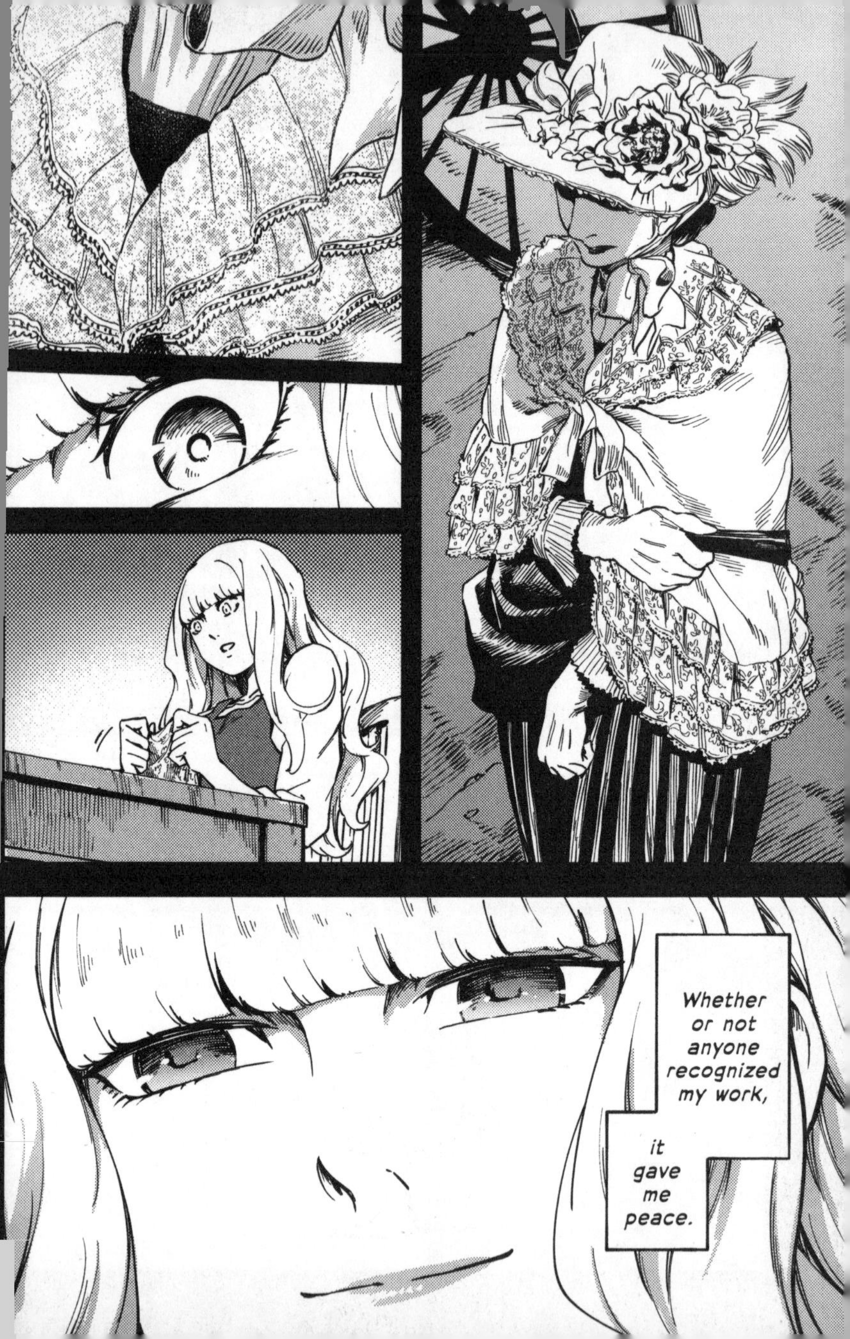
Whether or not anyone recognized my work,
it gave me peace.

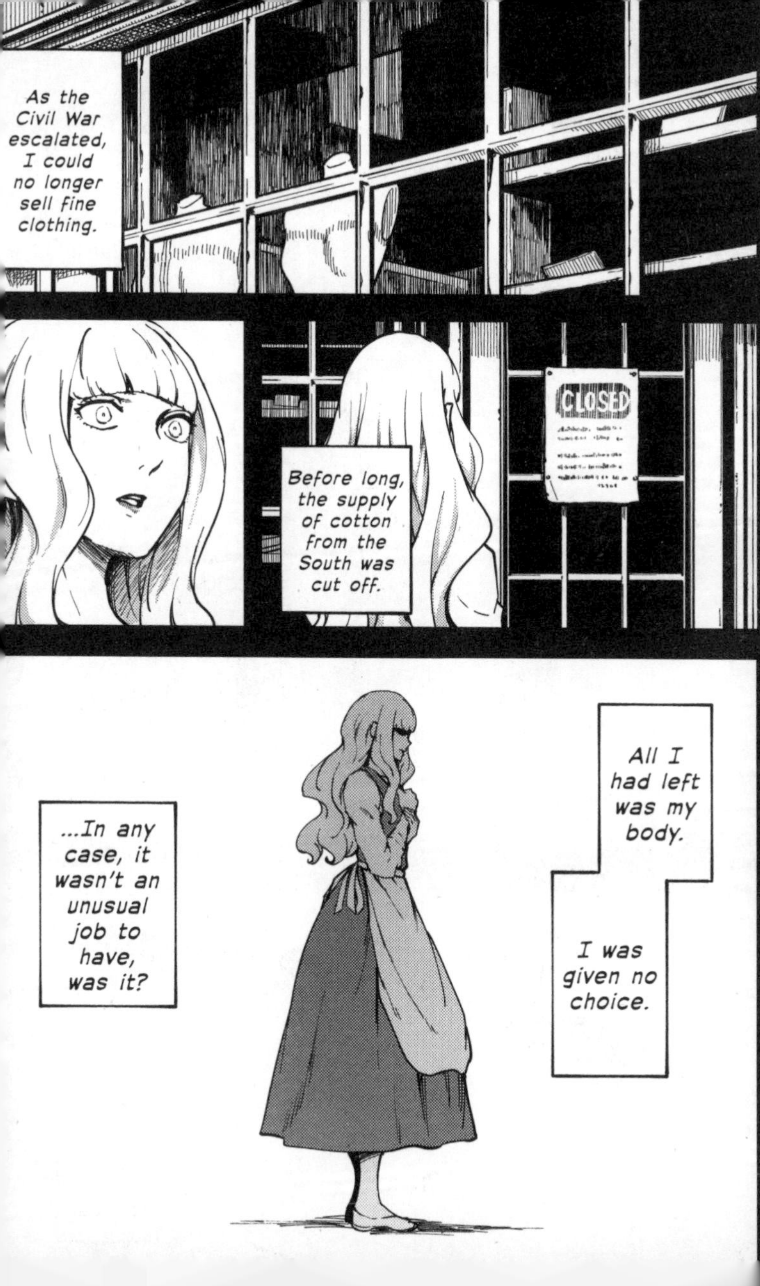
As the Civil War escalated, I could no longer sell fine clothing.
CLOSED
Before long, the supply of cotton from the South was cut off.
All I had left was my body.
I was given no choice.
...In any case, it wasn't an unusual job to have, was it?

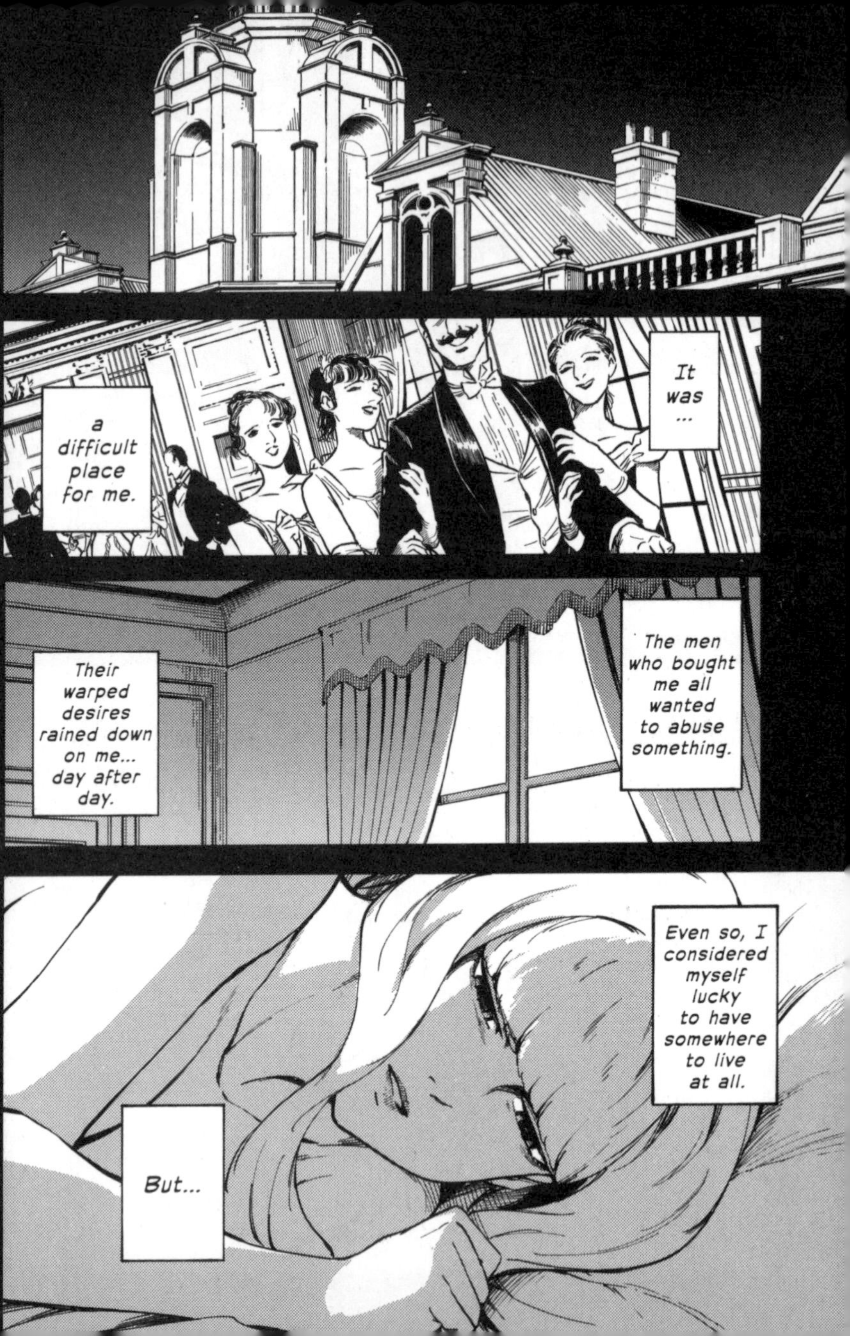
It was...
a difficult place for me.
The men who bought me all wanted to abuse something.
Their warped desires rained down on me... day after day.
Even so, I considered myself lucky to have somewhere to live at all.
But...

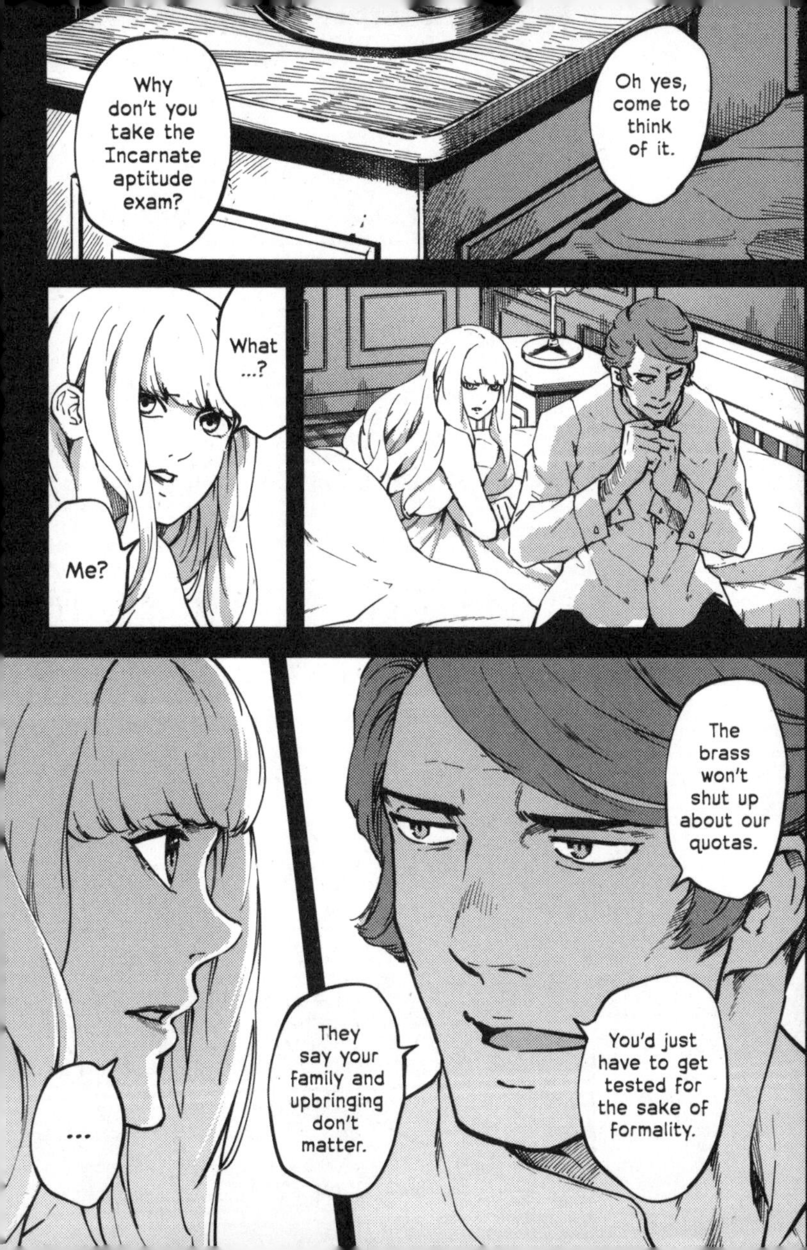
Oh yes, come to think of it.
Why don't you take the Incarnate aptitude exam?
What ...?
Me?
The brass won't shut up about our quotas.
You'd just have to get tested for the sake of formality.
They say your family and upbringing don't matter.
...

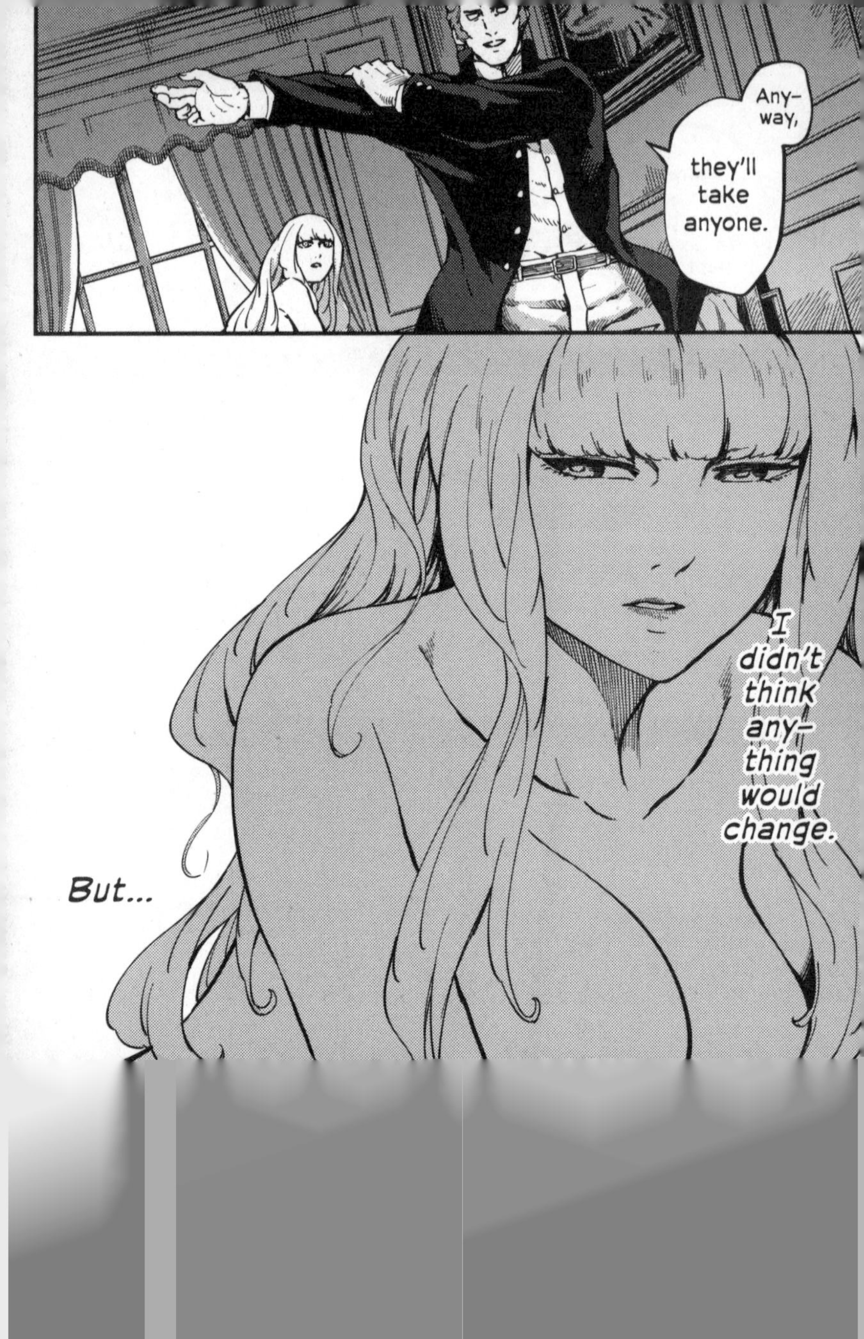
Any-way, they'll take anyone.
I didn't think any-thing would change.
But...

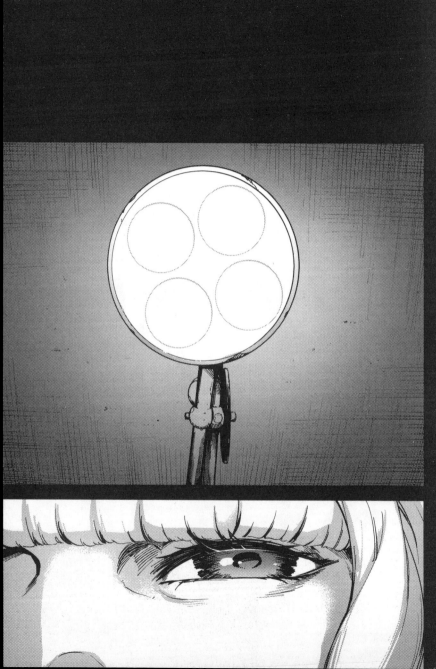

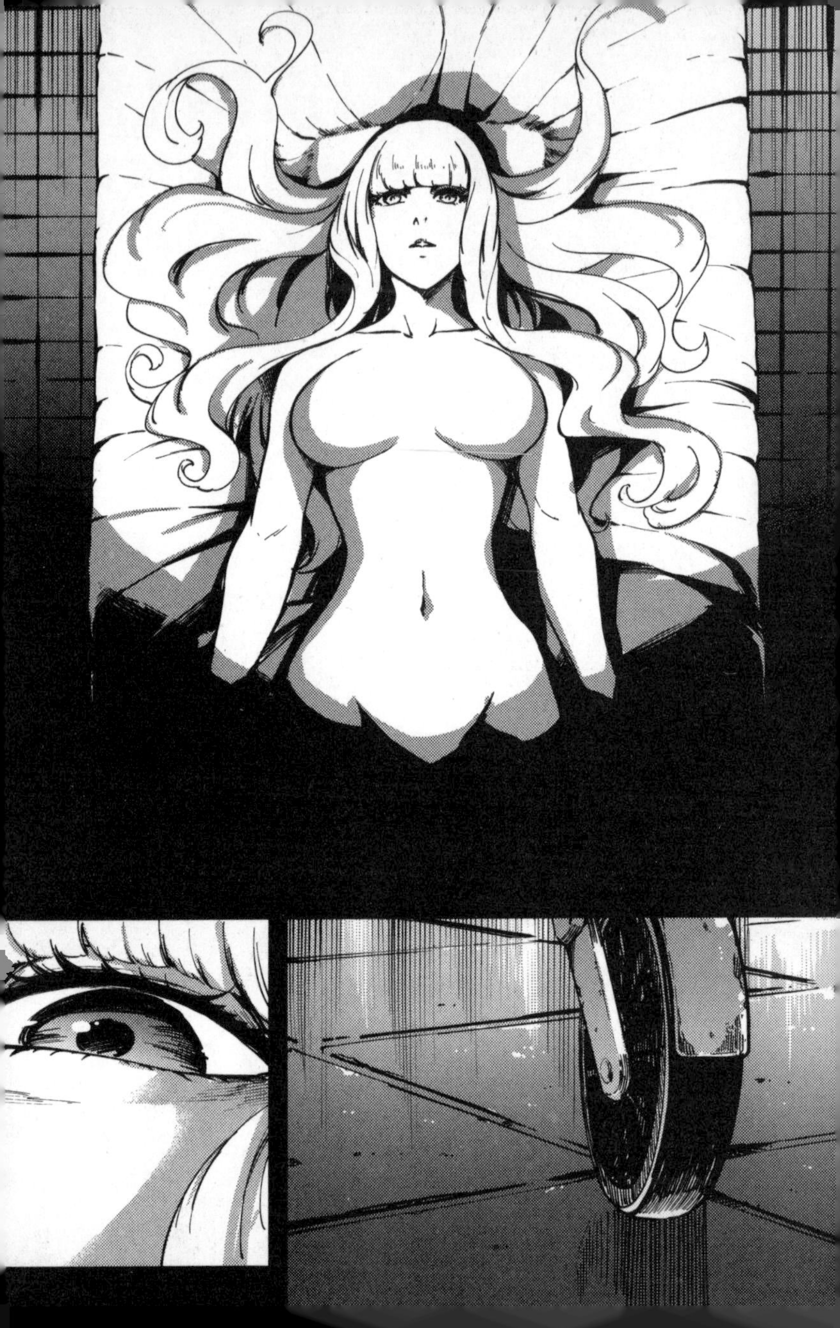

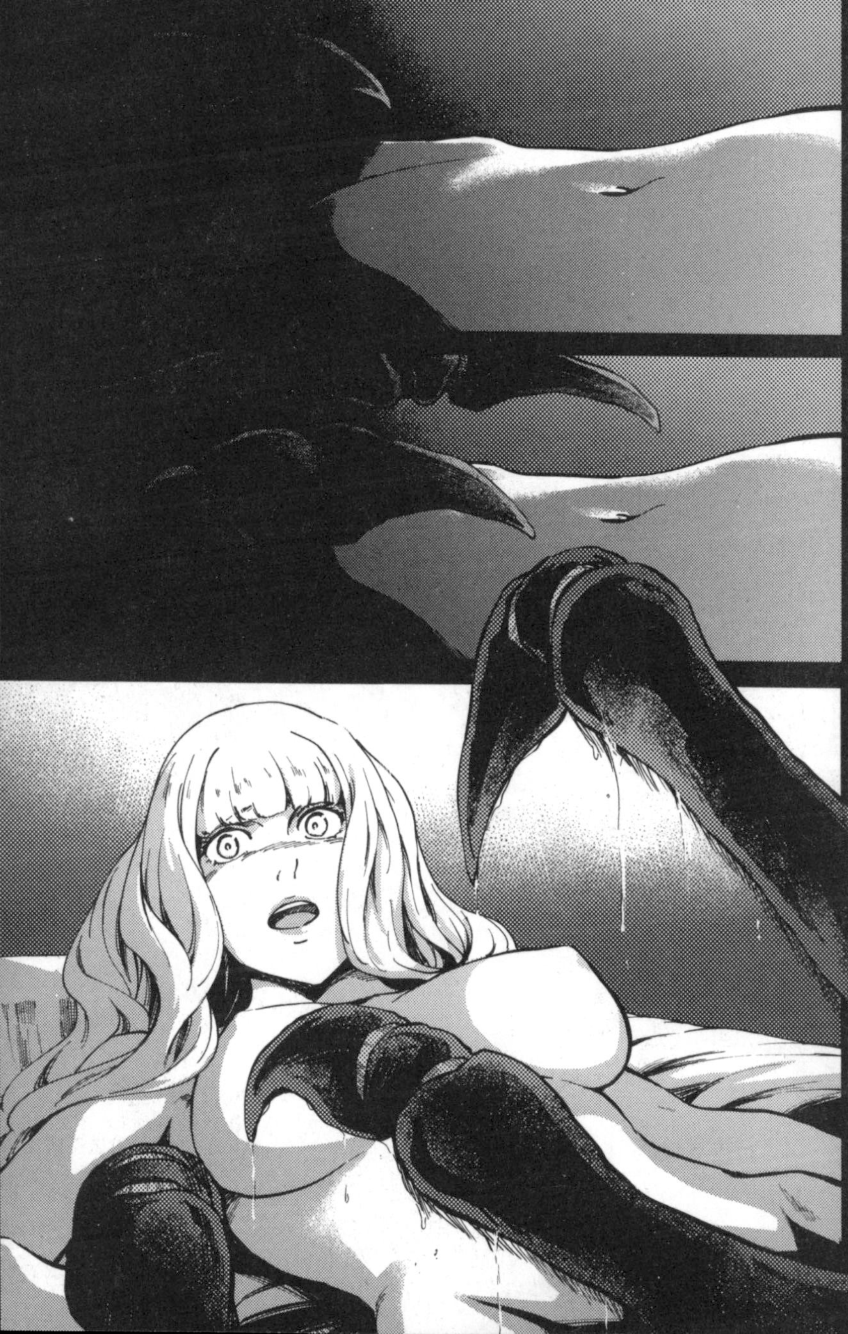

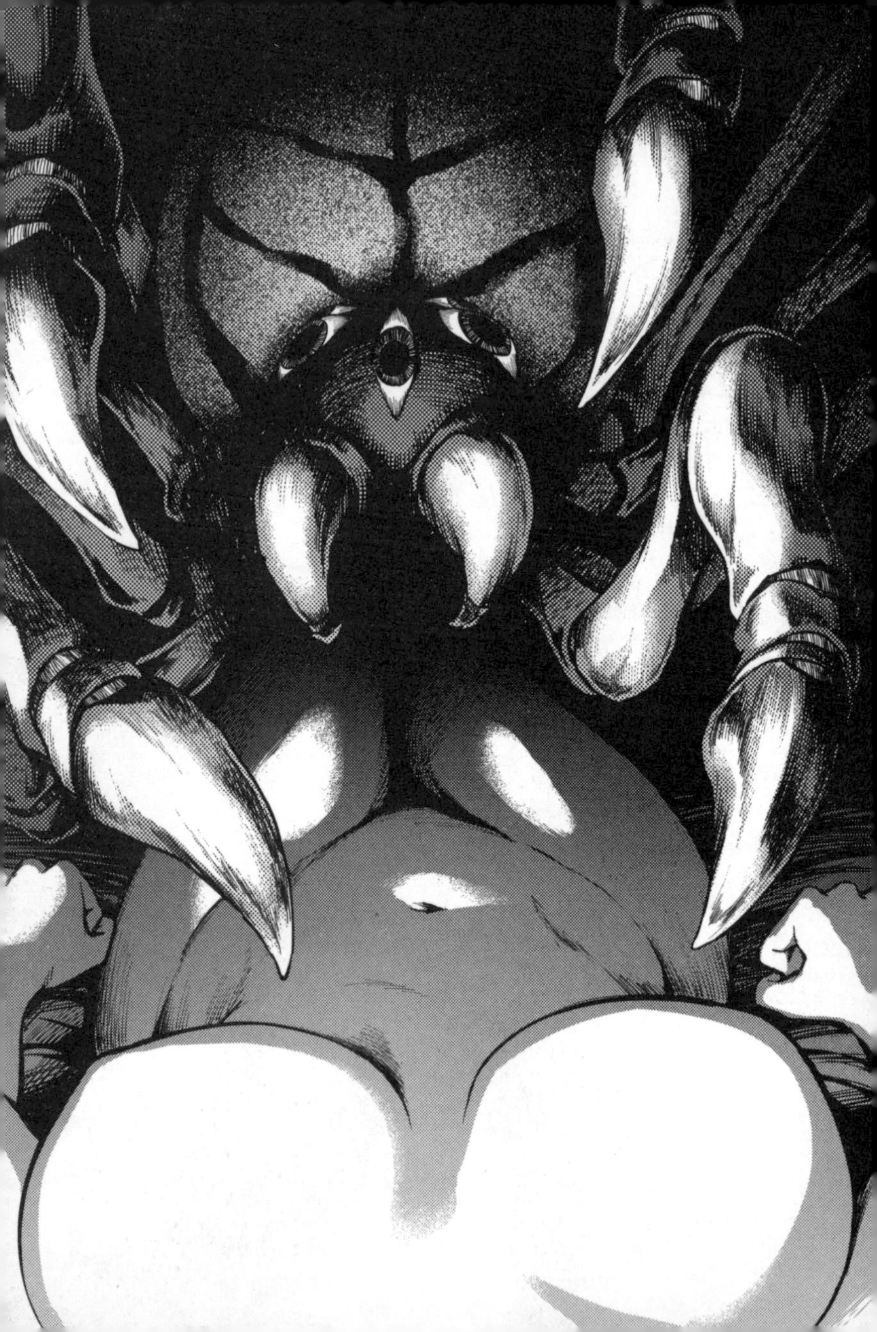

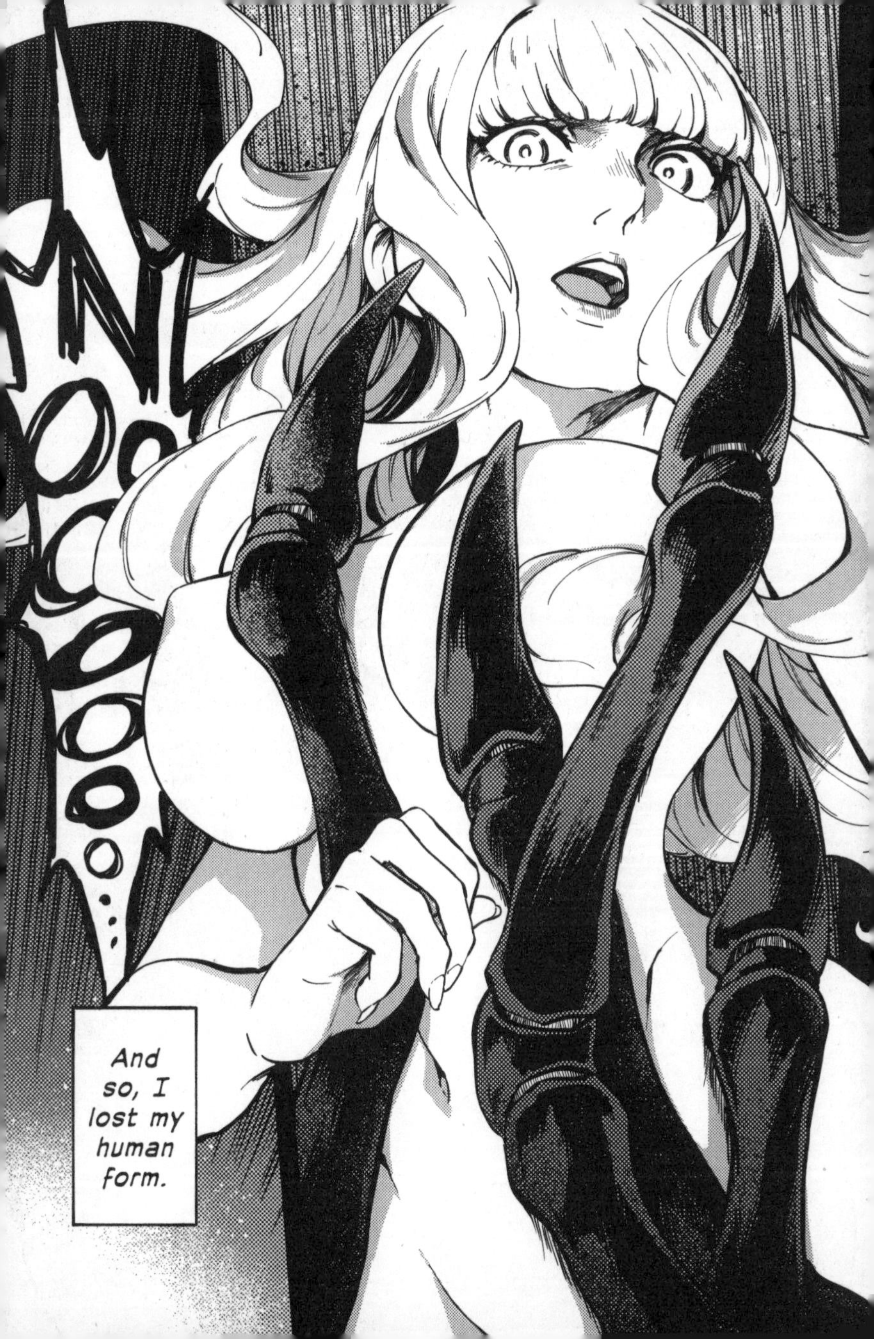
NOOOOOOOO...
And so, I lost my human form.

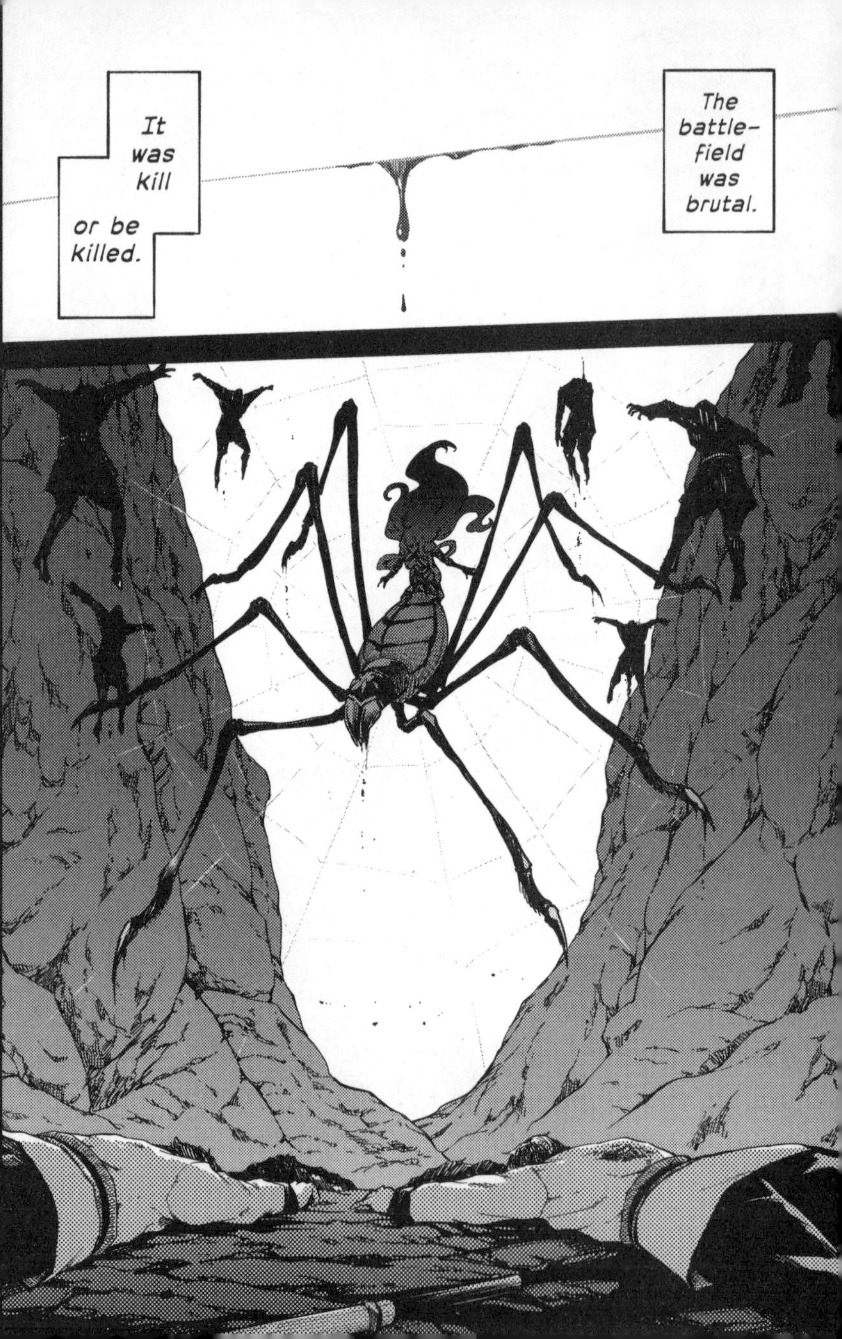
The battle-field was brutal.
It was kill or be killed.

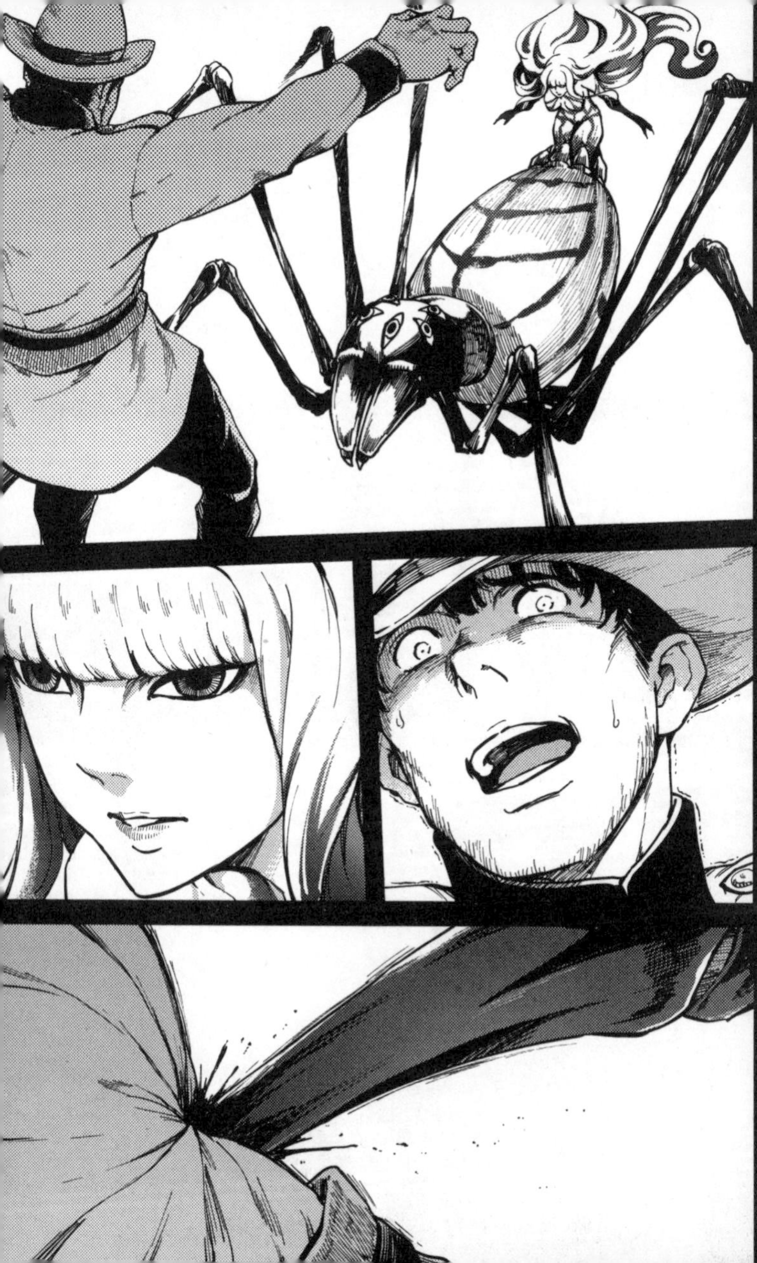

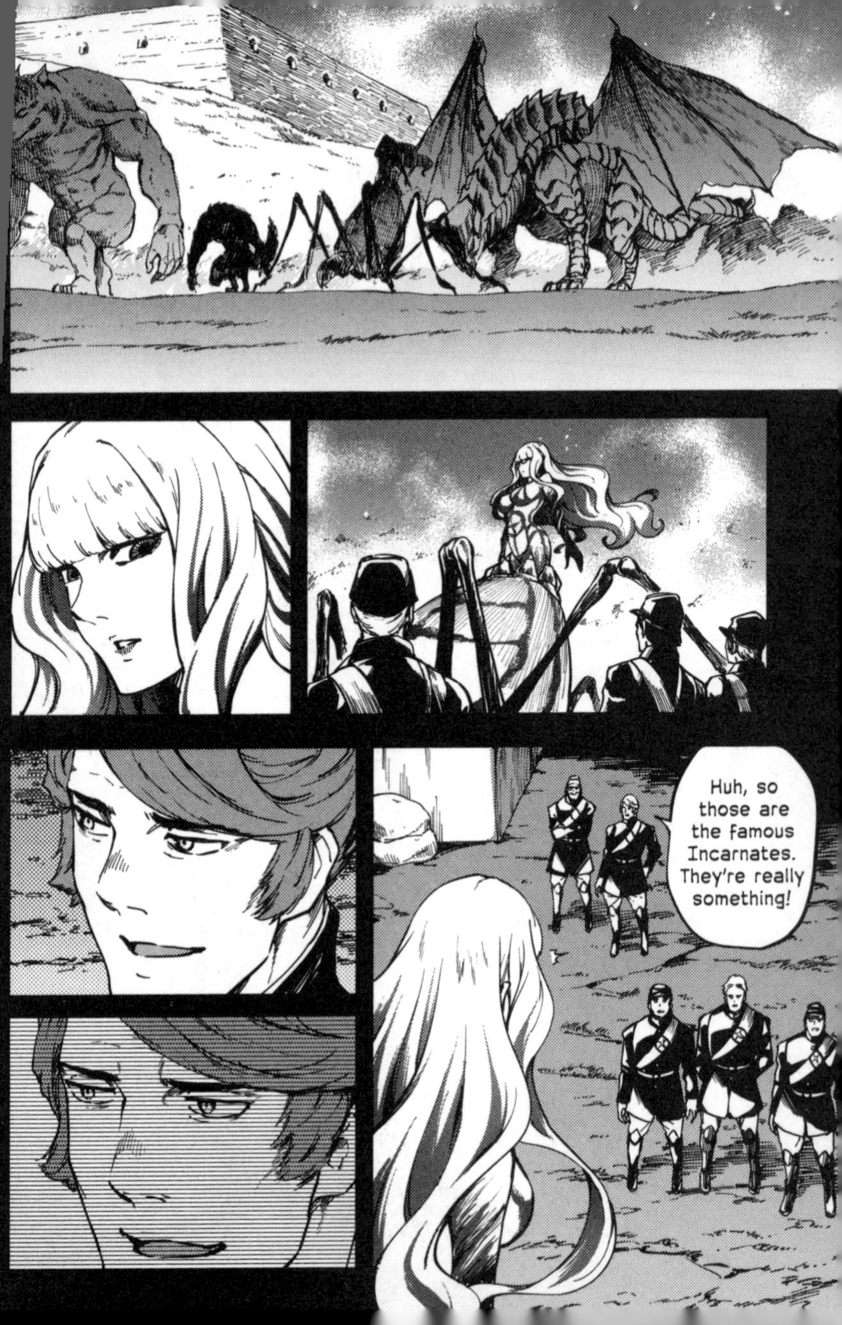
Huh, so those are the famous Incarnates. They're really something!

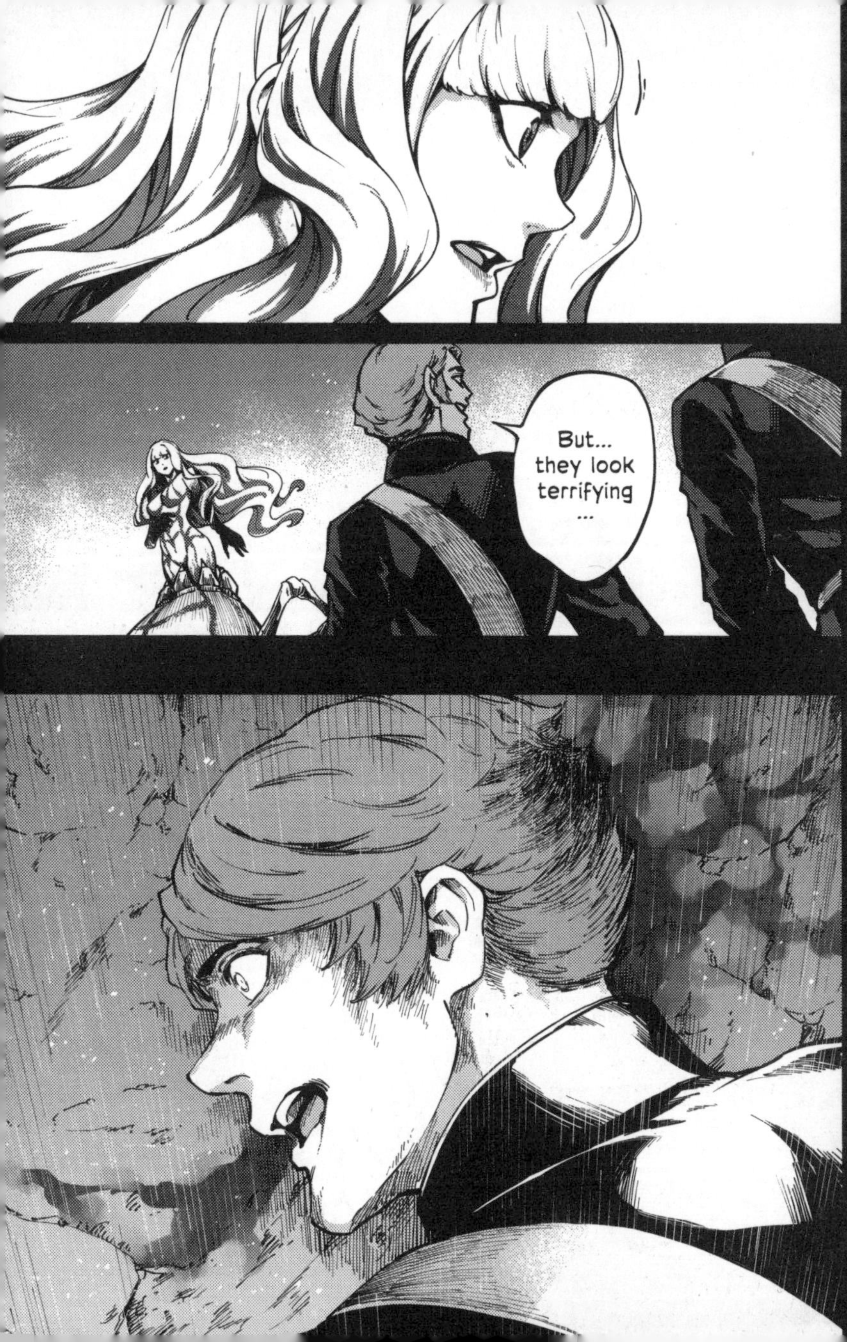
But... they look terrifying ...

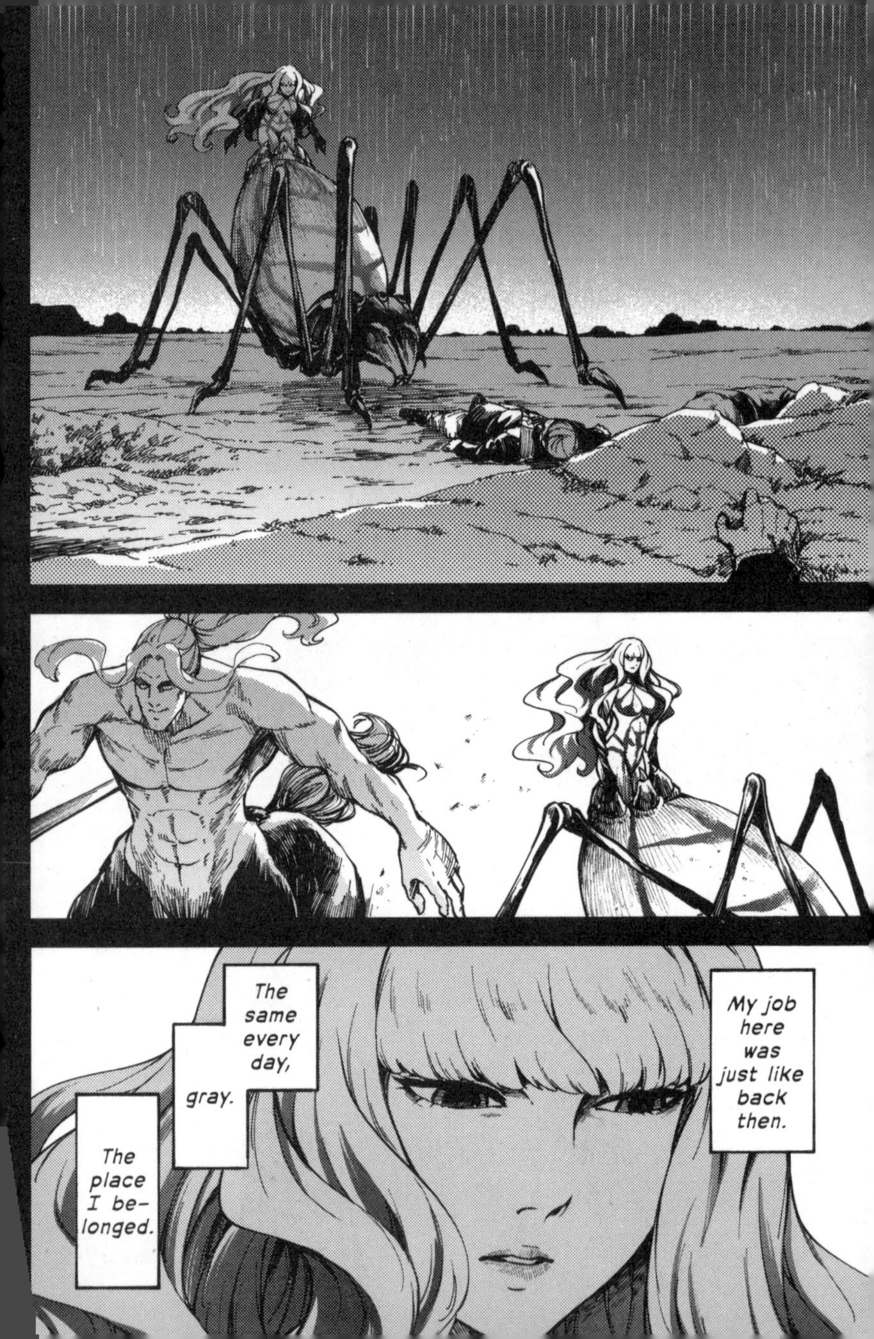
My job here was just like back then.
The same every day,
gray.
The place I be-longed.

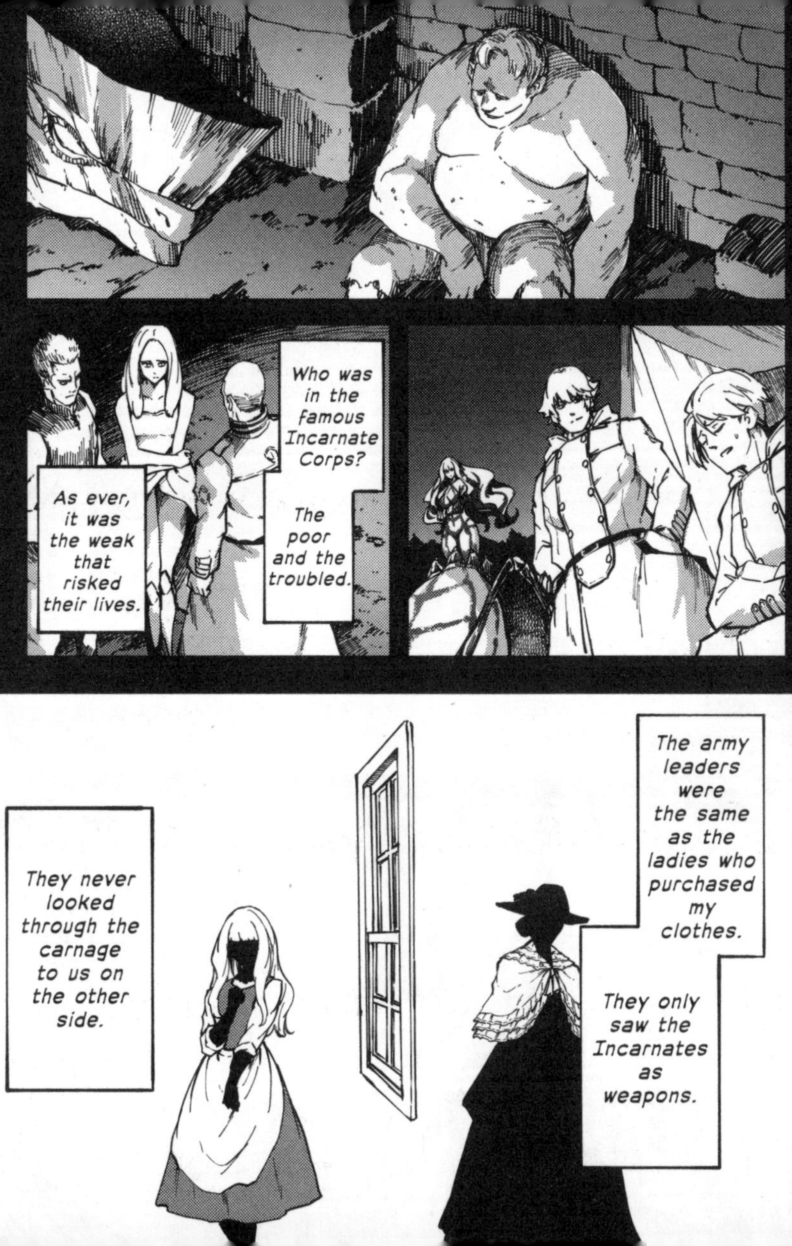

Who was in the famous Incarnate Corps?
The poor and the troubled.
As ever, it was the weak that risked their lives.
The army leaders were the same as the ladies who purchased my clothes.
They only saw the Incarnates as weapons.
They never looked through the carnage to us on the other side.

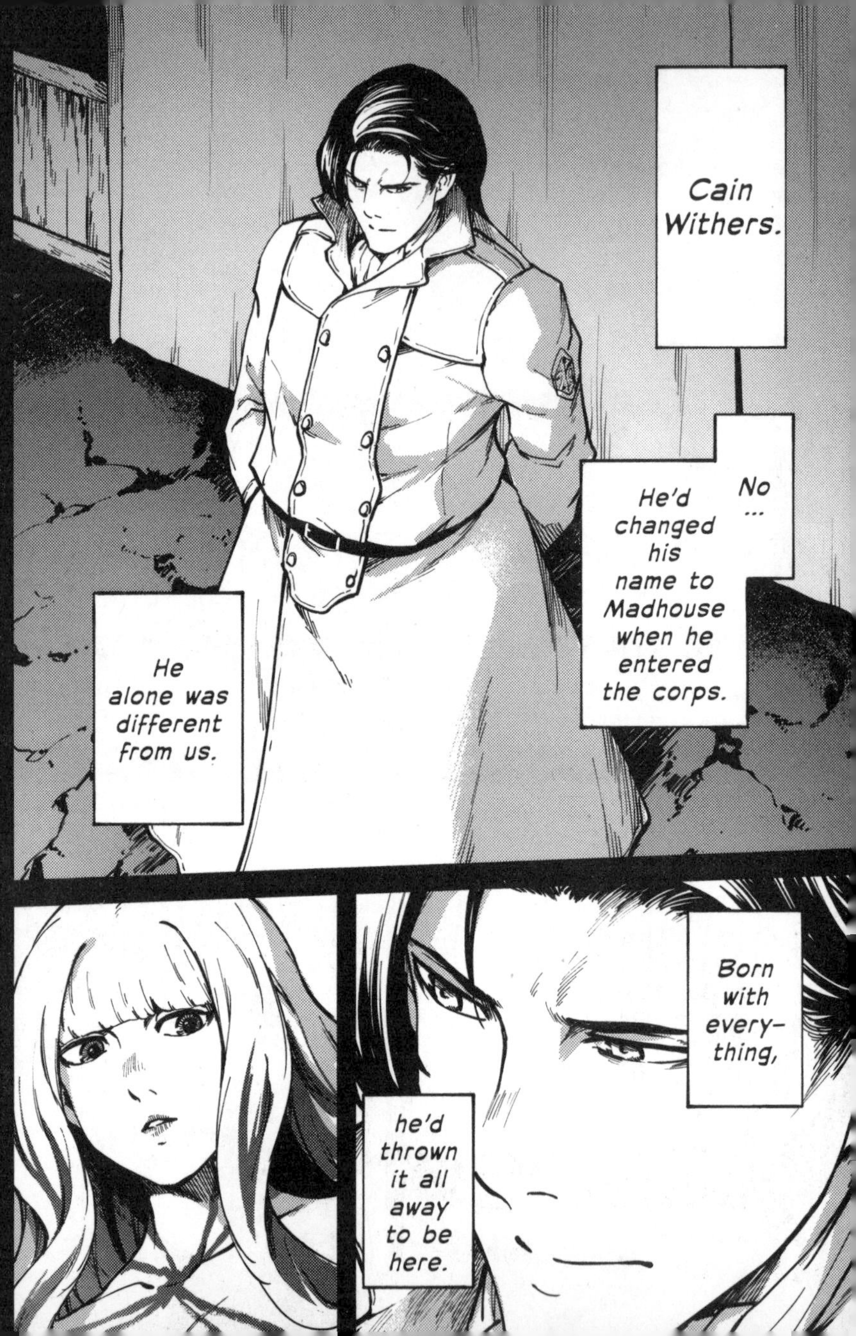
Cain Withers.
No ...
He'd changed his name to Madhouse when he entered the corps.
He alone was different from us.
Born with every-thing,
he'd thrown it all away to be here.

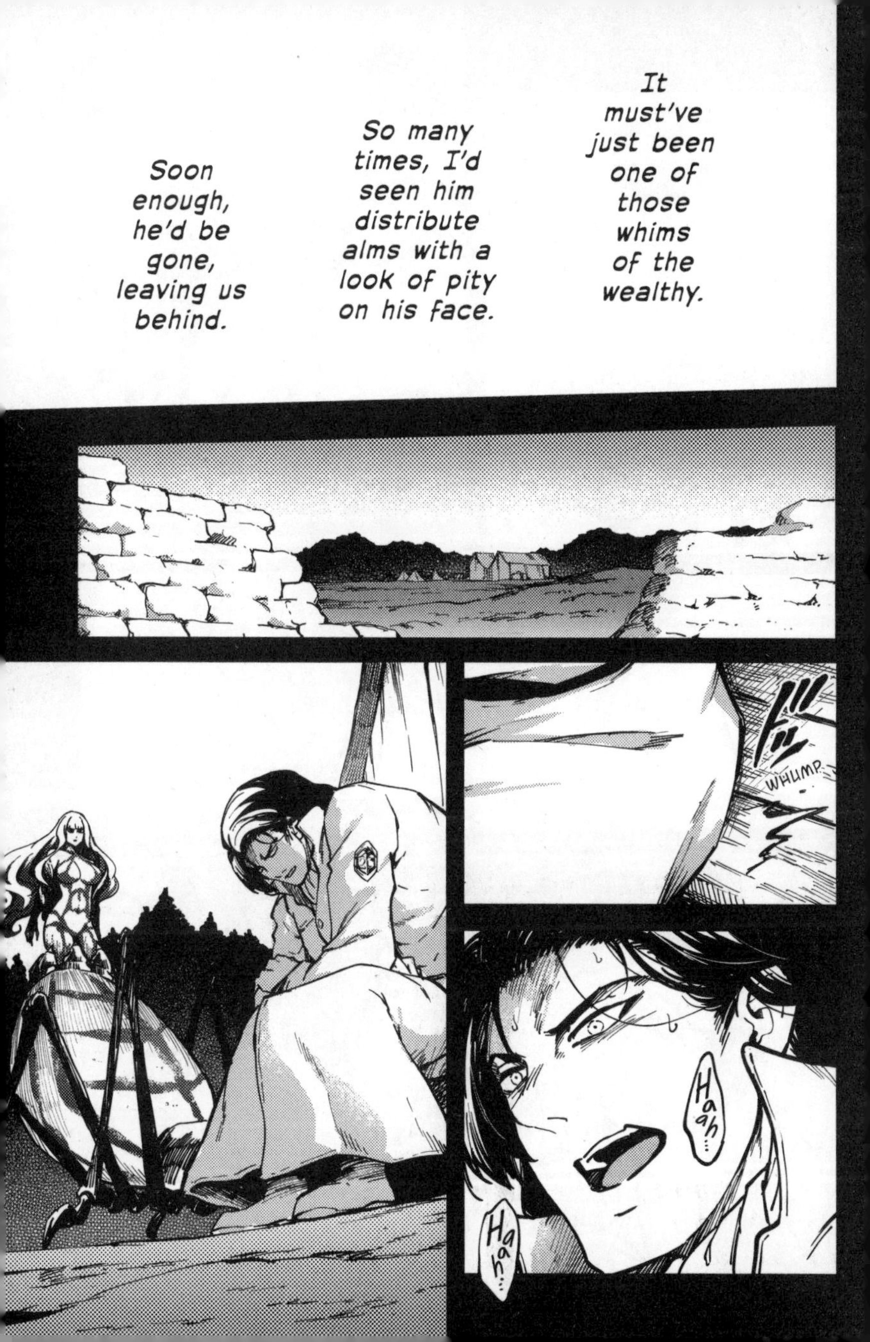
It must've just been one of those whims of the wealthy.
So many times, I'd seen him distribute alms with a look of pity on his face.
Soon enough, he'd be gone, leaving us behind.
WHUMP
Haah...
Haah...

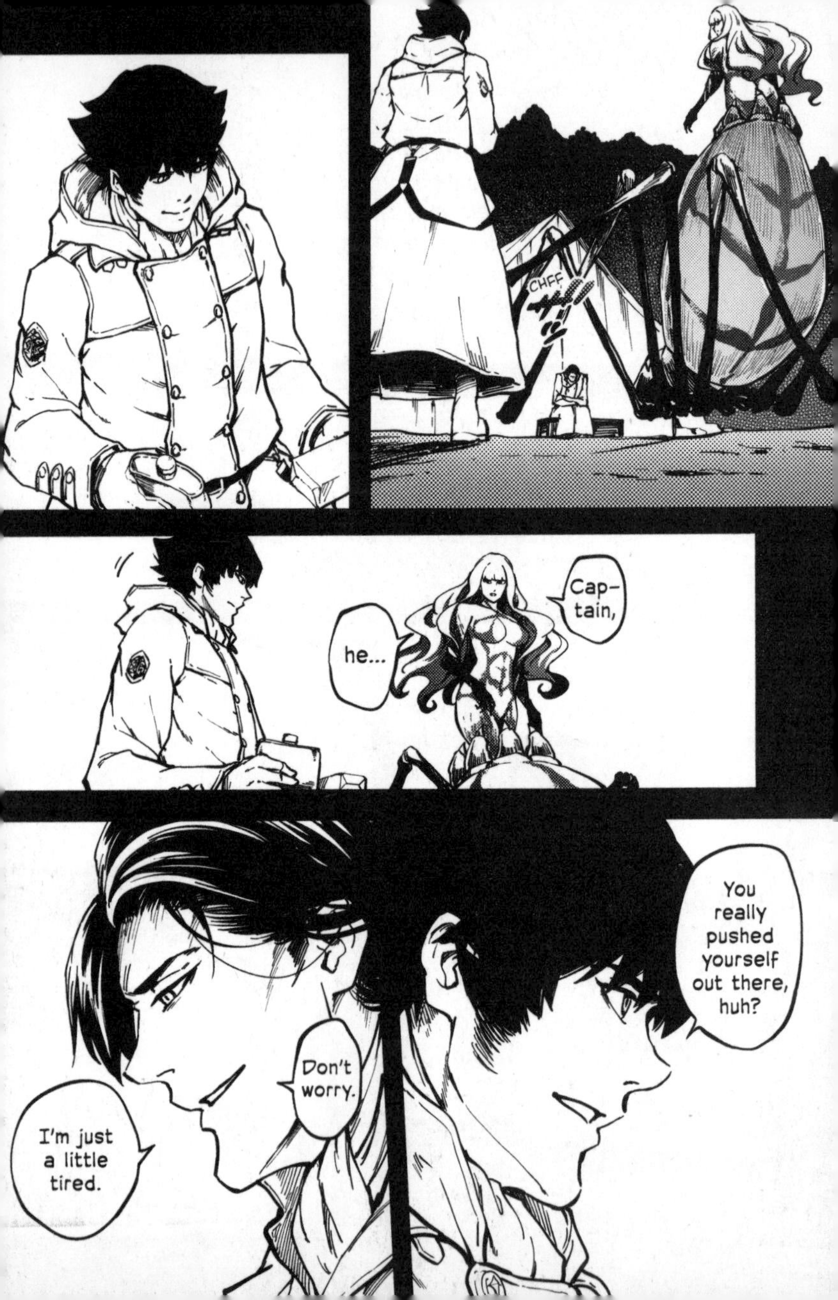
CHFF
Cap-tain,
he...
You really pushed yourself out there, huh?
Don't worry.
I'm just a little tired.

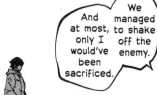
We managed to shake off the enemy.

And at most, only I would've been sacrificed.

It was more than a fair gamble compared to losing all of you.

Sorry.

...Fine.

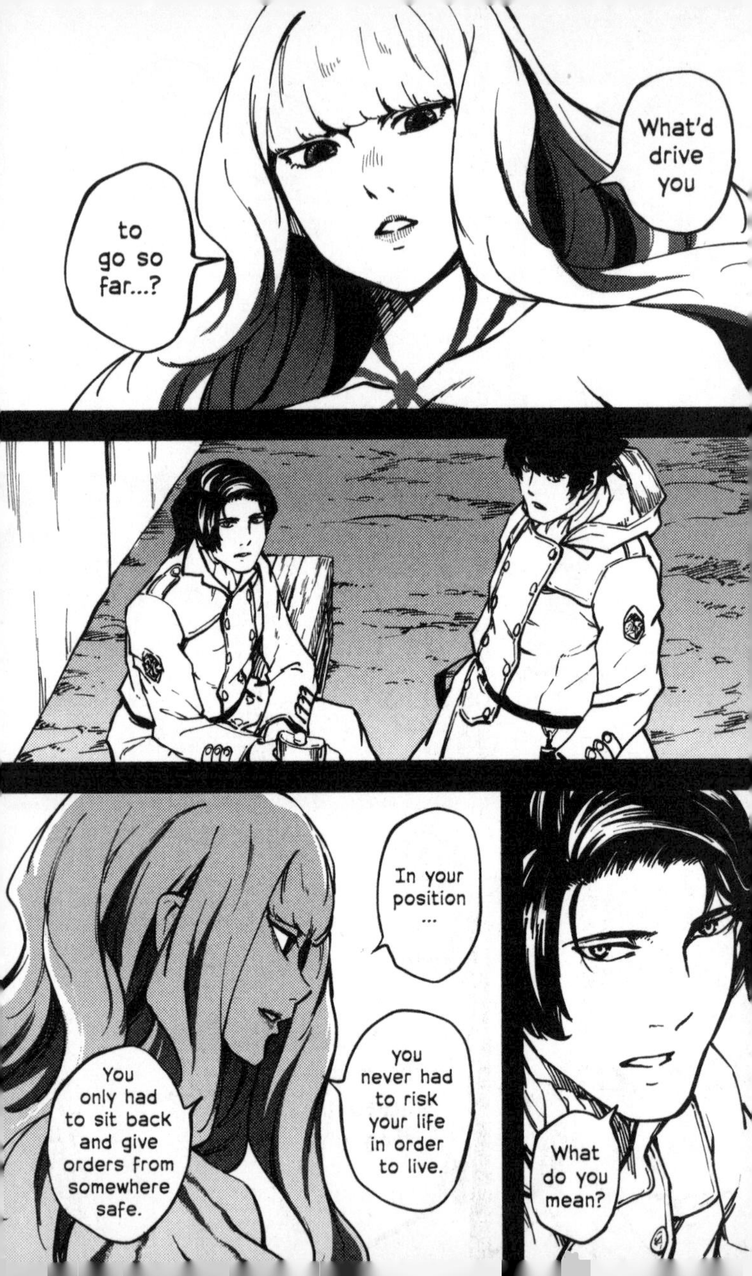
What'd drive you
to go so far...?
What do you mean?
In your position ...
you never had to risk your life in order to live.
You only had to sit back and give orders from somewhere safe.

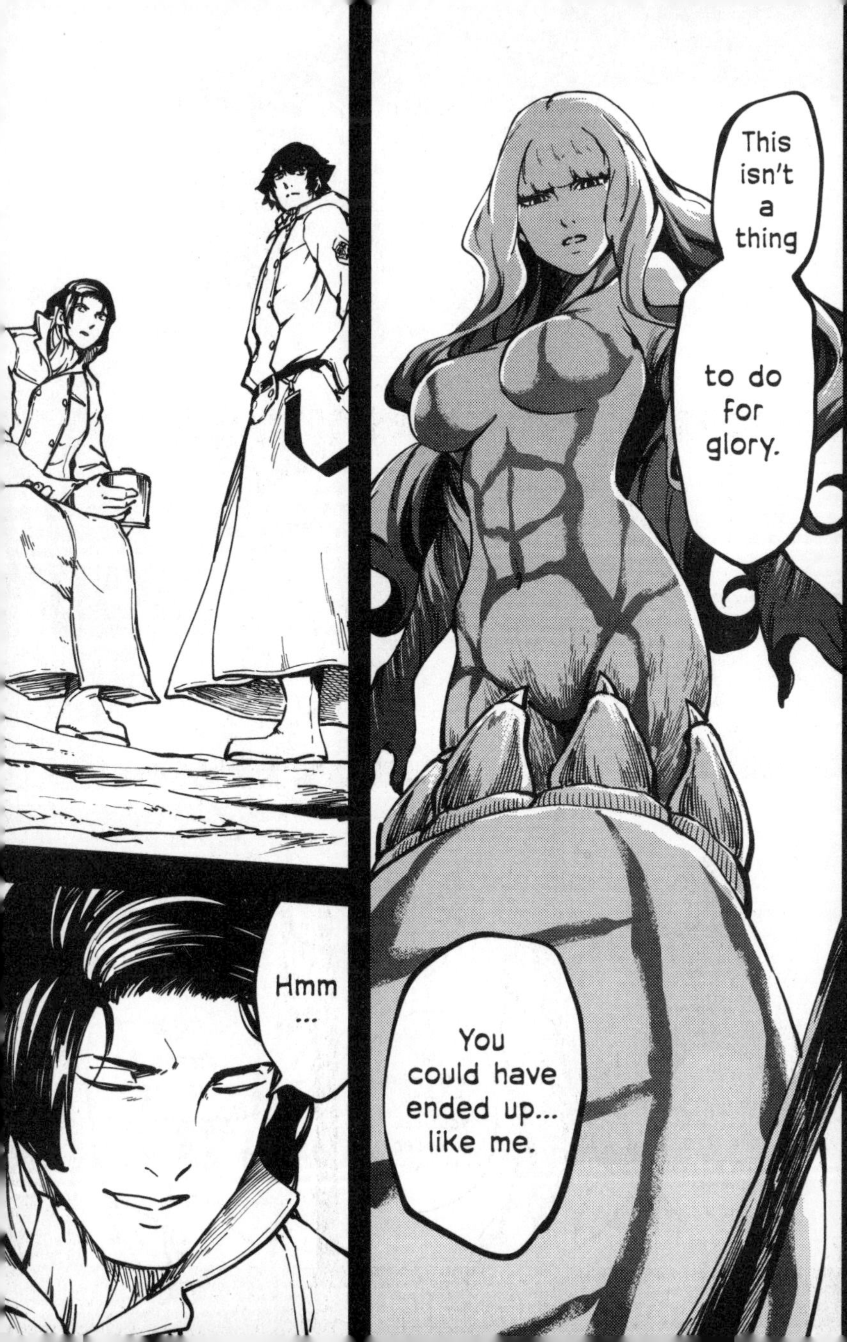
This isn't a thing to do for glory.
You could have ended up... like me.
Hmm ...

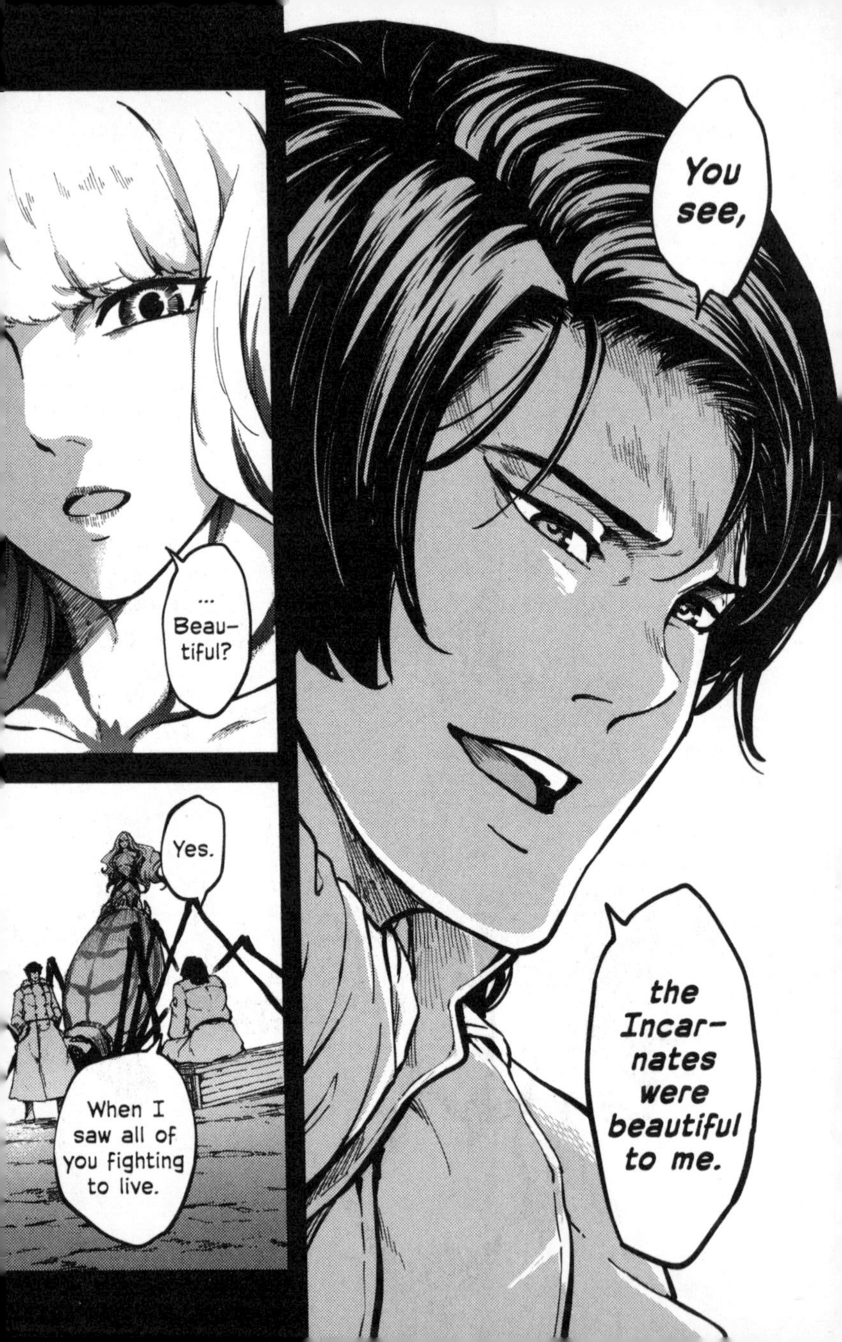
You see,
the Incarnates were beautiful to me.
... Beautiful?
Yes.
When I saw all of you fighting to live.

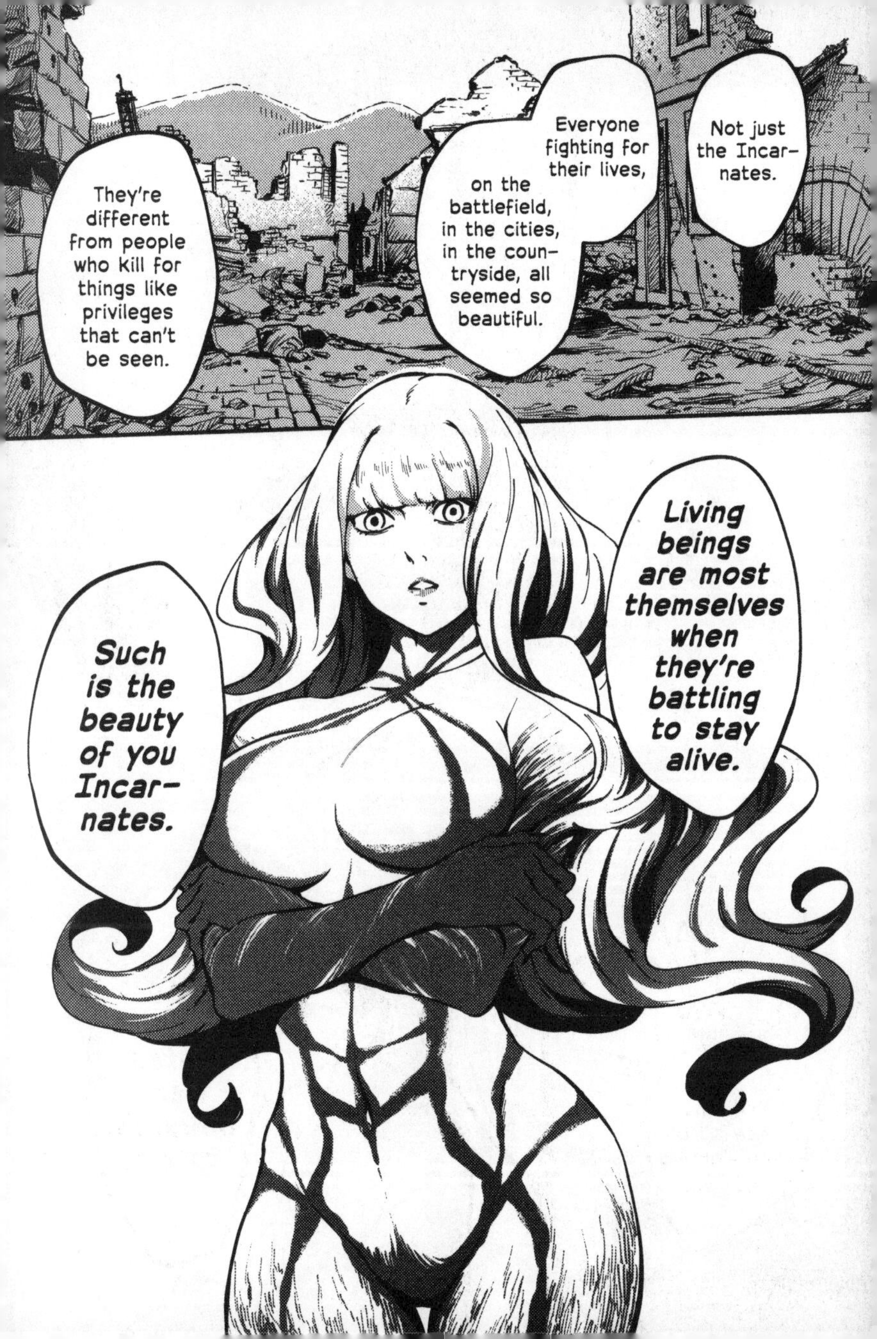
Not just the Incar- nates.
Everyone fighting for their lives,
on the battlefield, in the cities, in the coun- tryside, all seemed so beautiful.
They're different from people who kill for things like privileges that can't be seen.
Living beings are most themselves when they're battling to stay alive.
Such is the beauty of you Incar- nates.

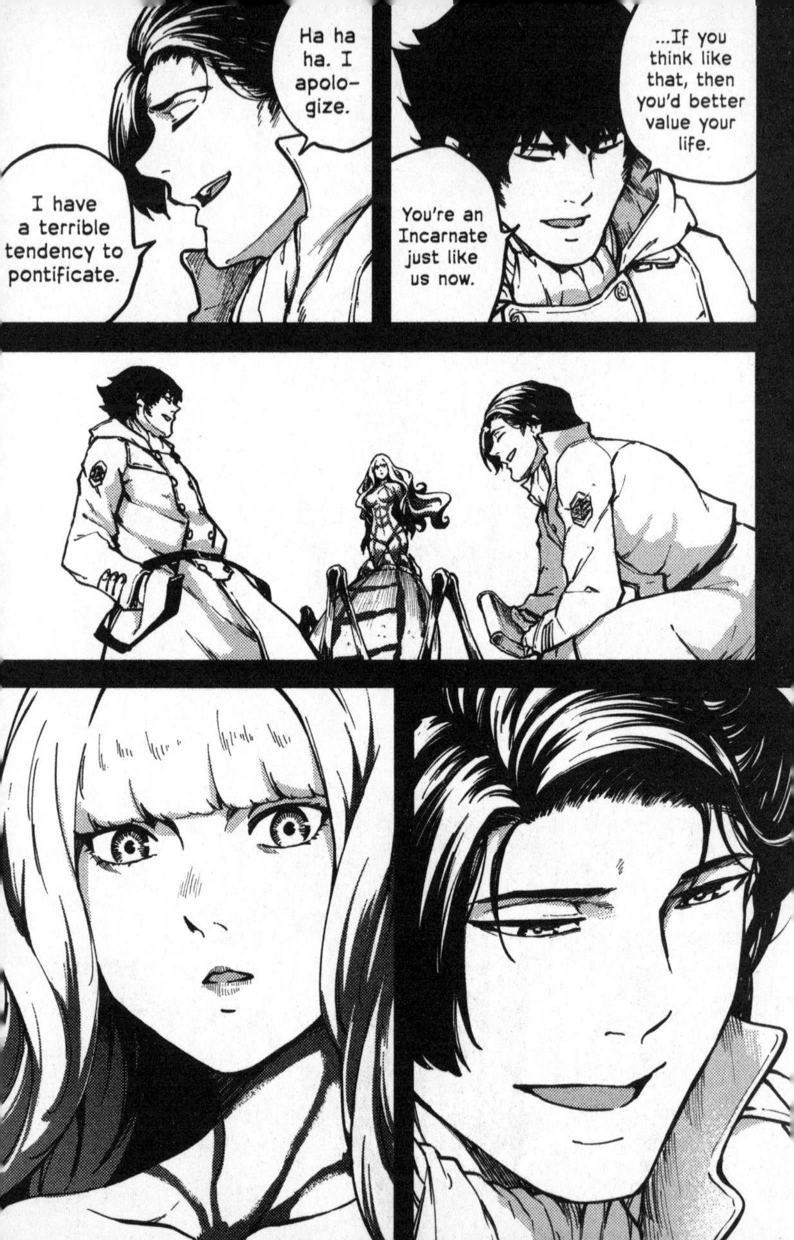
...If you think like that, then you'd better value your life.
You're an Incarnate just like us now.
Ha ha ha. I apologize.
I have a terrible tendency to pontificate.

To the Abandoned
Sacred Beasts

To the Abandoned
Sacred Beasts

Chapter 69: The Arachne's Threads (Pt. 2)

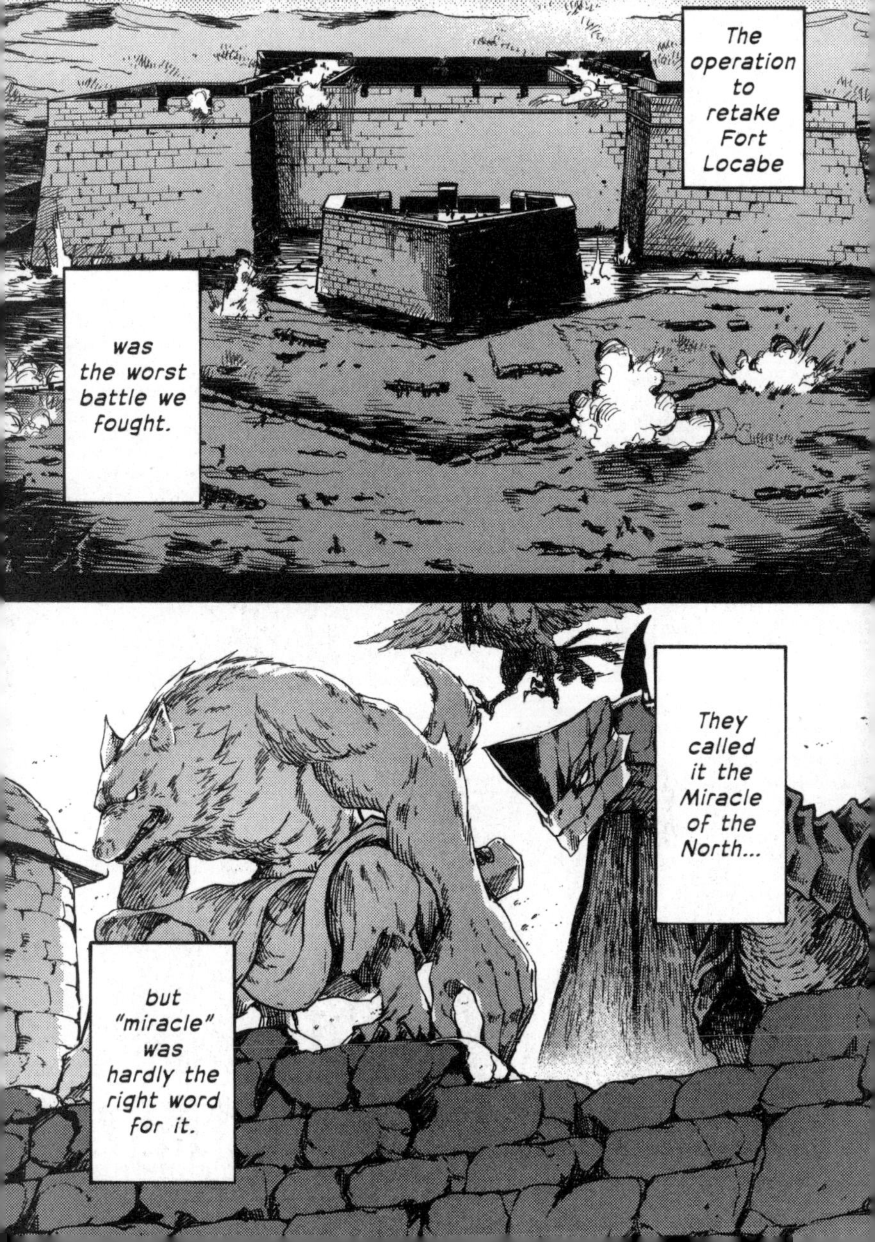
The operation to retake Fort Locabe
was the worst battle we fought.
They called it the Miracle of the North...
but "miracle" was hardly the right word for it.

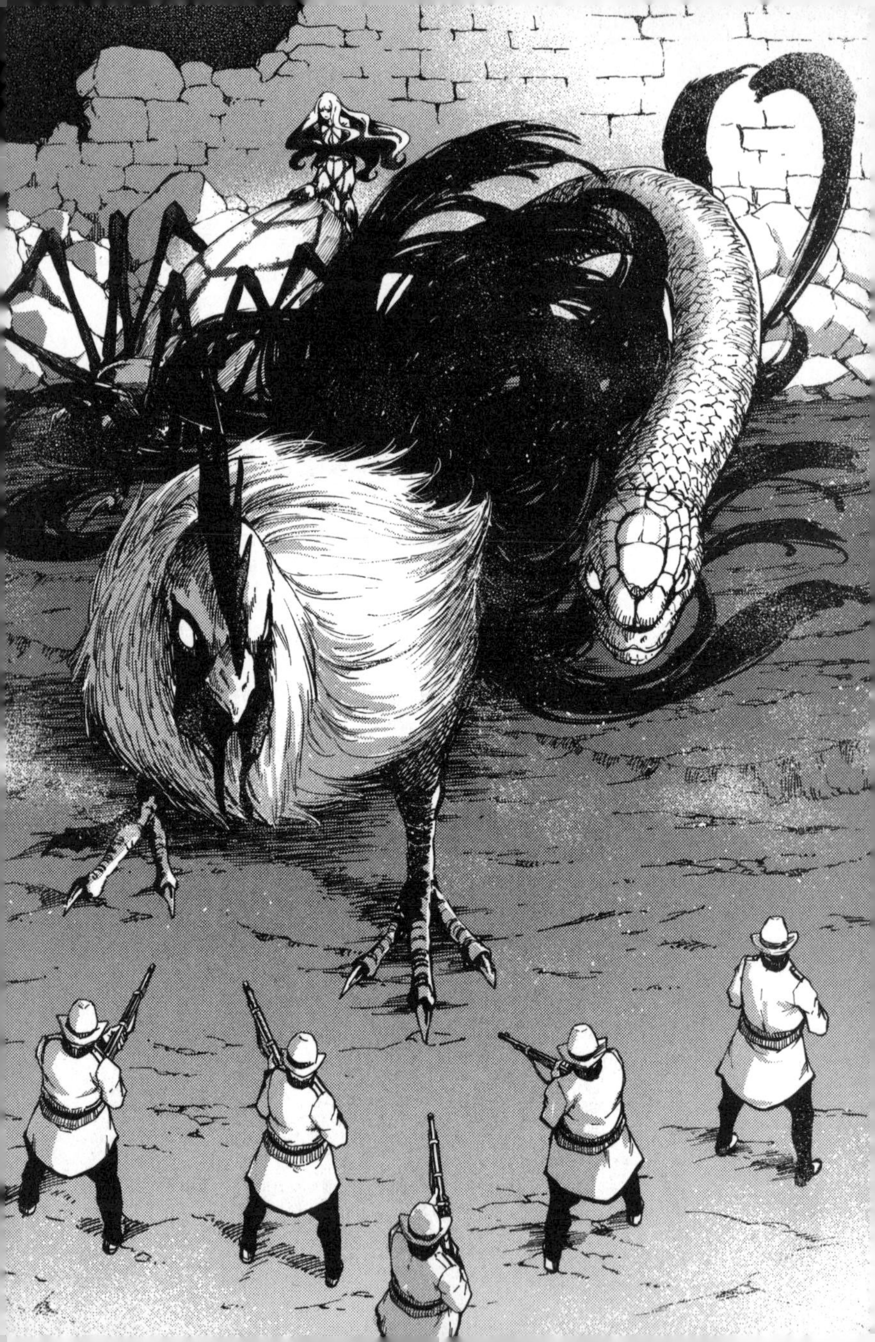

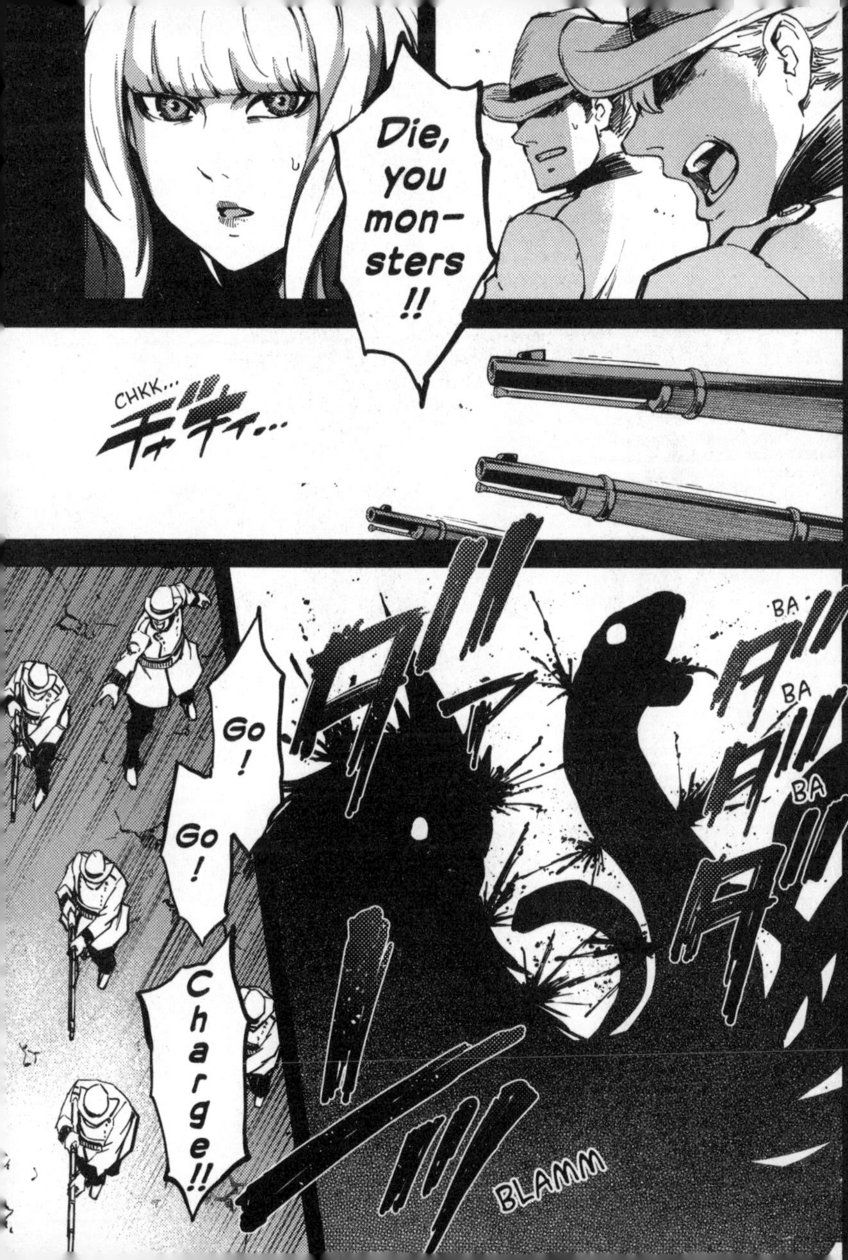
Die, you mon-sters!!
CHKK...
チャキィ...
BA
BA
BA
Go!
Go!
Charge!!
BLAMM

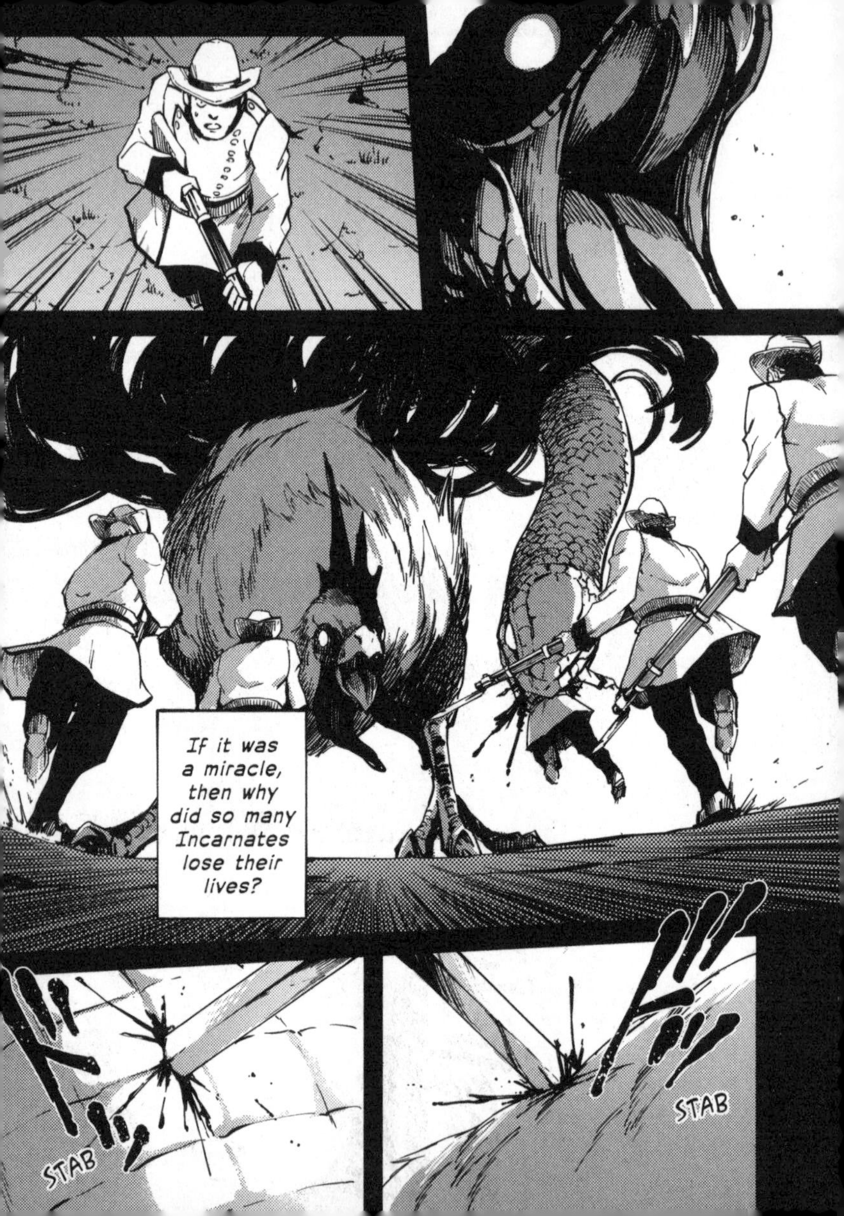
If it was a miracle, then why did so many Incarnates lose their lives?
STAB
STAB

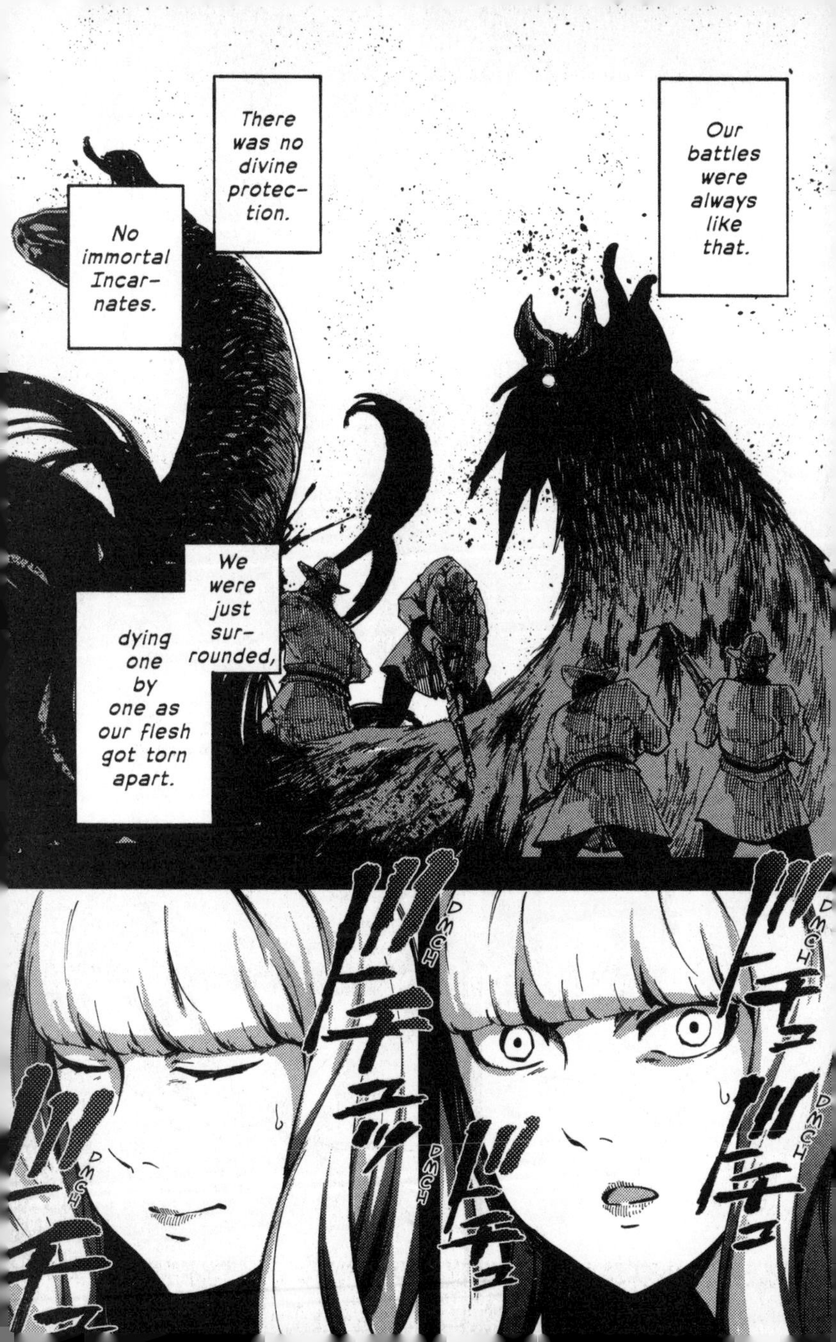
Our battles were always like that.
There was no divine protection.
No immortal Incarnates.
We were just surrounded,
dying one by one as our flesh got torn apart.
DMCH
DMCH
DMCH
DMCH

Still
...

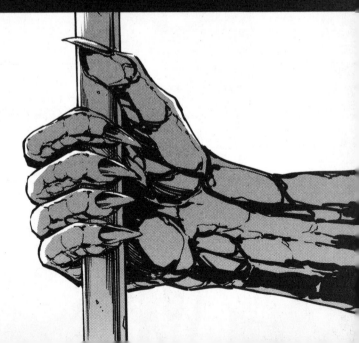

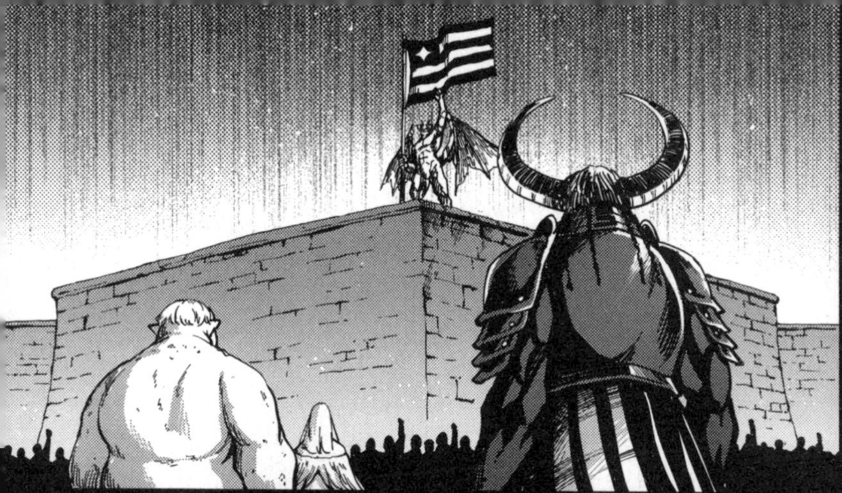
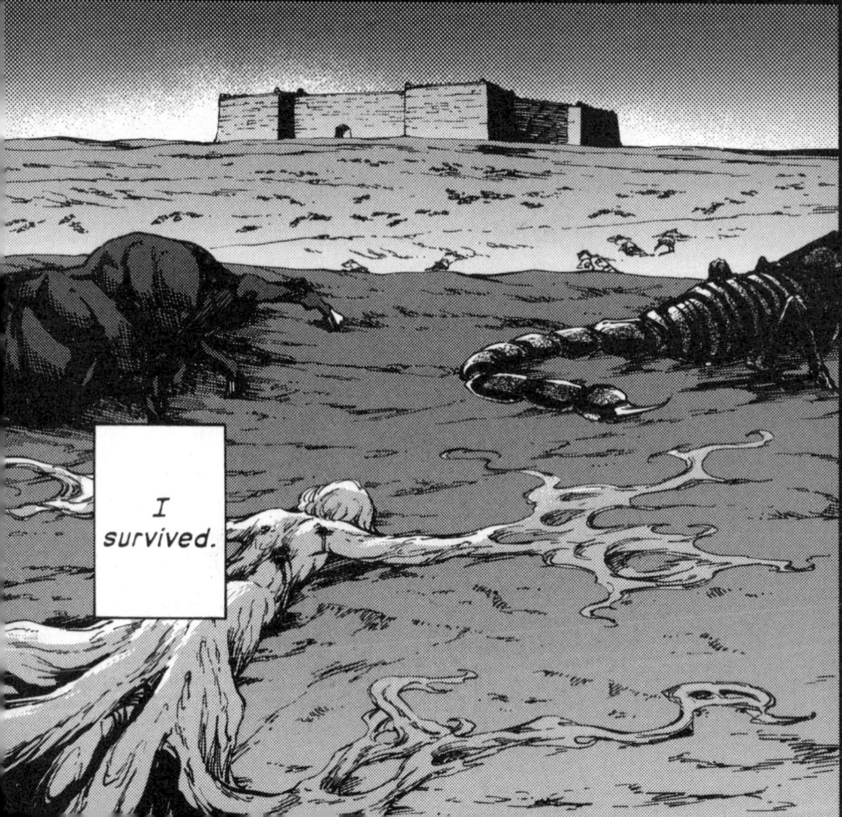
I survived.

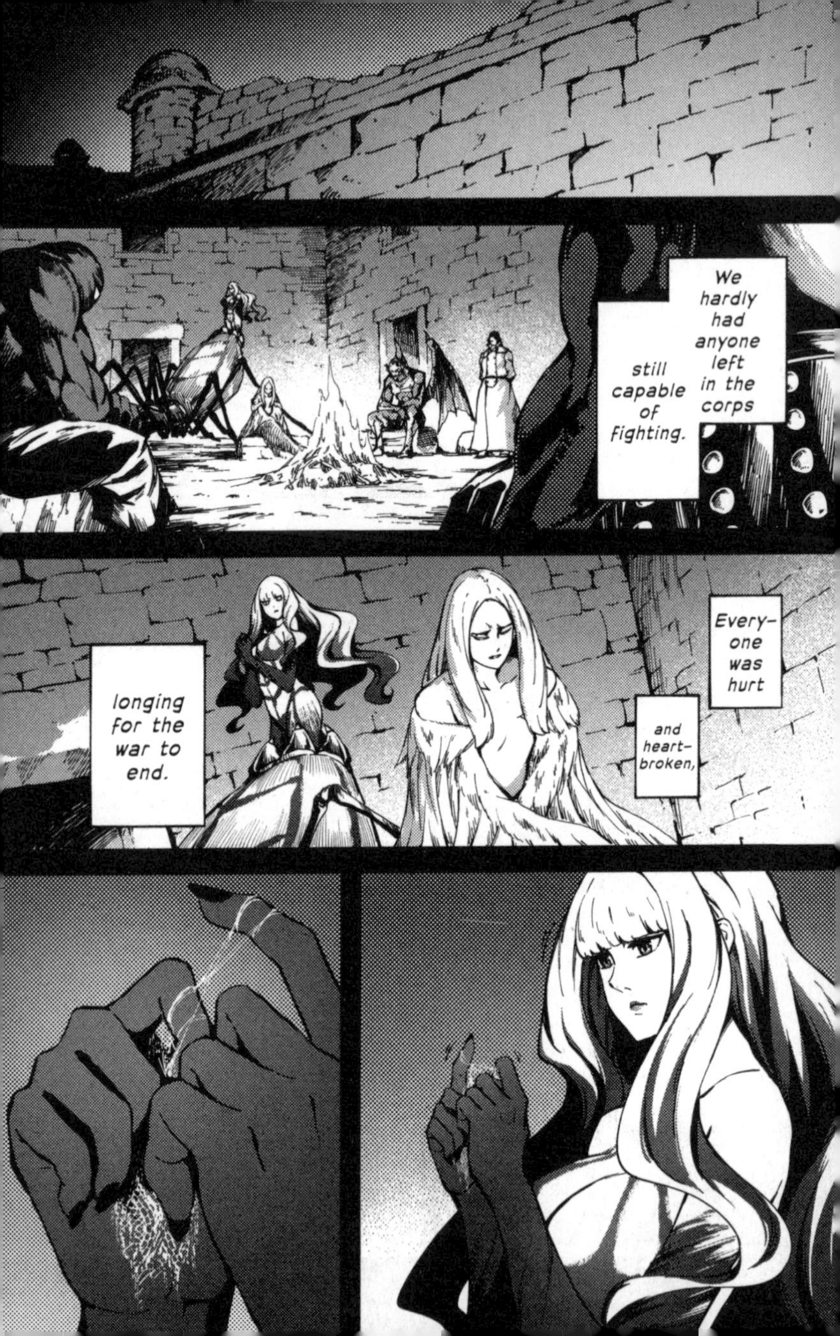
We hardly had anyone left in the corps
still capable of fighting.
Every-one was hurt
and heart-broken,
longing for the war to end.

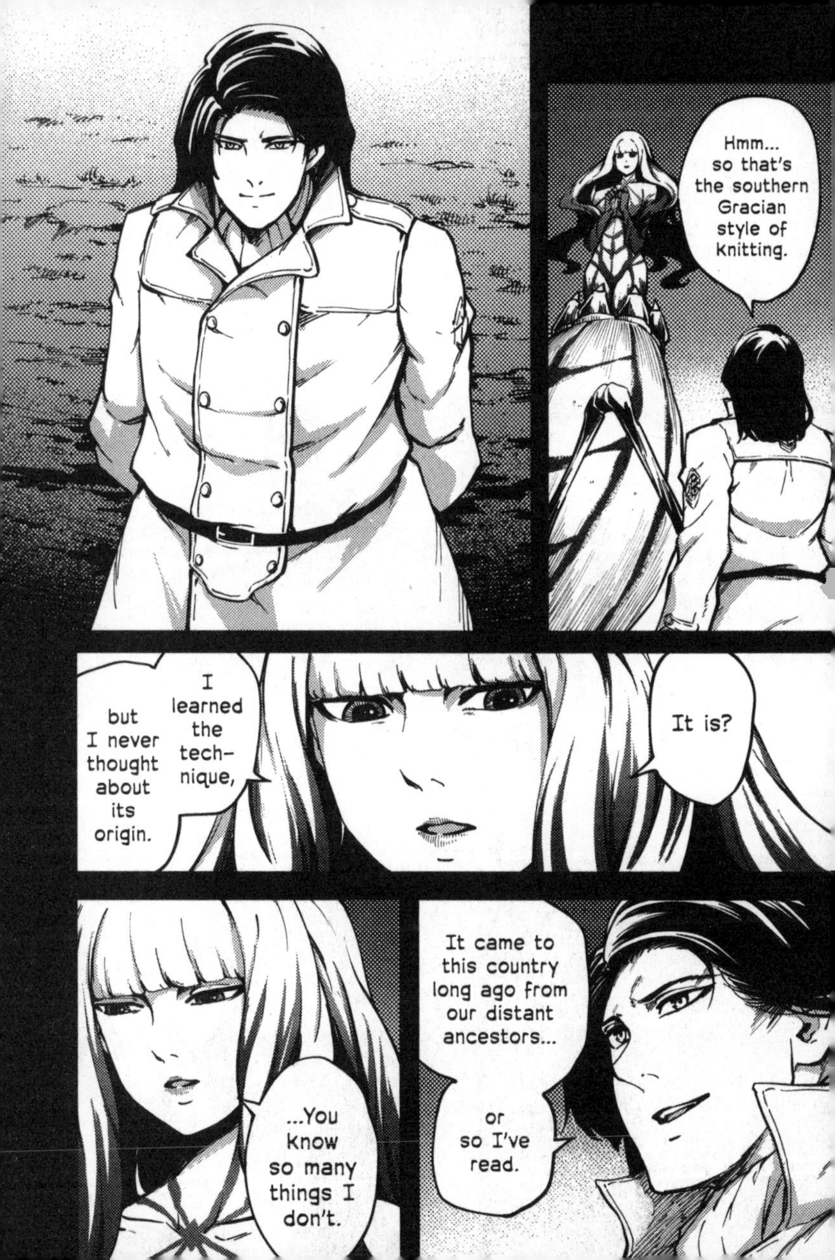
Hmm... so that's the southern Gracian style of knitting.
It is?
I learned the tech-nique,
but I never thought about its origin.
It came to this country long ago from our distant ancestors...
or so I've read.
...You know so many things I don't.

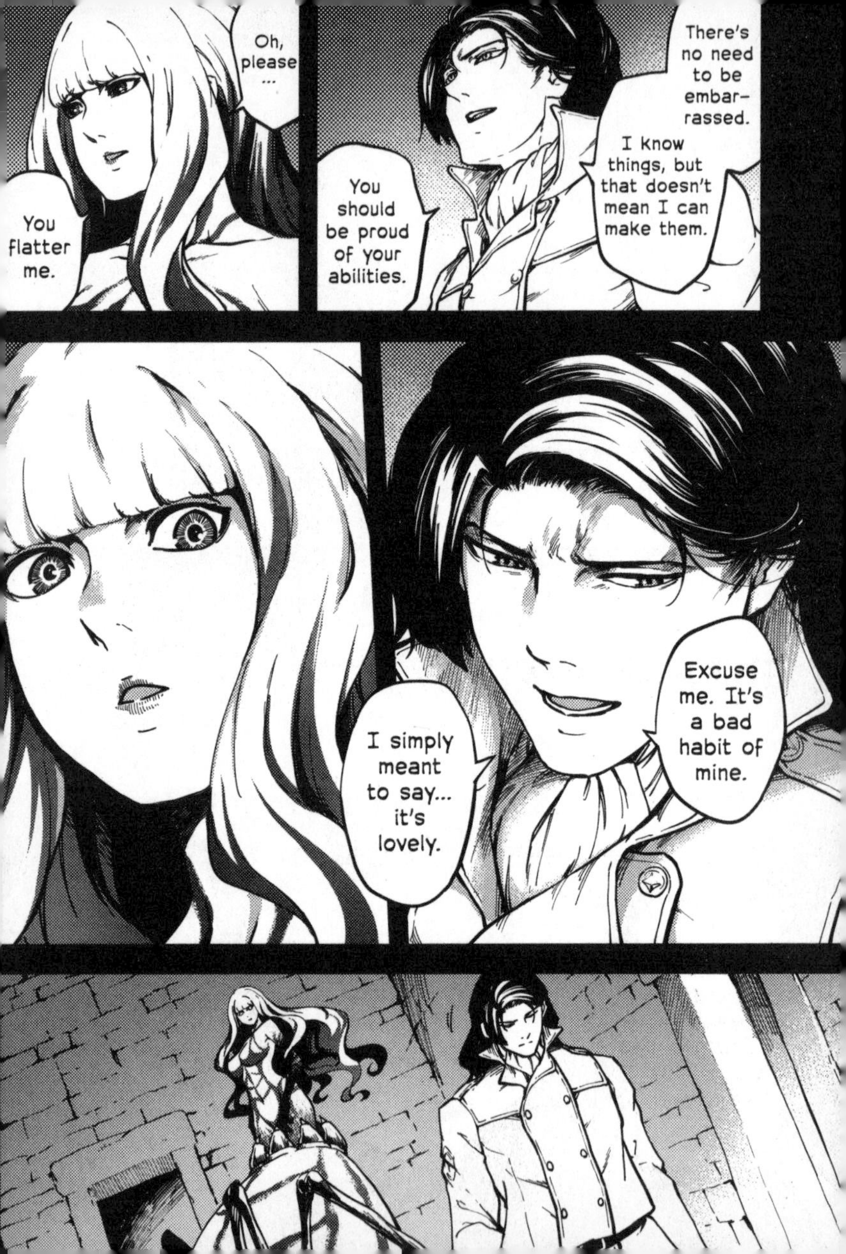
There's no need to be embarrassed.
I know things, but that doesn't mean I can make them.
You should be proud of your abilities.
Oh, please...
You flatter me.
Excuse me. It's a bad habit of mine.
I simply meant to say... it's lovely.

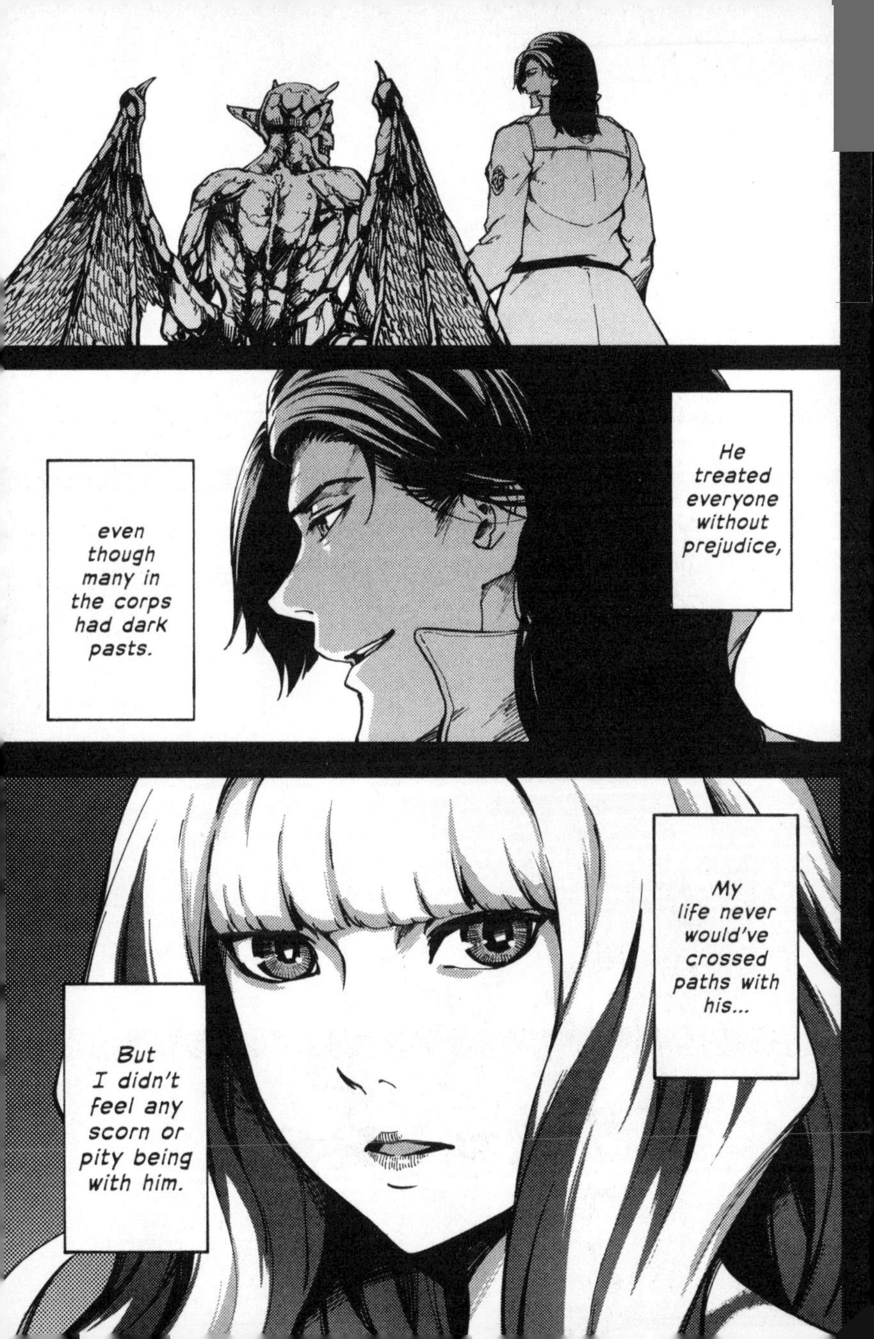
He treated everyone without prejudice,
even though many in the corps had dark pasts.
My life never would've crossed paths with his...
But I didn't feel any scorn or pity being with him.

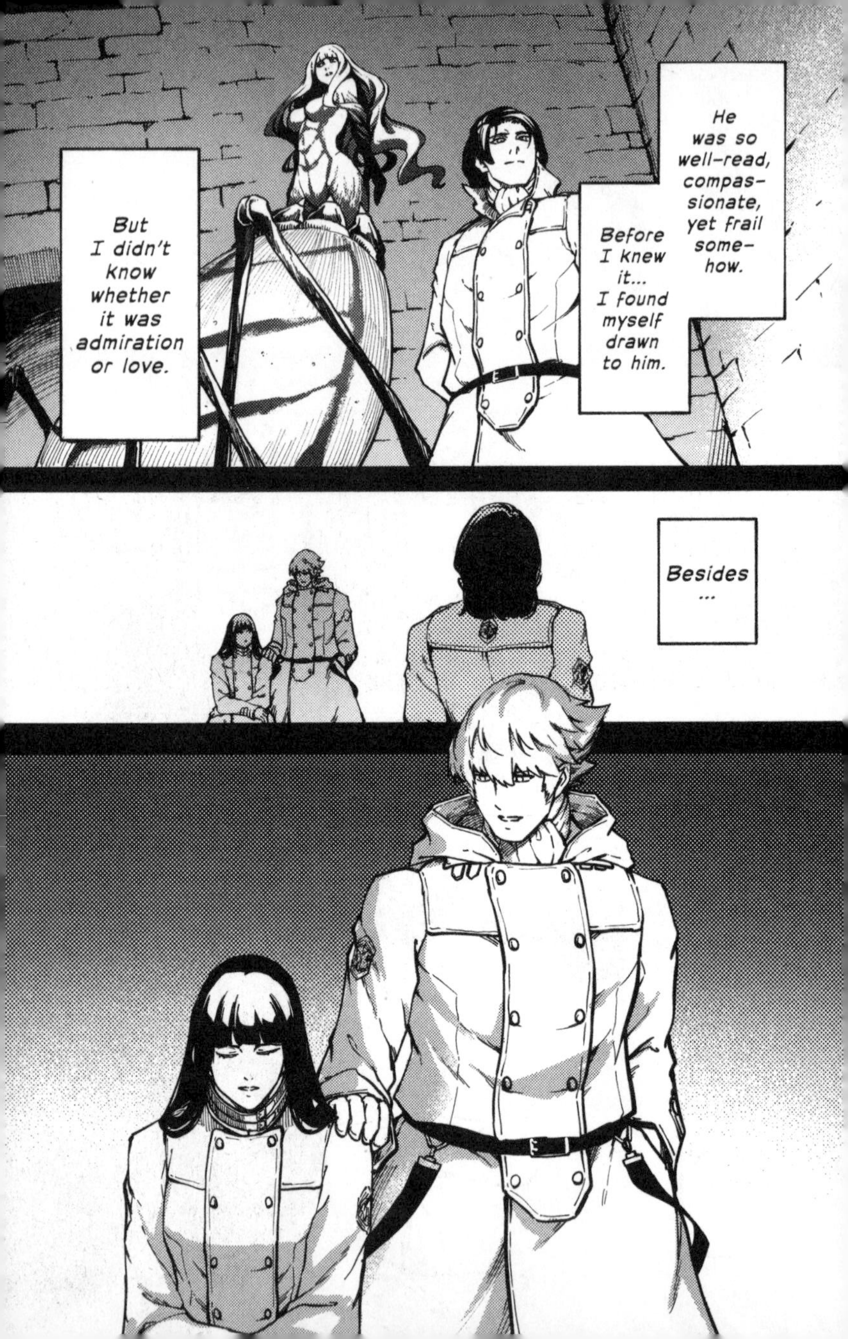
He was so well-read, compassionate, yet frail somehow.
Before I knew it... I found myself drawn to him.
But I didn't know whether it was admiration or love.
Besides
...

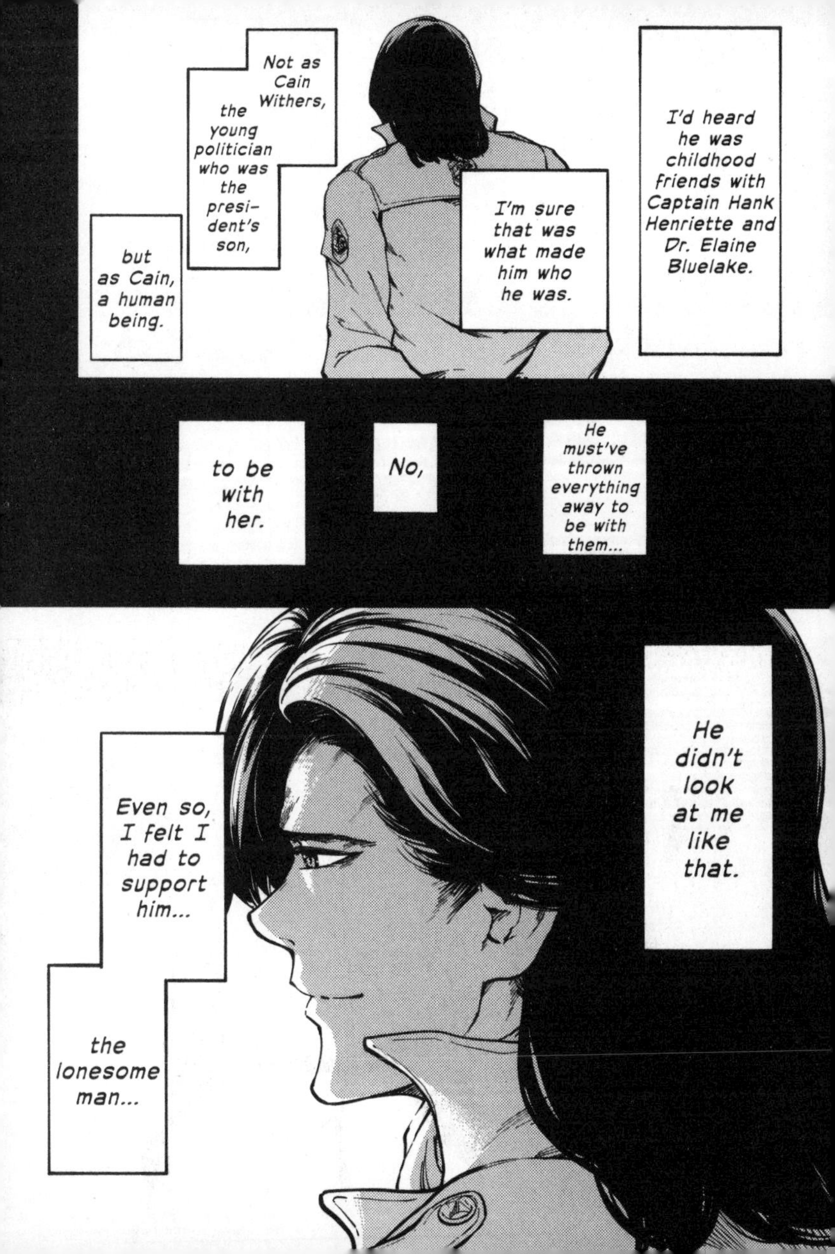
I'd heard he was childhood friends with Captain Hank Henriette and Dr. Elaine Bluelake.
I'm sure that was what made him who he was.
Not as Cain Withers,
the young politician who was the president's son,
but as Cain, a human being.
He must've thrown everything away to be with them...
No,
to be with her.
He didn't look at me like that.
Even so, I felt I had to support him...
the lonesome man...

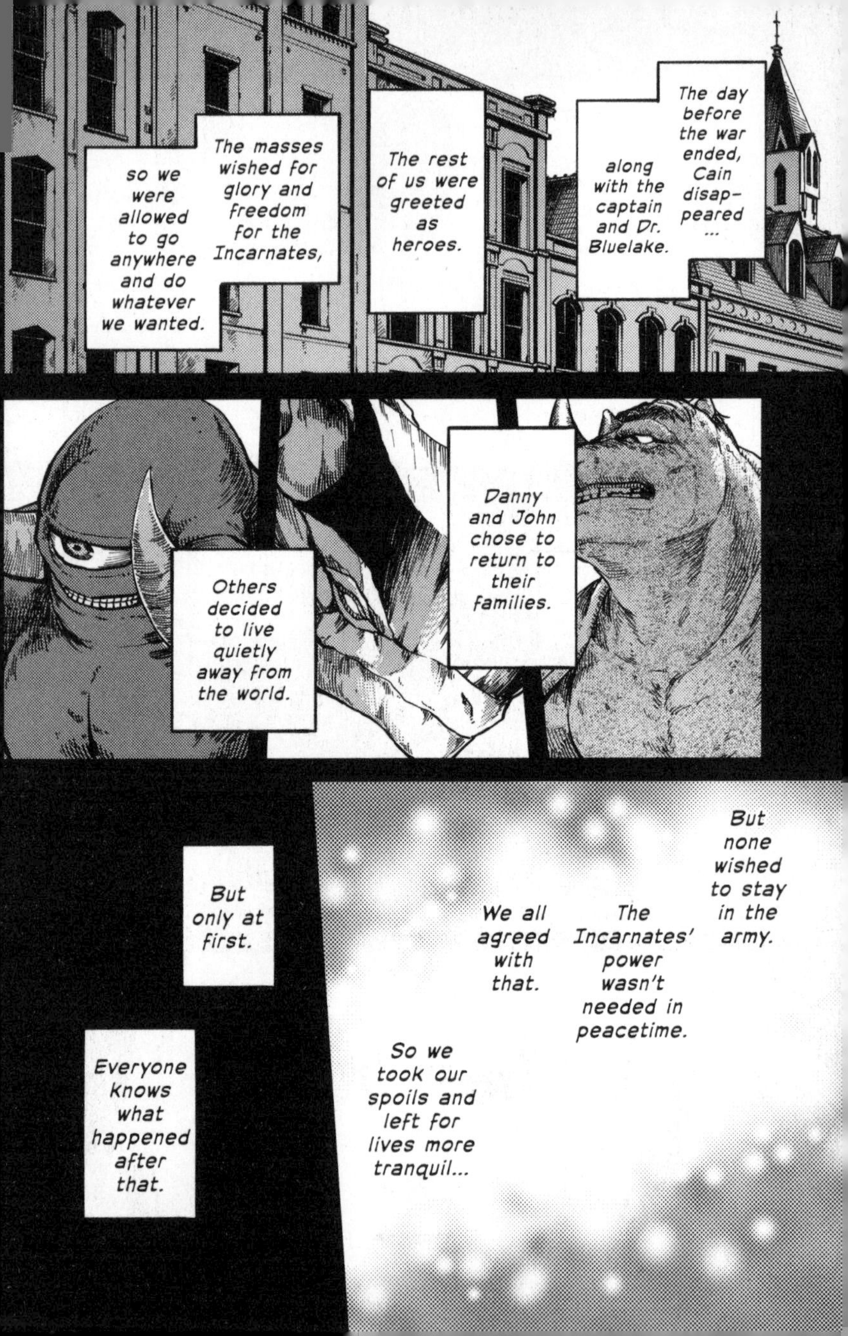
The day before the war ended, Cain disap-peared ...
along with the captain and Dr. Bluelake.
The rest of us were greeted as heroes.
The masses wished for glory and freedom for the Incarnates,
so we were allowed to go anywhere and do whatever we wanted.
Danny and John chose to return to their families.
Others decided to live quietly away from the world.
But none wished to stay in the army.
The Incarnates' power wasn't needed in peacetime.
We all agreed with that.
So we took our spoils and left for lives more tranquil...
But only at first.
Everyone knows what happened after that.

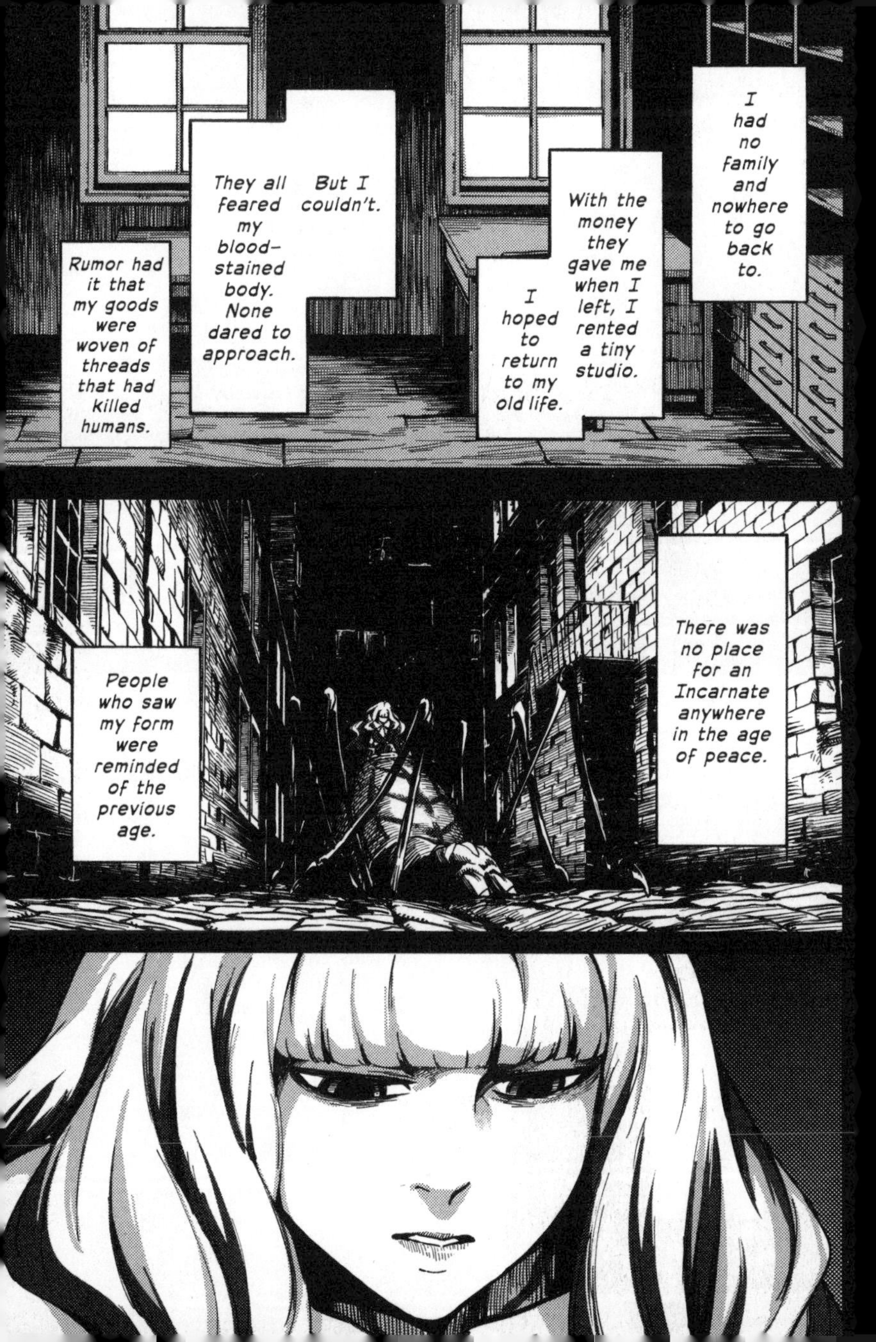
I had no family and nowhere to go back to.
With the money they gave me when I left, I rented a tiny studio.
I hoped to return to my old life.
But I couldn't.
They all feared my blood-stained body. None dared to approach.
Rumor had it that my goods were woven of threads that had killed humans.
There was no place for an Incarnate anywhere in the age of peace.
People who saw my form were reminded of the previous age.

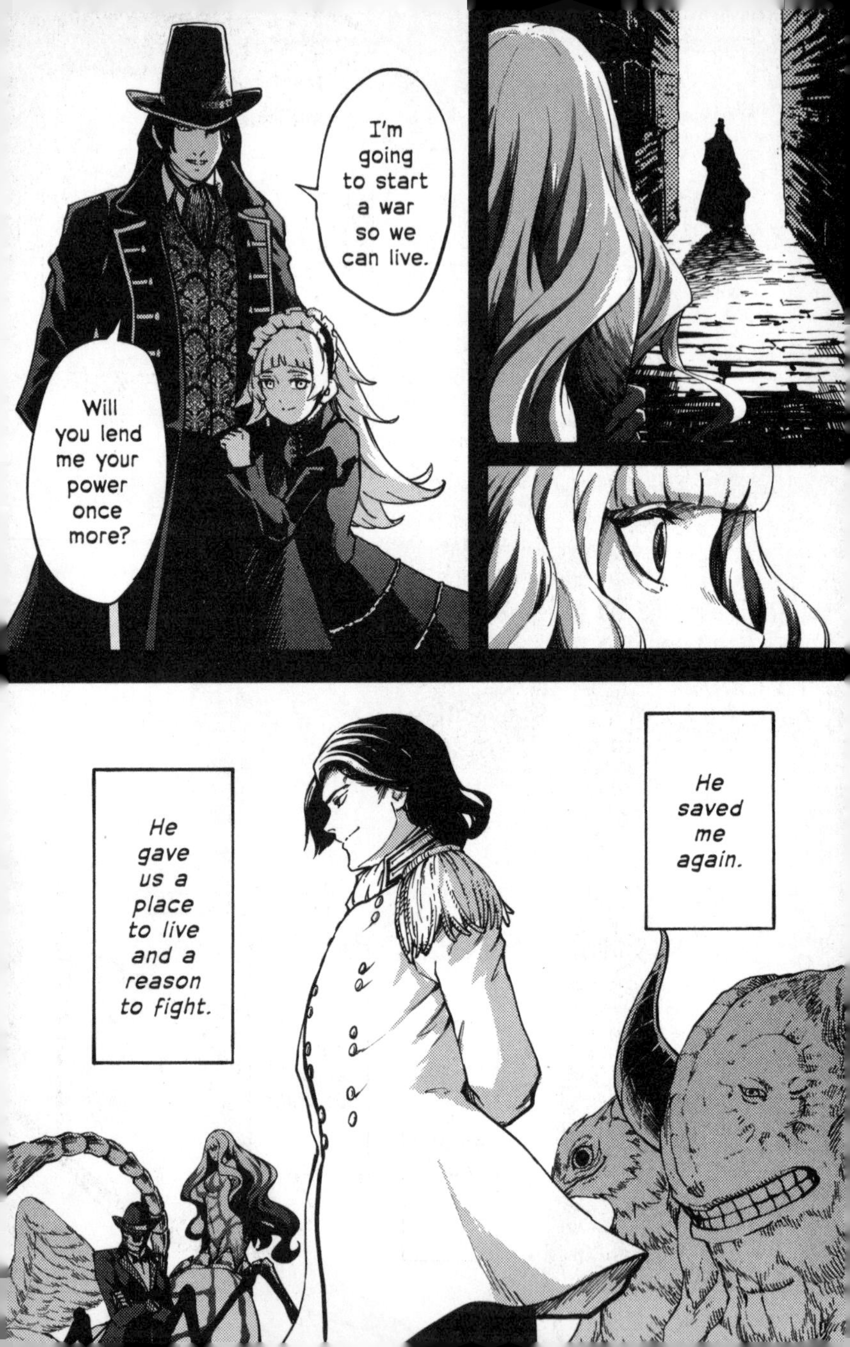
I'm going to start a war so we can live.
Will you lend me your power once more?
He saved me again.
He gave us a place to live and a reason to fight.

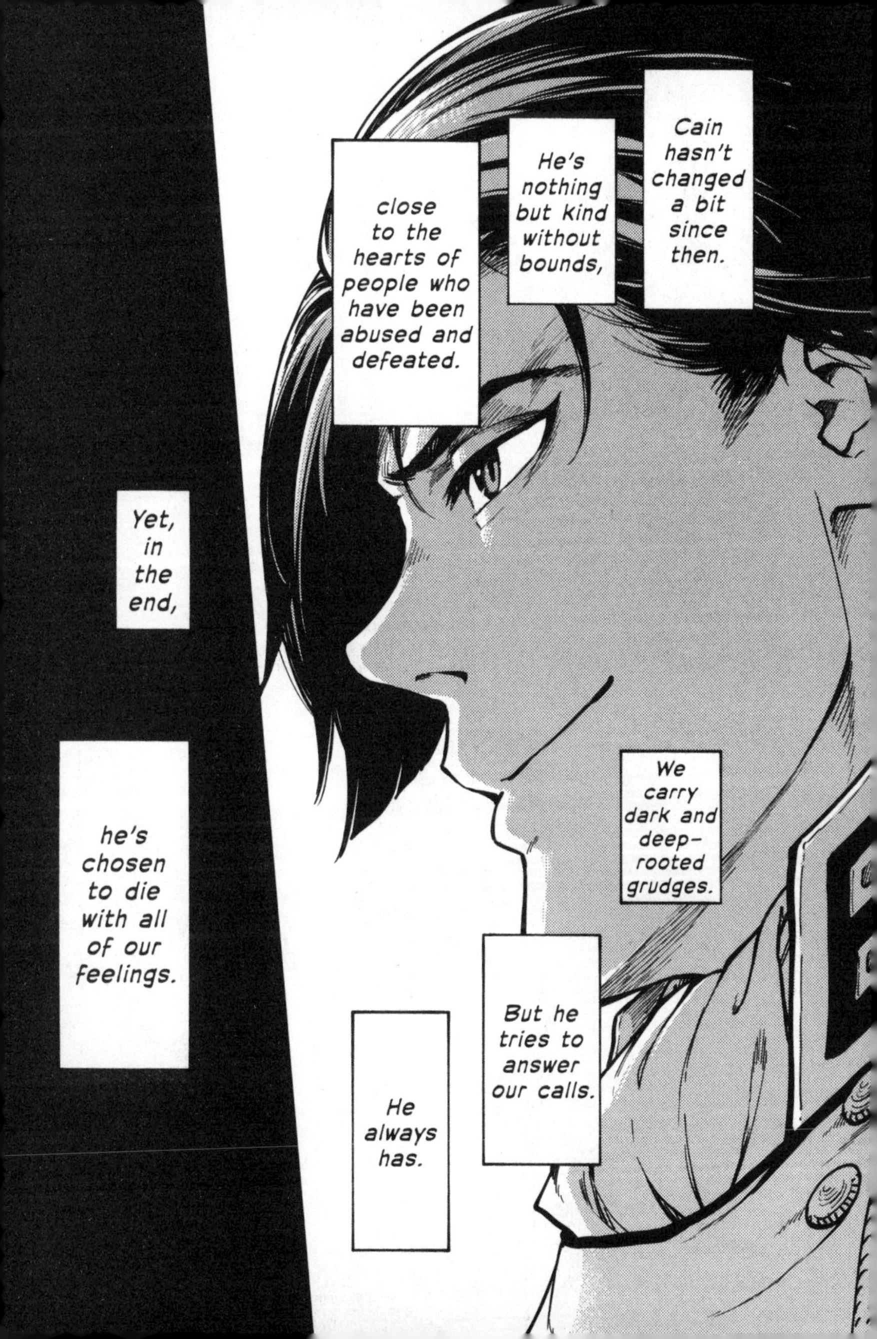
Cain hasn't changed a bit since then.
He's nothing but kind without bounds,
close to the hearts of people who have been abused and defeated.
We carry dark and deep-rooted grudges.
But he tries to answer our calls.
He always has.
Yet, in the end,
he's chosen to die with all of our feelings.

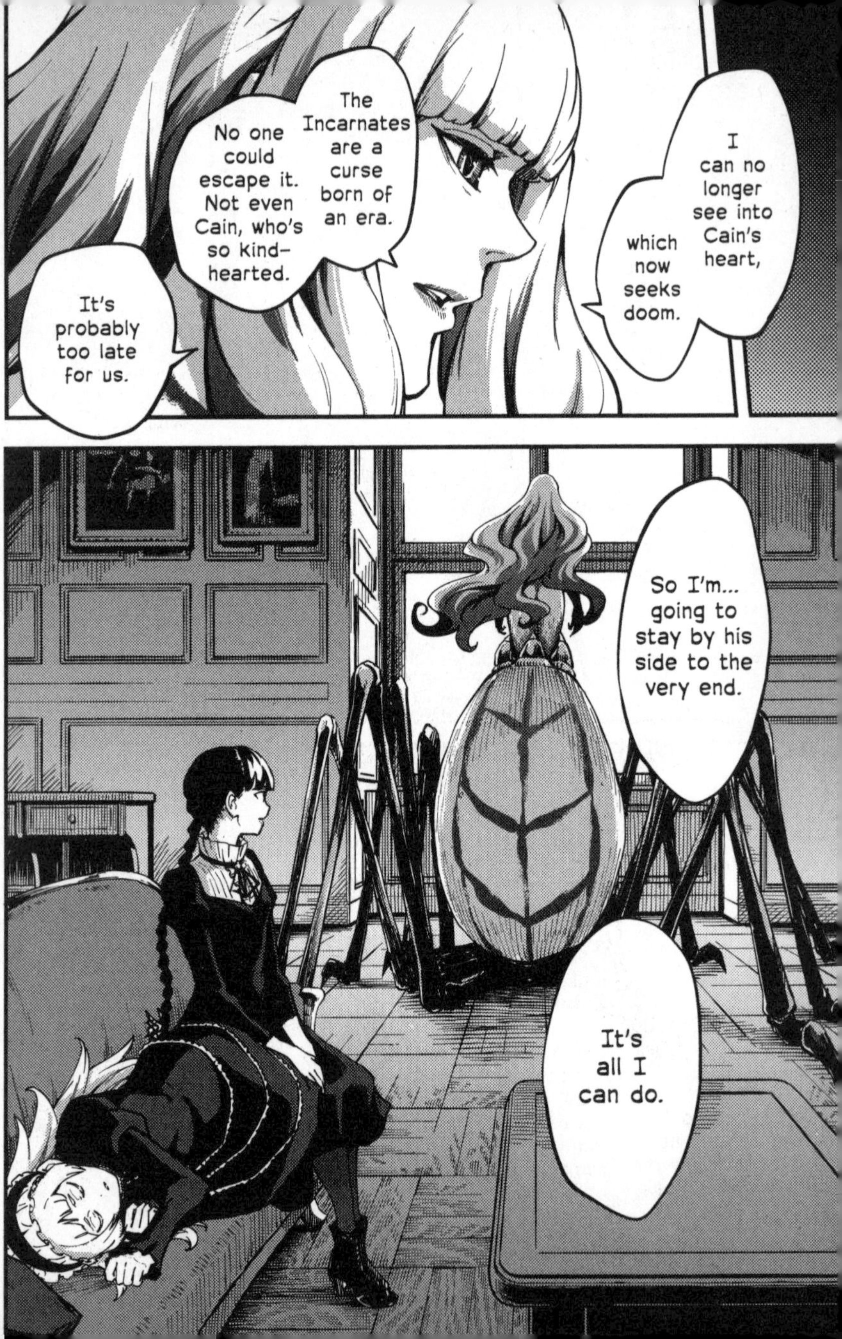
I can no longer see into Cain's heart,
which now seeks doom.
The Incarnates are a curse born of an era.
No one could escape it. Not even Cain, who's so kind-hearted.
It's probably too late for us.
So I'm... going to stay by his side to the very end.
It's all I can do.

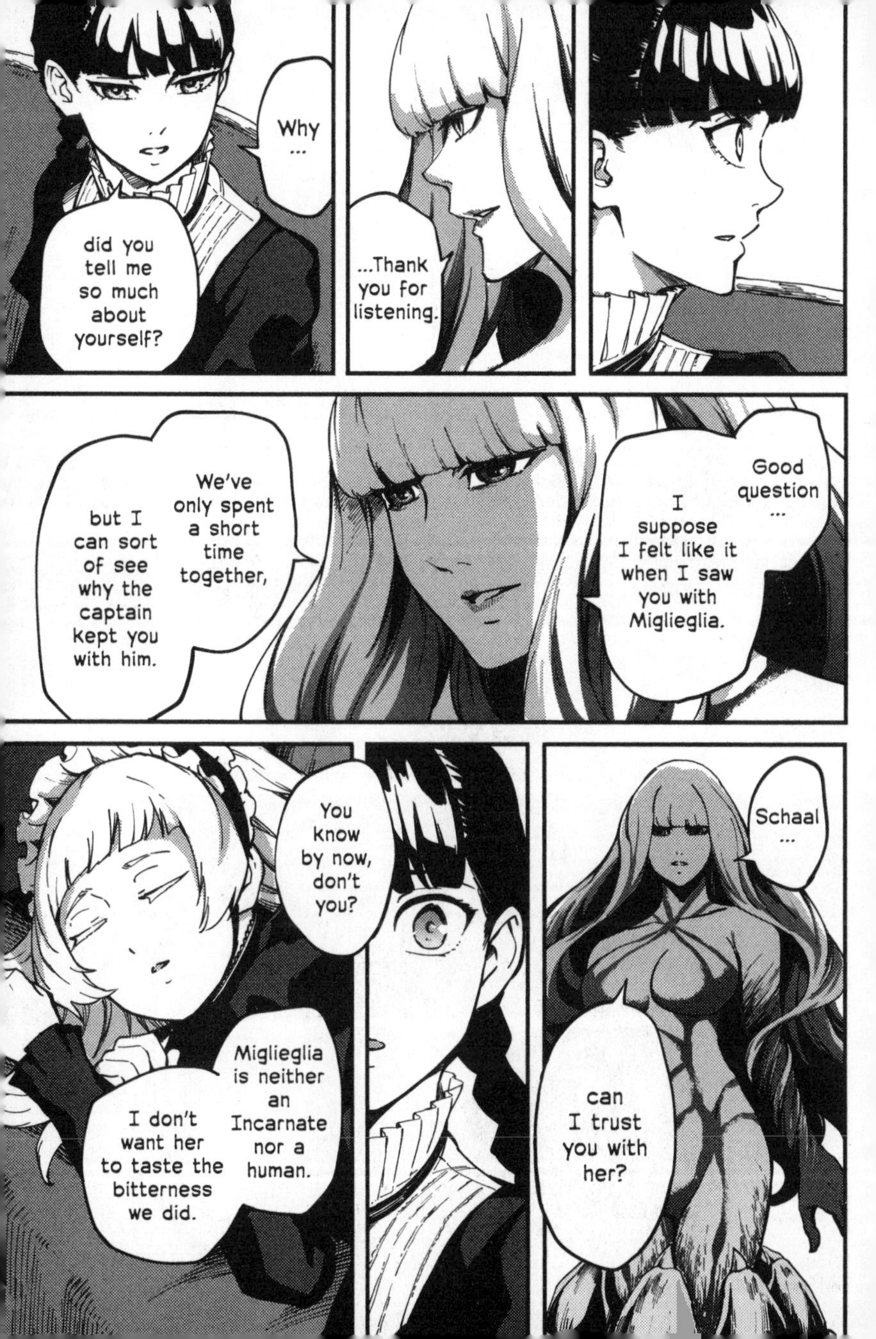
...Thank you for listening.
Why ...
did you tell me so much about yourself?
Good question ...
I suppose I felt like it when I saw you with Miglieglia.
We've only spent a short time together,
but I can sort of see why the captain kept you with him.
Schaal ...
can I trust you with her?
You know by now, don't you?
Miglieglia is neither an Incarnate nor a human.
I don't want her to taste the bitterness we did.

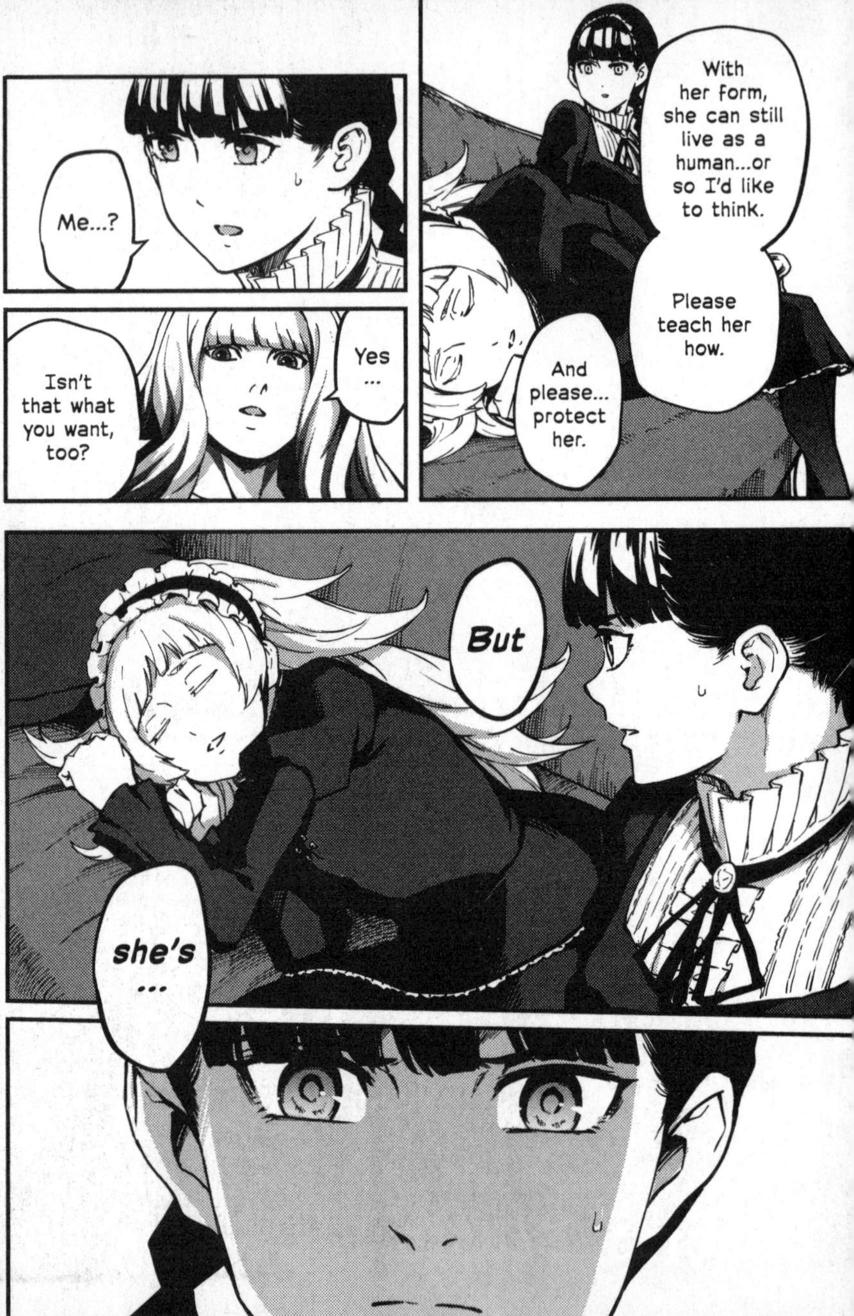
With her form, she can still live as a human...or so I'd like to think.
Please teach her how.
And please... protect her.
Me...?
Yes...
Isn't that what you want, too?
But
she's...

To the Abandoned
Sacred Beasts

To the Abandoned
Sacred Beasts

Chapter 70: Encounter (Pt. 1)

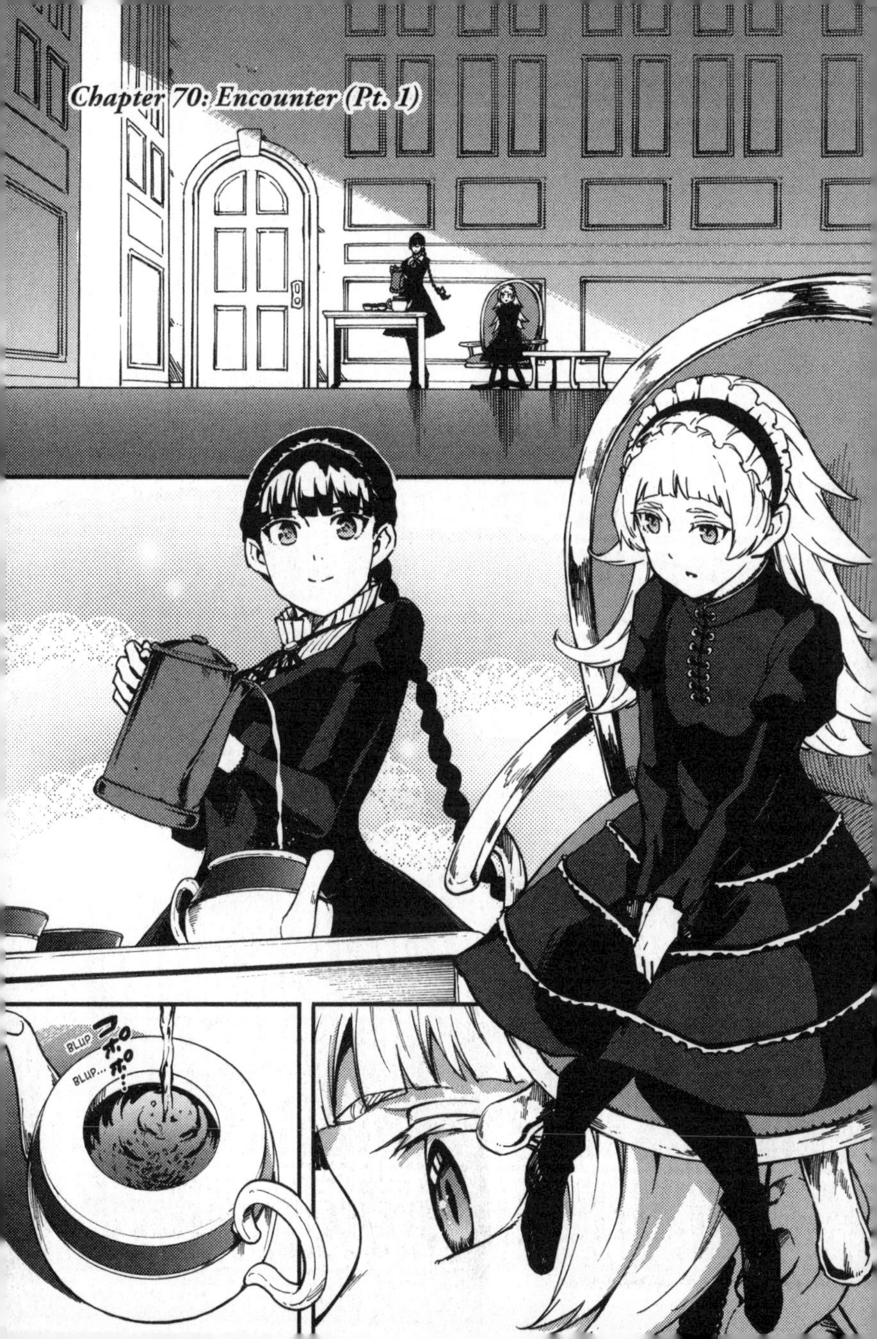
コポポ…
BLUP
BLUP...

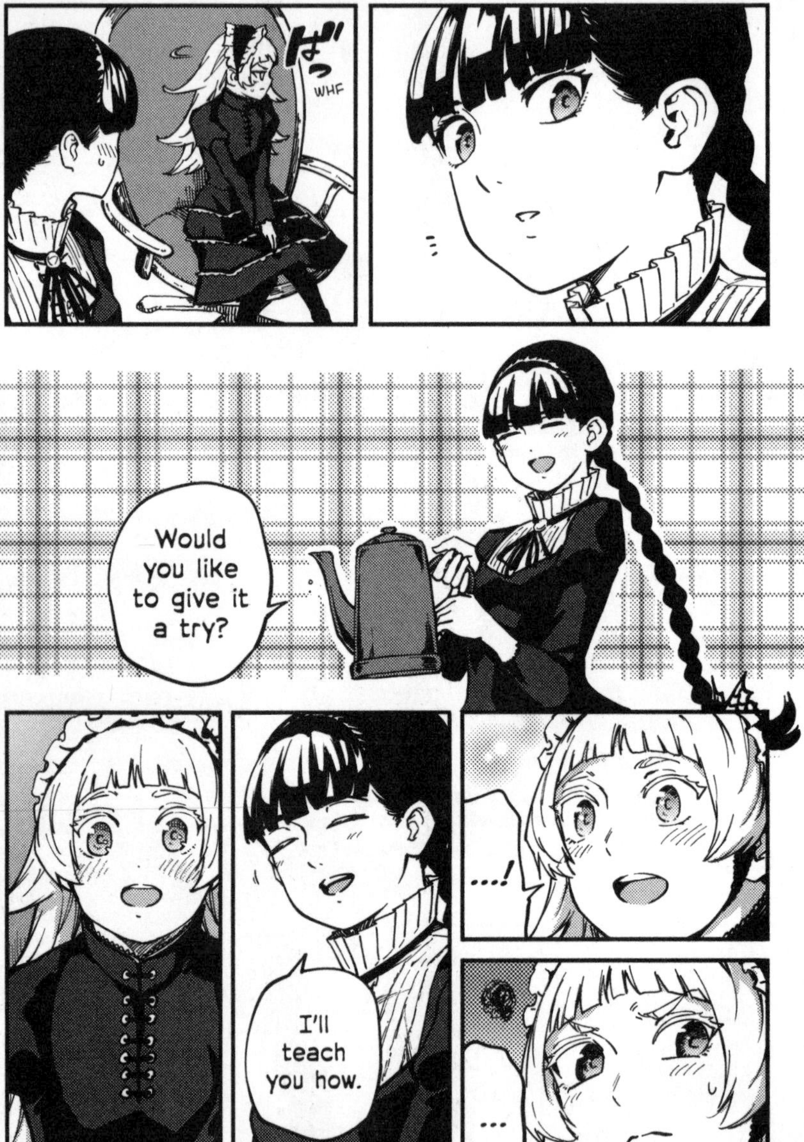
ばっ
WHF
Would you like to give it a try?
...!
...
I'll teach you how.

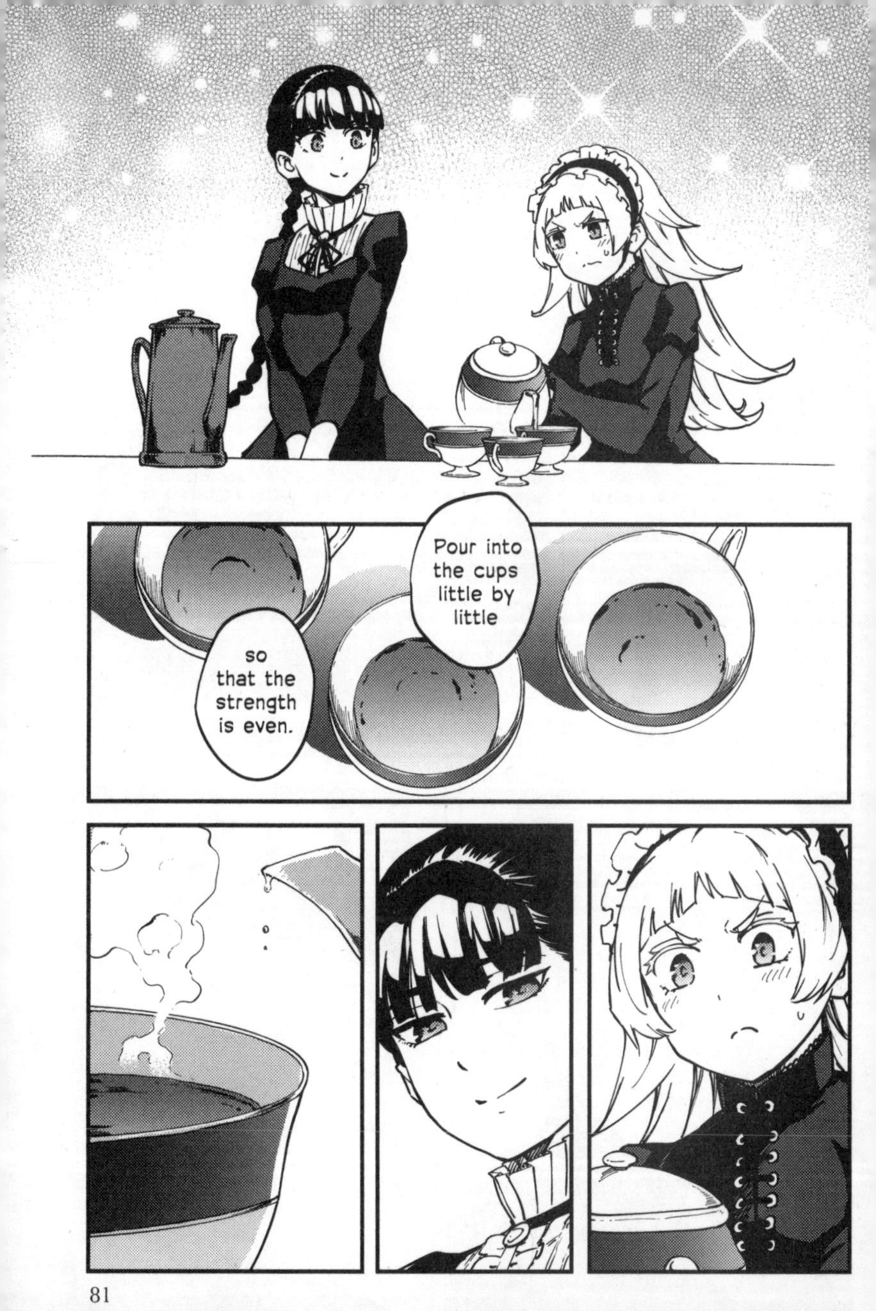
Pour into the cups little by little
so that the strength is even.

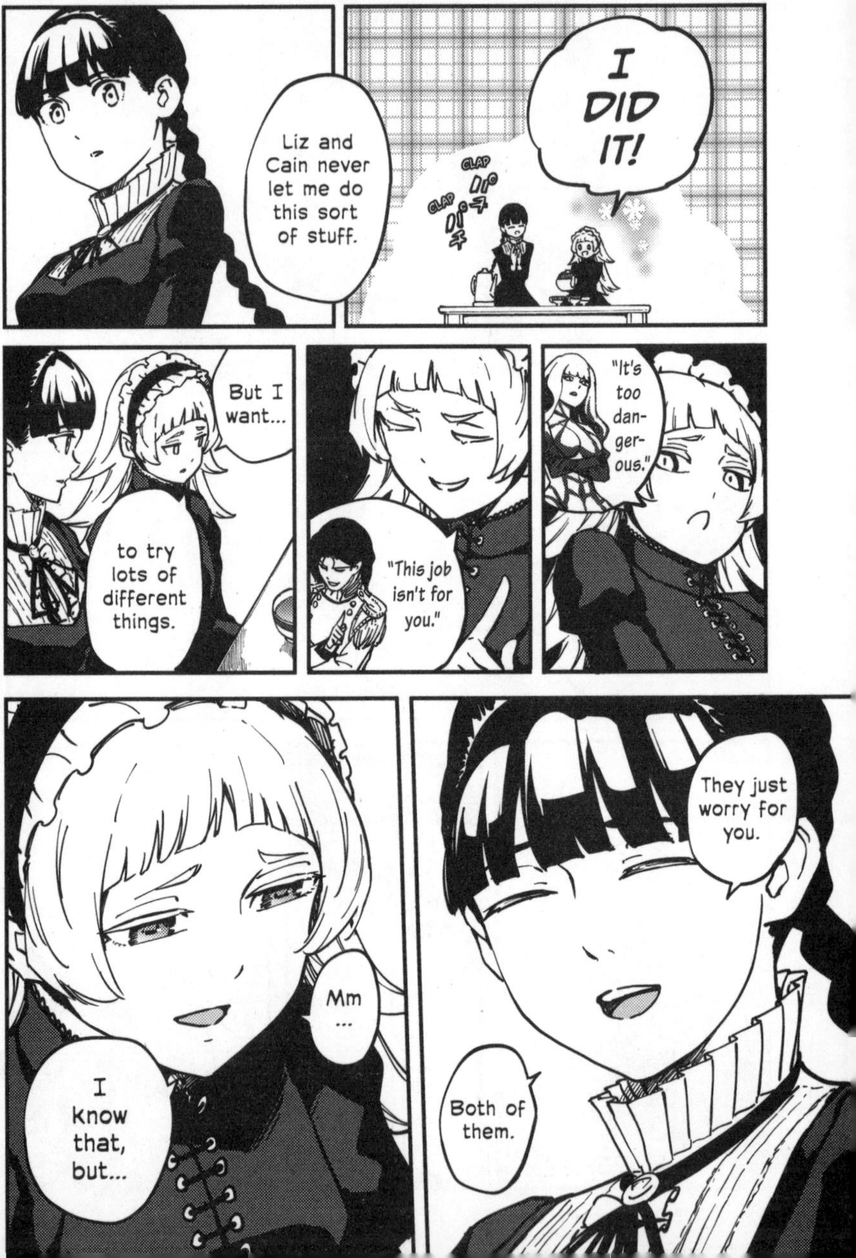
I DID IT!
CLAP
CLAP
Liz and Cain never let me do this sort of stuff.
"It's too dan-ger-ous."
"This job isn't for you."
But I want...
to try lots of different things.
They just worry for you.
Both of them.
Mm...
I know that, but...

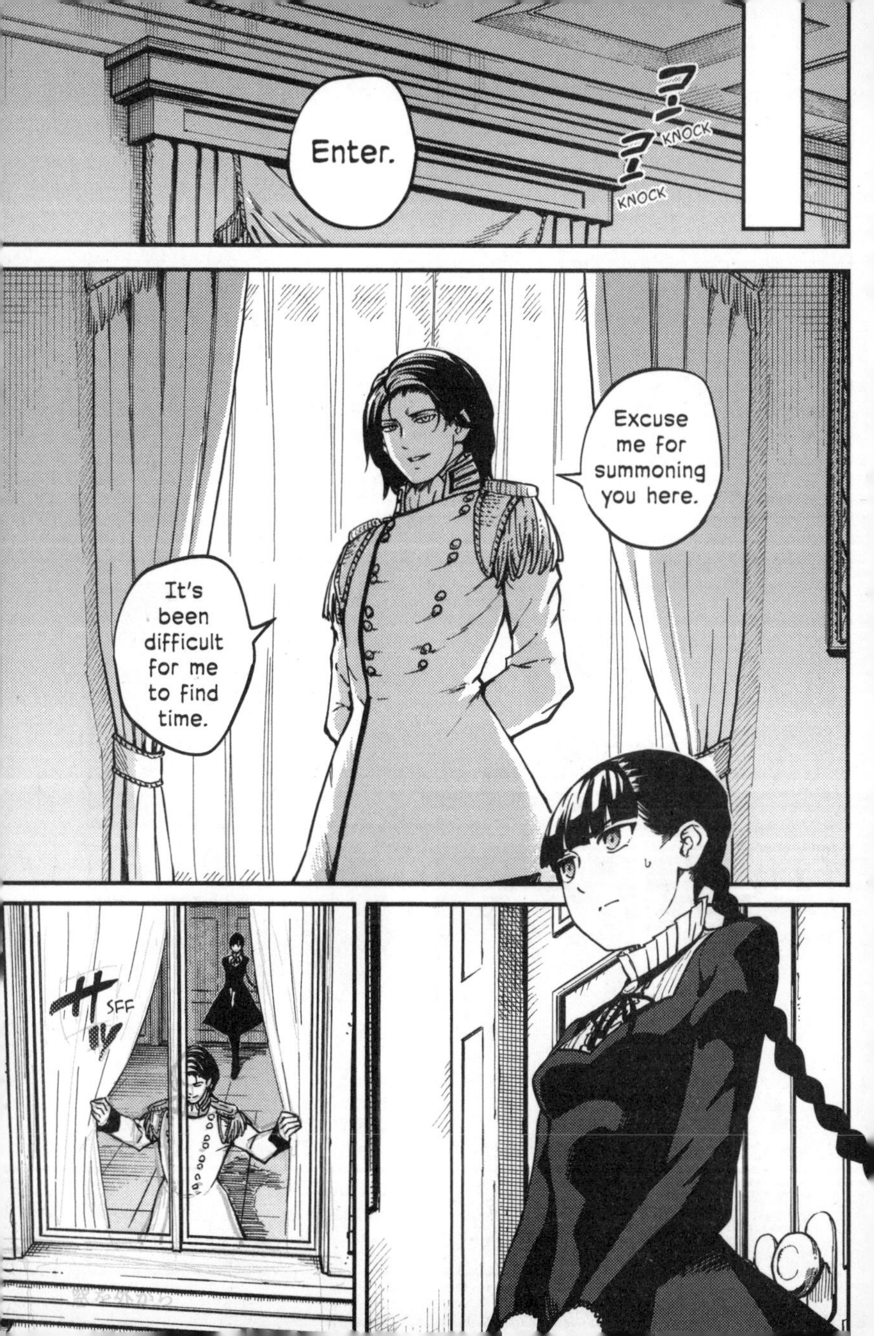
KNOCK
KNOCK
Enter.
Excuse me for summoning you here.
It's been difficult for me to find time.
SFF

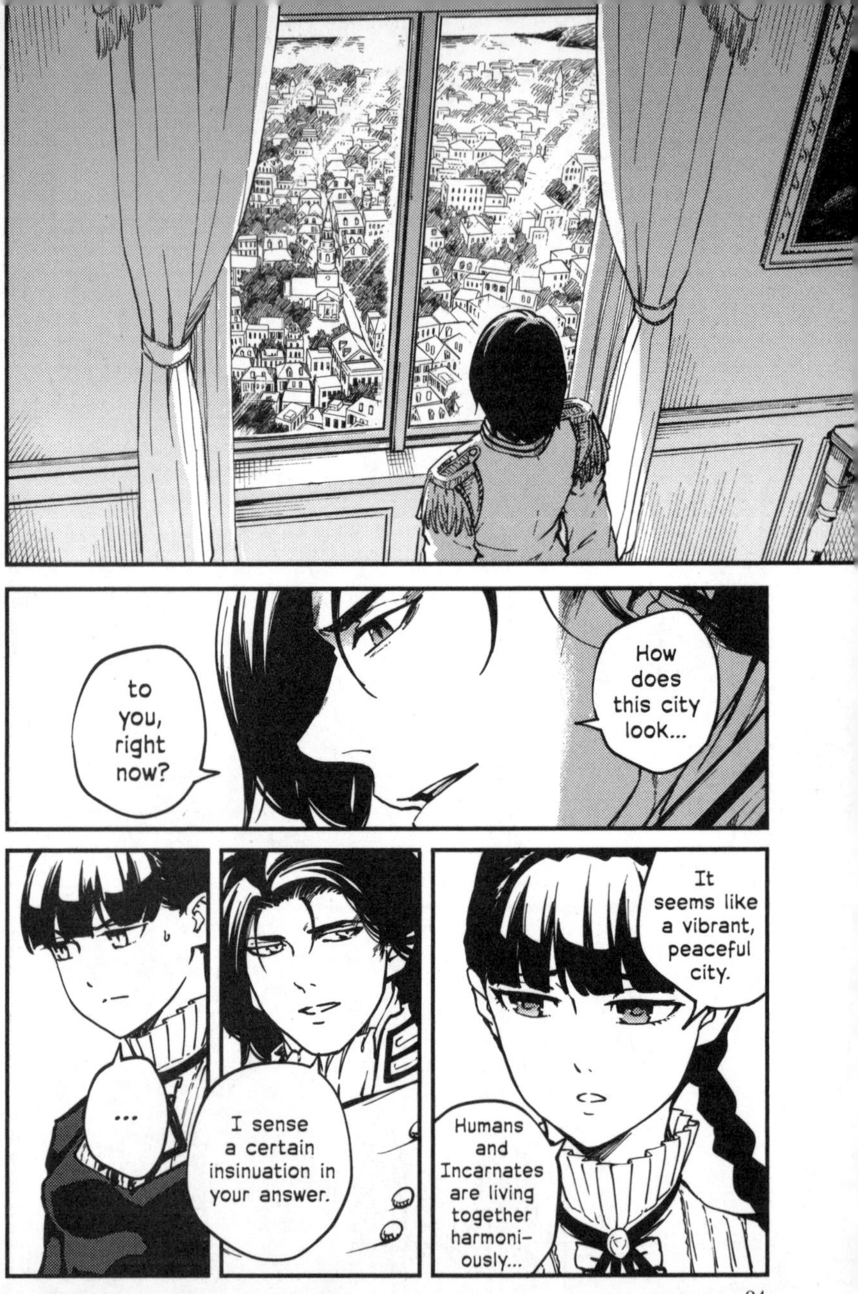
How does this city look...
to you, right now?
It seems like a vibrant, peaceful city.
Humans and Incarnates are living together harmoniously...
I sense a certain insinuation in your answer.
...

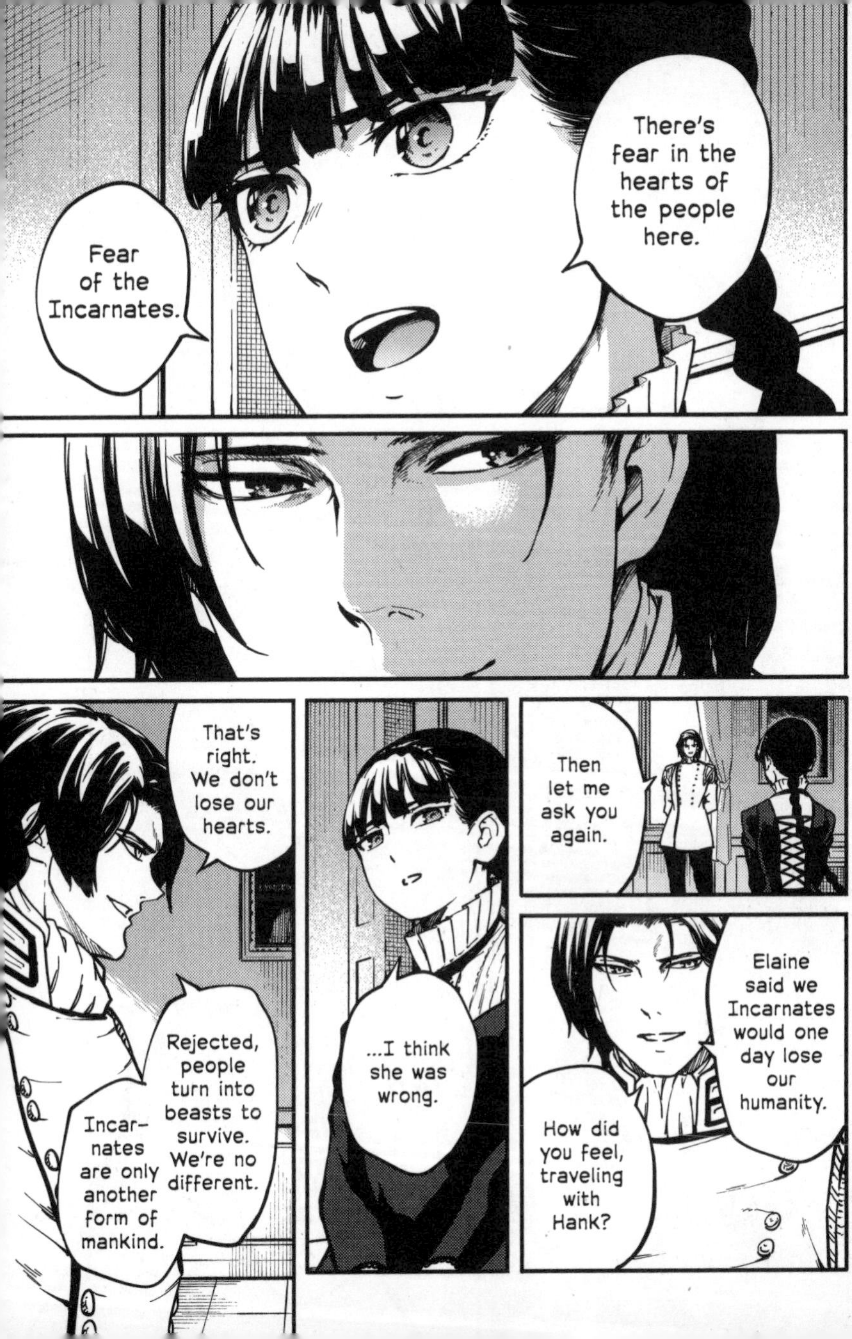
There's fear in the hearts of the people here.
Fear of the Incarnates.
Then let me ask you again.
Elaine said we Incarnates would one day lose our humanity.
How did you feel, traveling with Hank?
...I think she was wrong.
That's right. We don't lose our hearts.
Rejected, people turn into beasts to survive. We're no different.
Incar-nates are only another form of mankind.

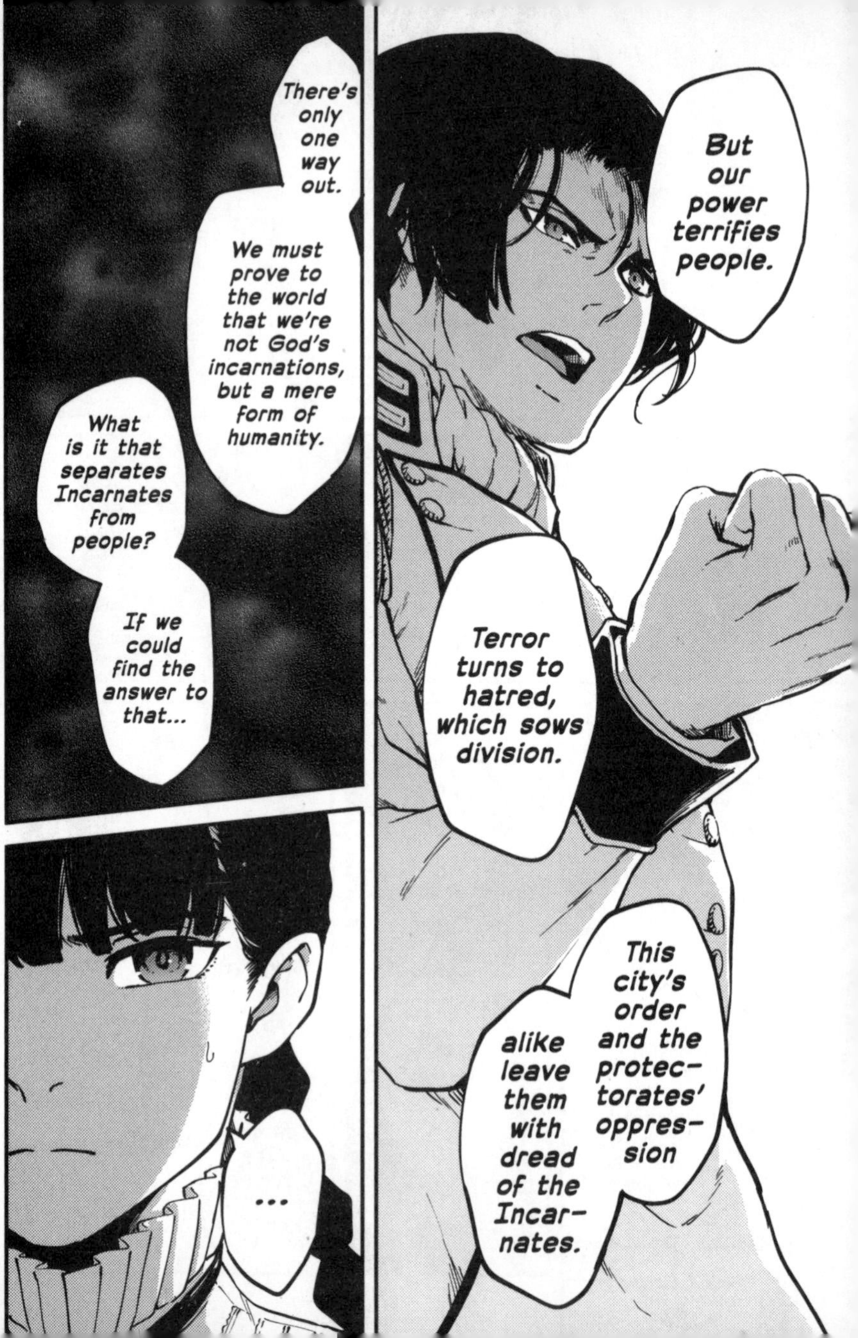
But our power terrifies people.
Terror turns to hatred, which sows division.
This city's order and the protectorates' oppression
alike leave them with dread of the Incarnates.
There's only one way out.
We must prove to the world that we're not God's incarnations, but a mere form of humanity.
What is it that separates Incarnates from people?
If we could find the answer to that...
...

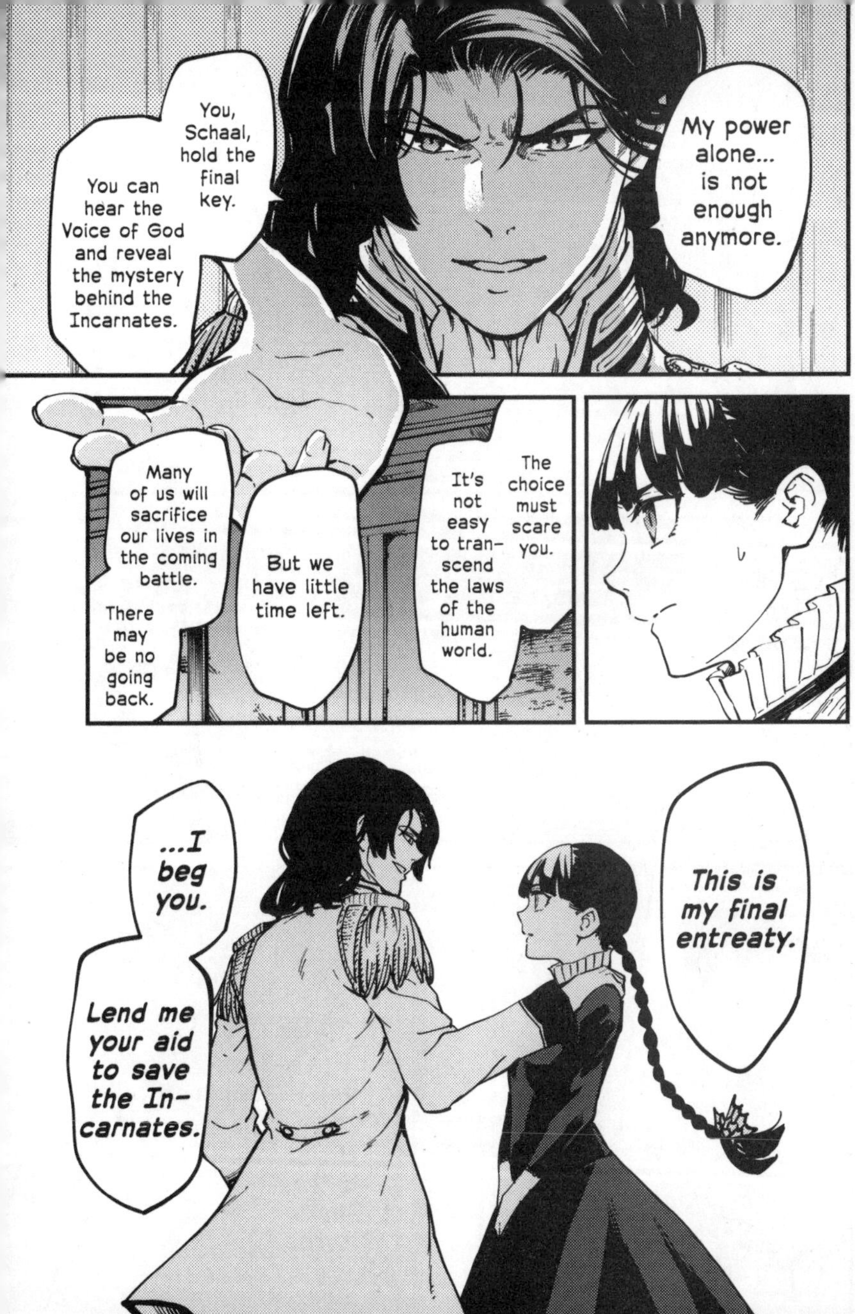
My power alone... is not enough anymore.
You, Schaal, hold the final key.
You can hear the Voice of God and reveal the mystery behind the Incarnates.
The choice must scare you.
It's not easy to transcend the laws of the human world.
But we have little time left.
Many of us will sacrifice our lives in the coming battle.
There may be no going back.
This is my final entreaty.
...I beg you.
Lend me your aid to save the Incarnates.

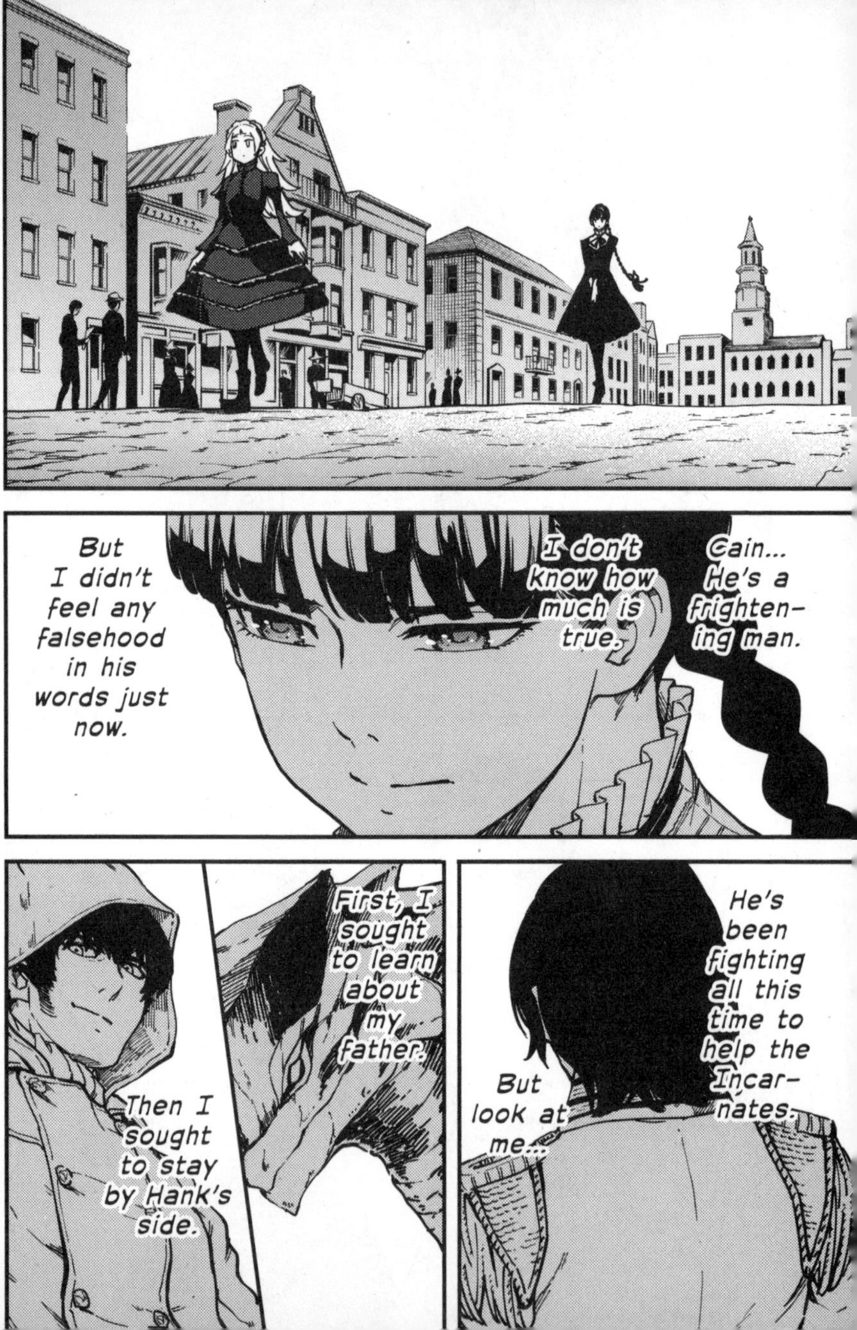
Cain... He's a frighten-ing man.
I don't know how much is true.
But I didn't feel any falsehood in his words just now.
He's been fighting all this time to help the Incar-nates.
But look at me...
First, I sought to learn about my father.
Then I sought to stay by Hank's side.

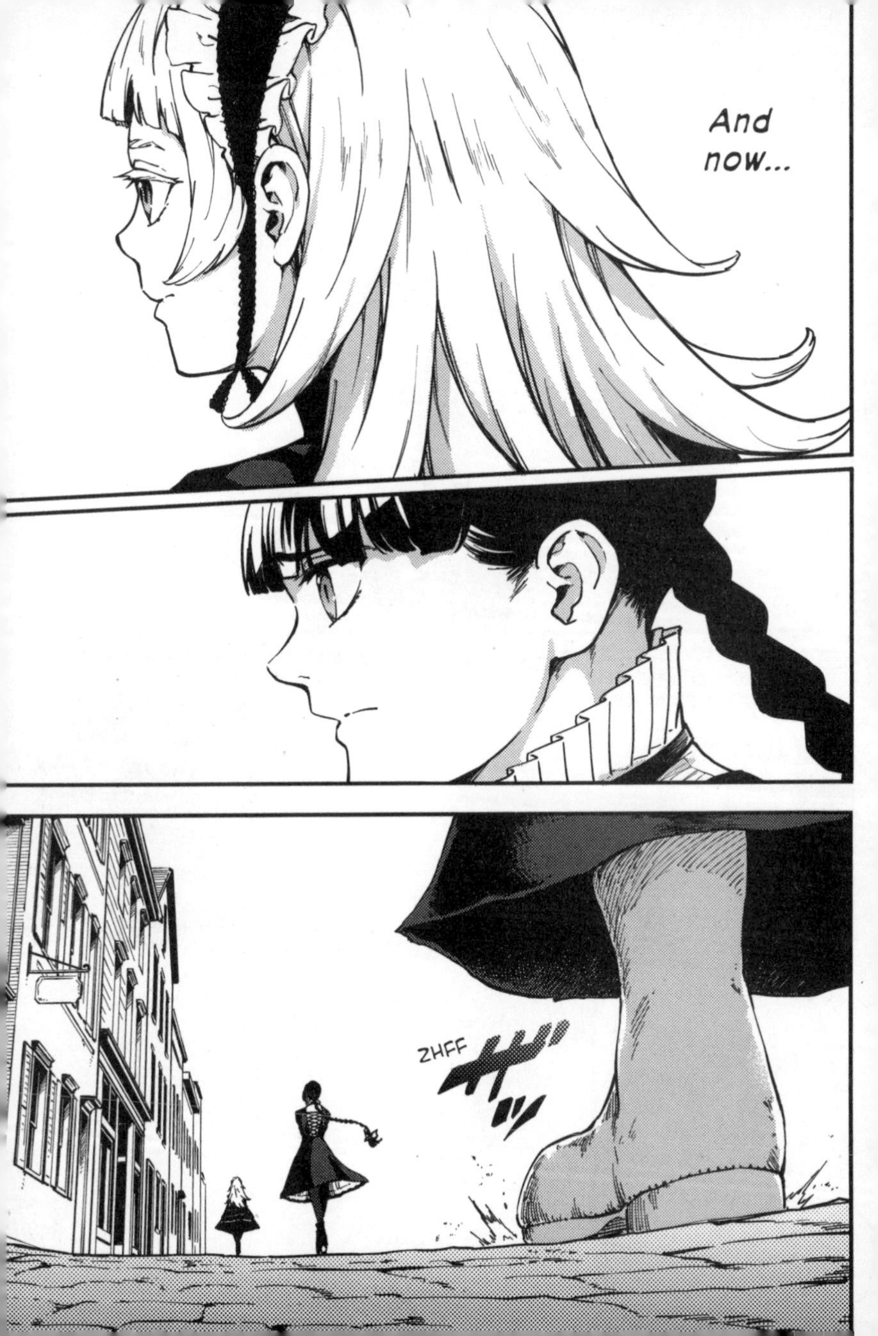
And now...
ZHFF

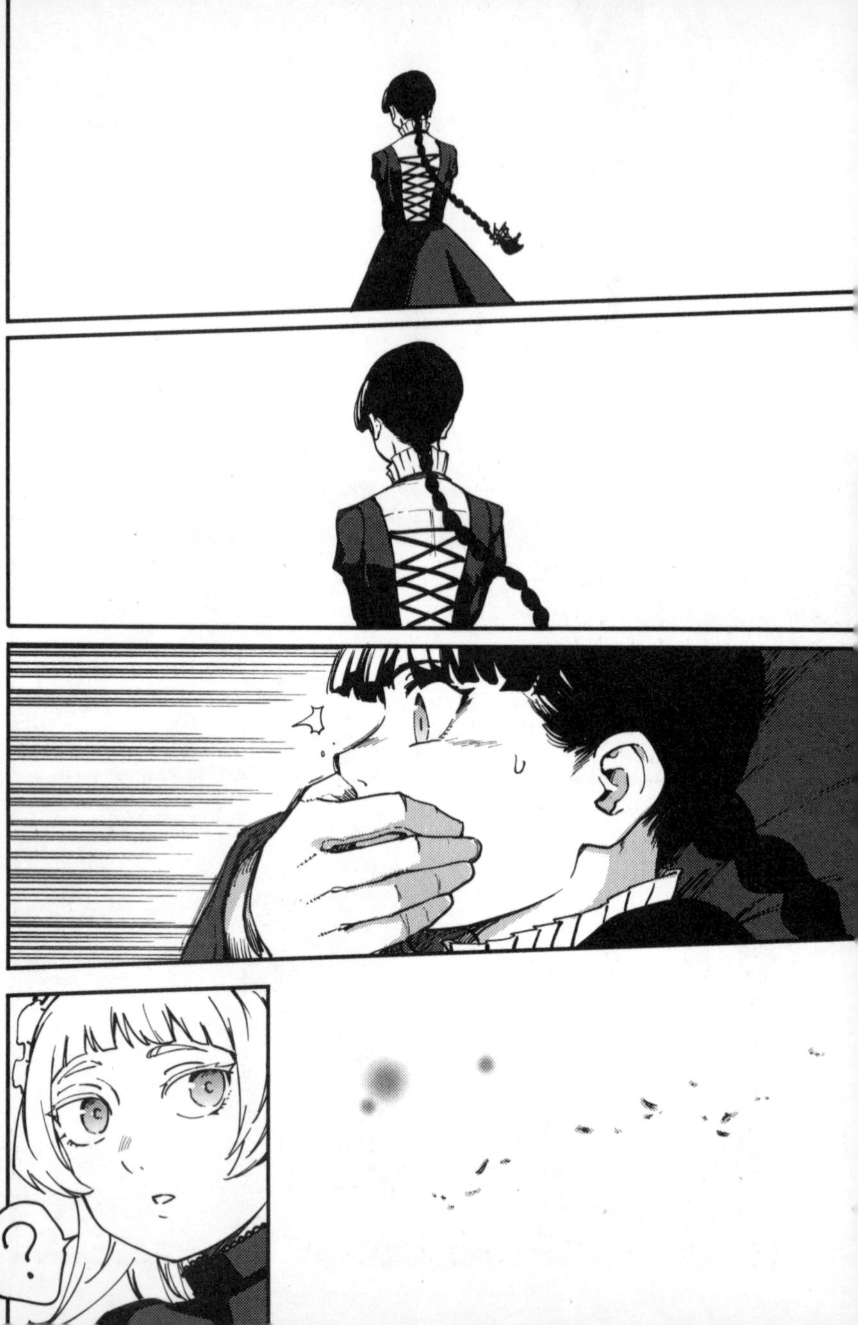
?

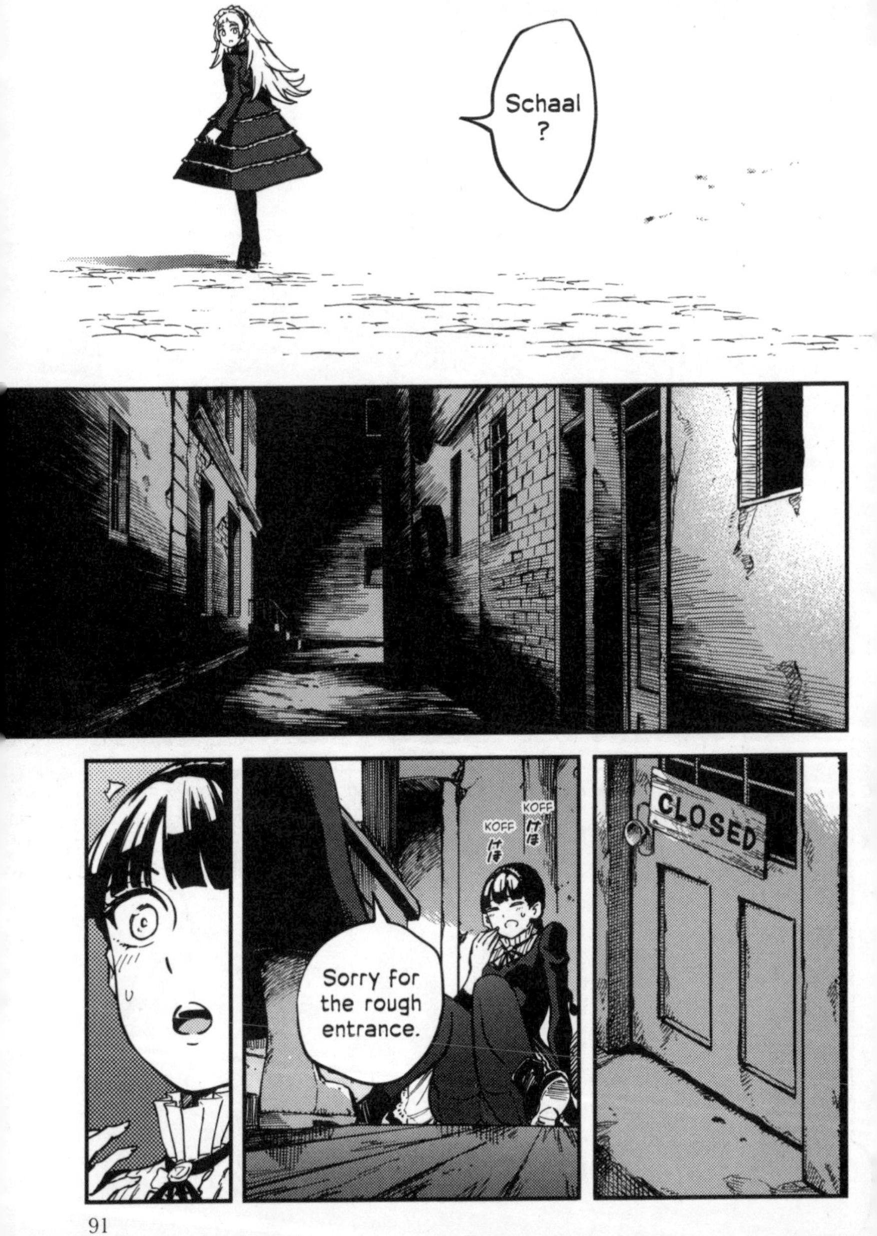
Schaal ?
CLOSED
KOFF けほ
KOFF けほ
Sorry for the rough entrance.

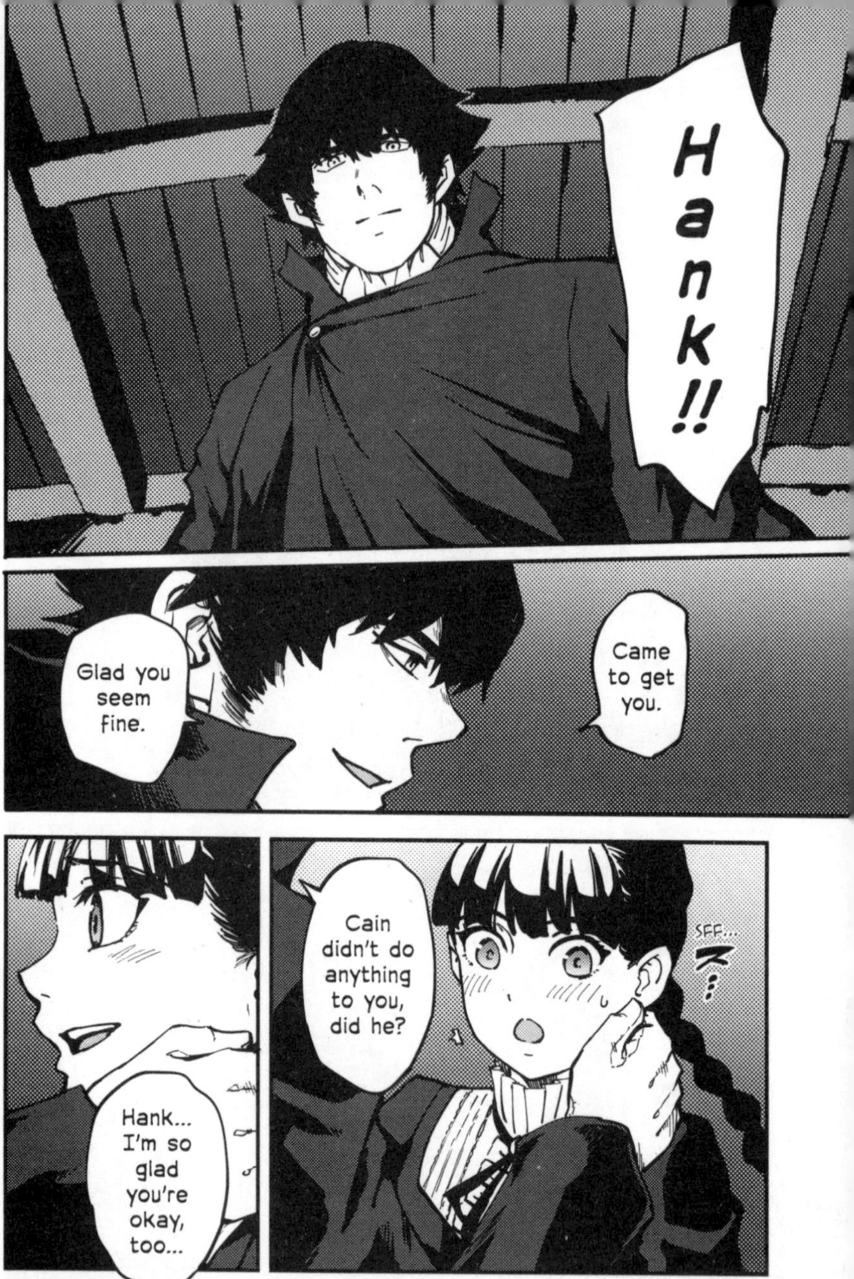
Hank!!
Came to get you.
Glad you seem fine.
Cain didn't do anything to you, did he?
SFF...
ス…
Hank... I'm so glad you're okay, too...

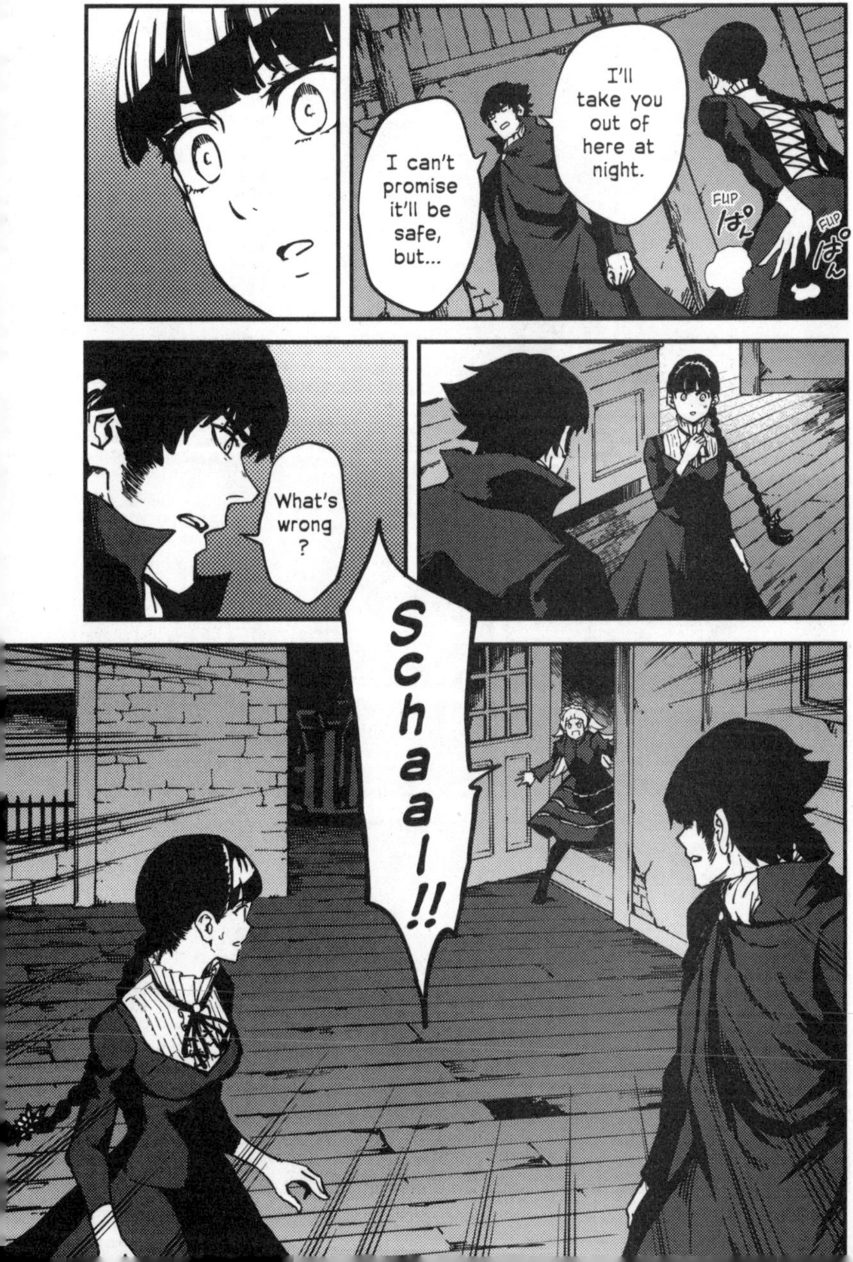

I'll take you out of here at night.
I can't promise it'll be safe, but...
FLIP ぱん
FLIP ぱ
What's wrong ?
Schaal!!

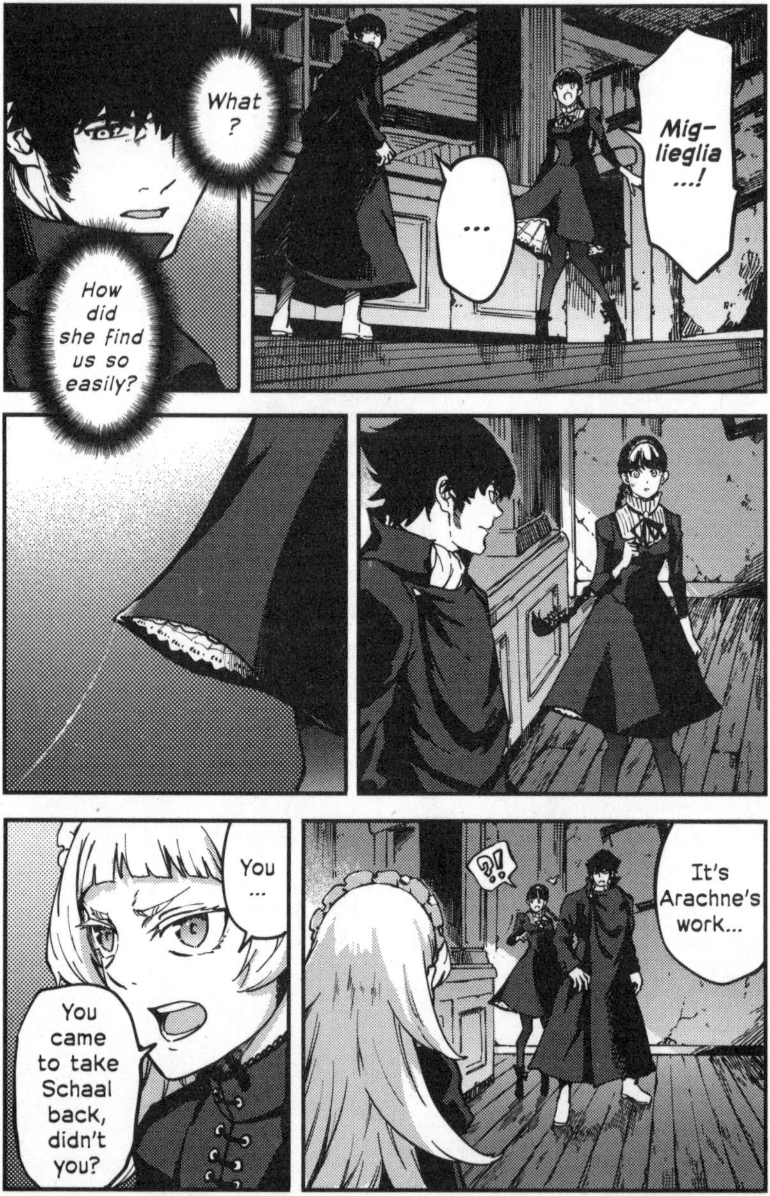
Mig-lieglia ...!
...
What?
How did she find us so easily?
It's Arachne's work...
?!
You...
You came to take Schaal back, didn't you?

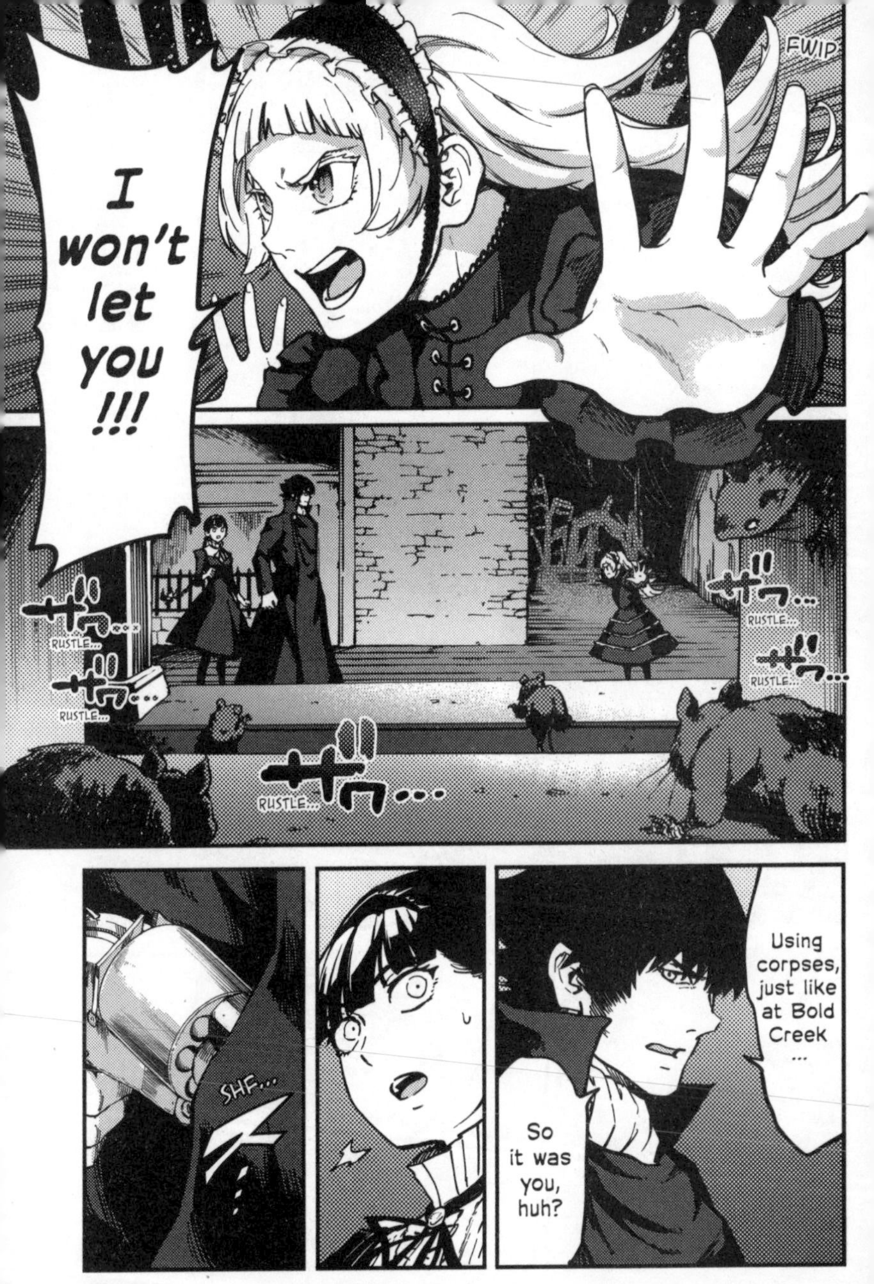
FWIP
I won't let you !!!
RUSTLE...
RUSTLE...
RUSTLE...
RUSTLE...
RUSTLE...
Using corpses, just like at Bold Creek ...
So it was you, huh?
SHF...

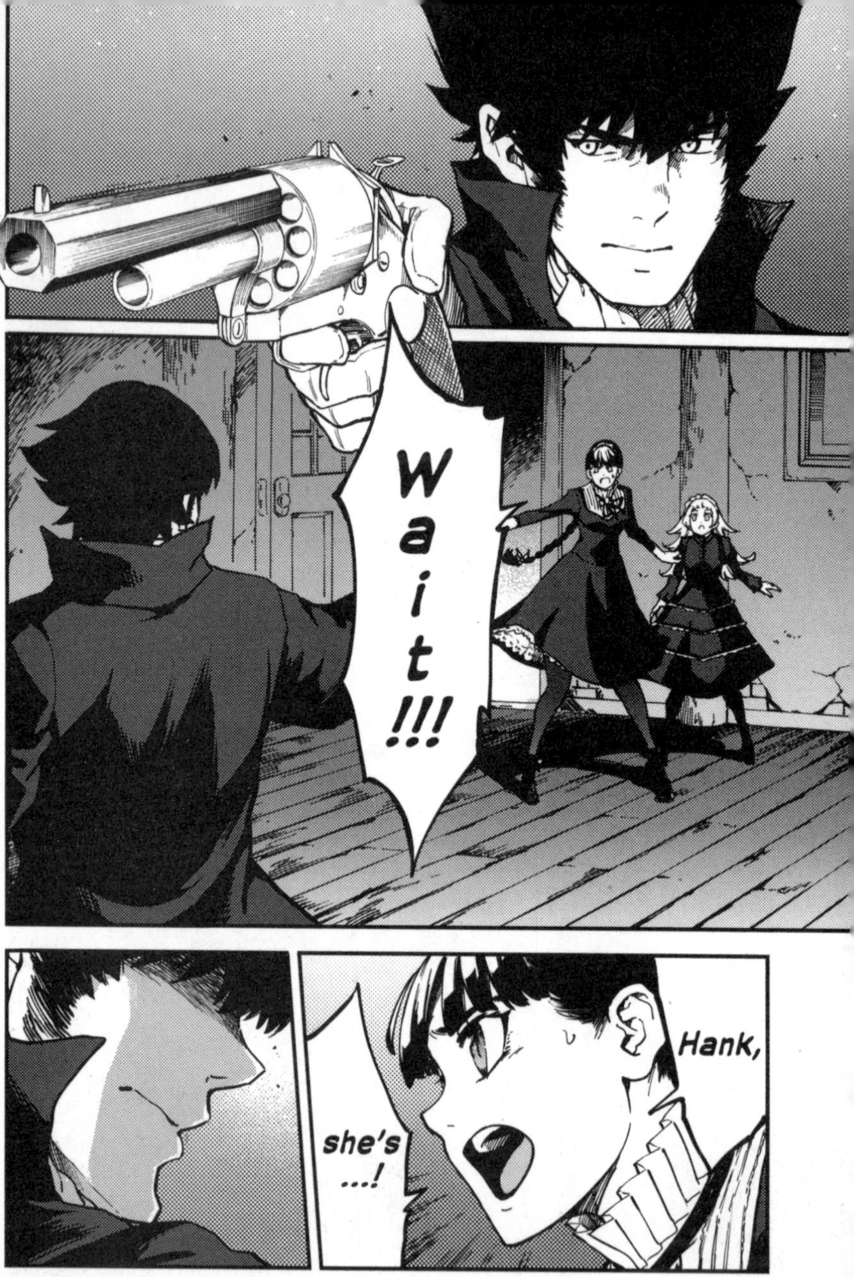
Wait!!!
Hank,
she's ...!

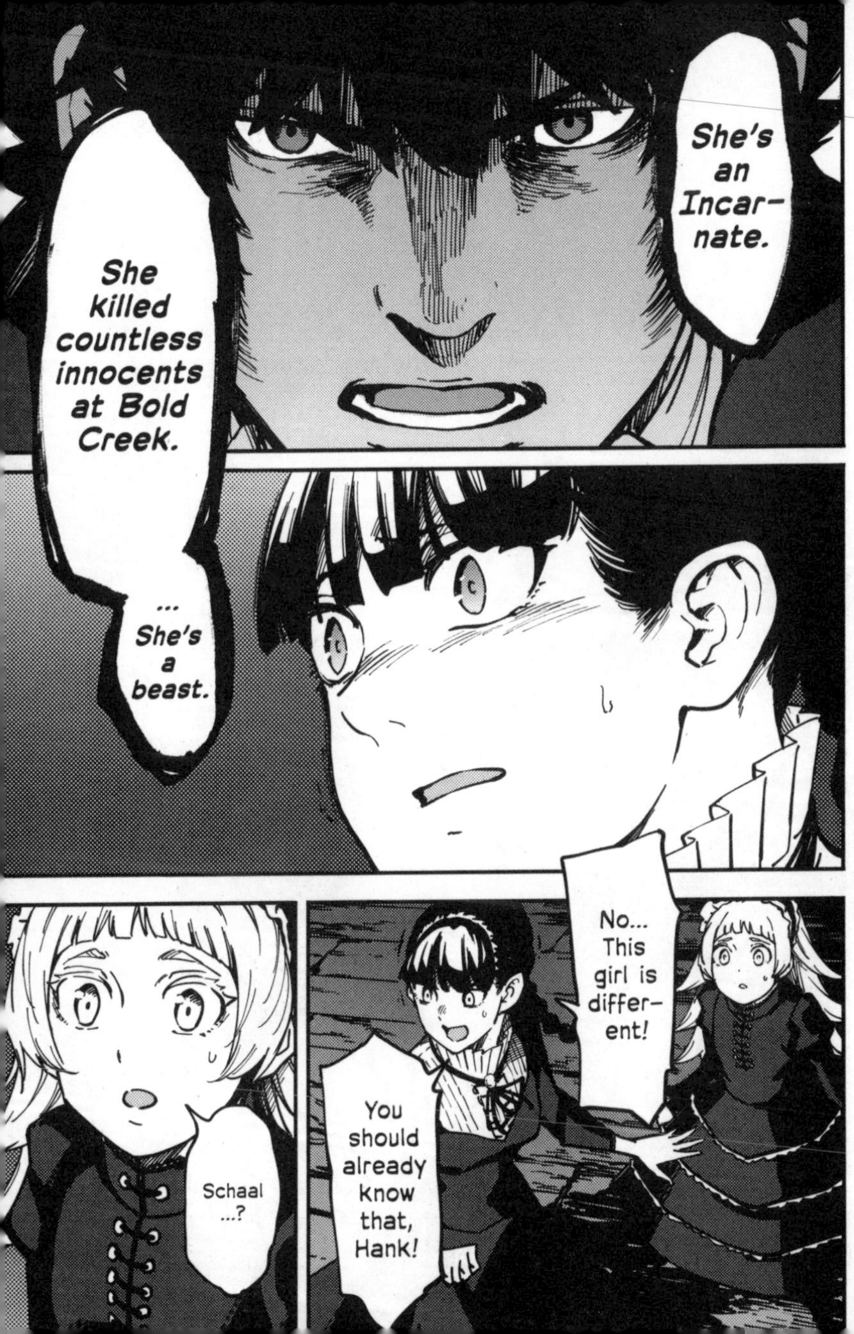
She's an Incar-nate.
She killed countless innocents at Bold Creek.
... She's a beast.
No... This girl is differ-ent!
You should already know that, Hank!
Schaal ...?

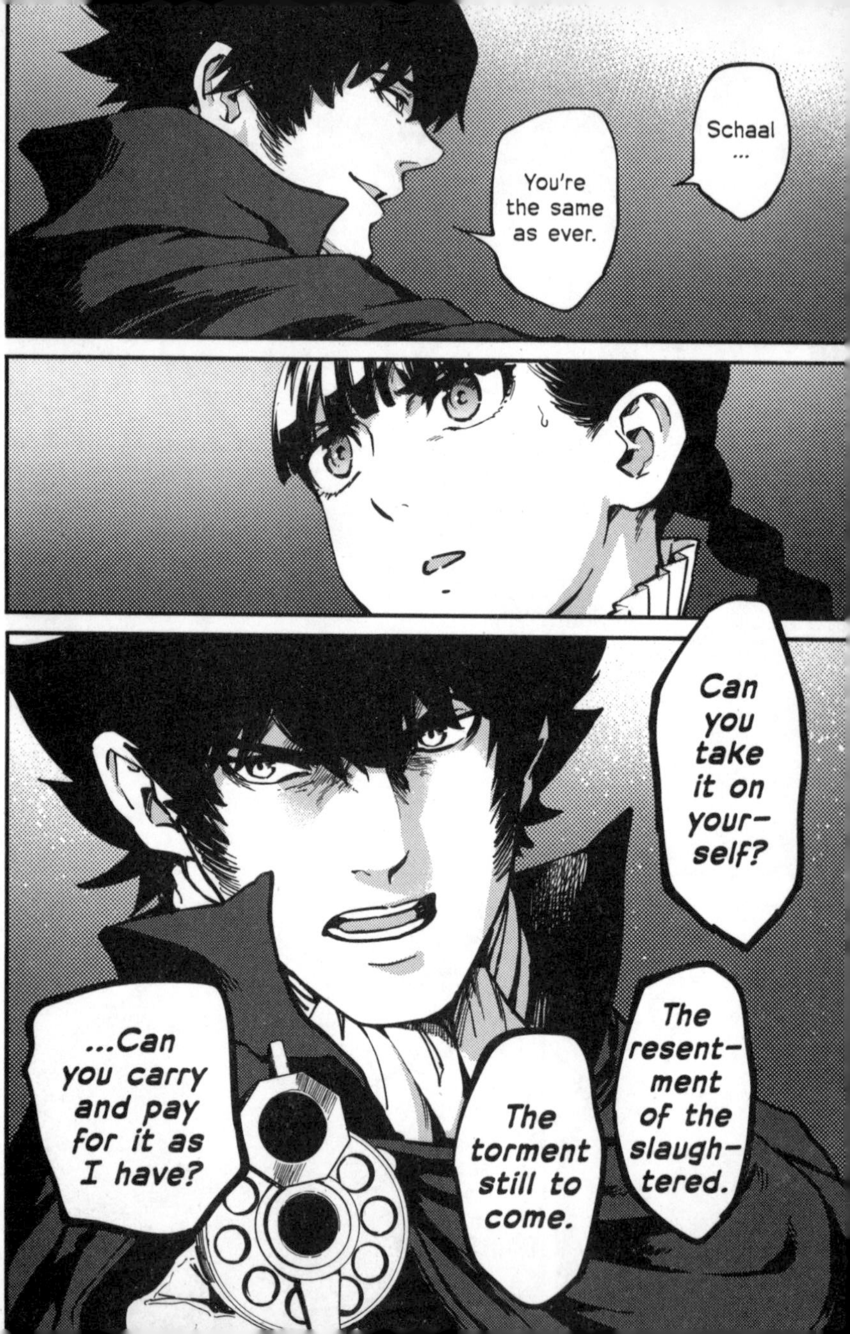
Schaal ...
You're the same as ever.
Can you take it on your-self?
The resent-ment of the slaugh-tered.
The torment still to come.
...Can you carry and pay for it as I have?

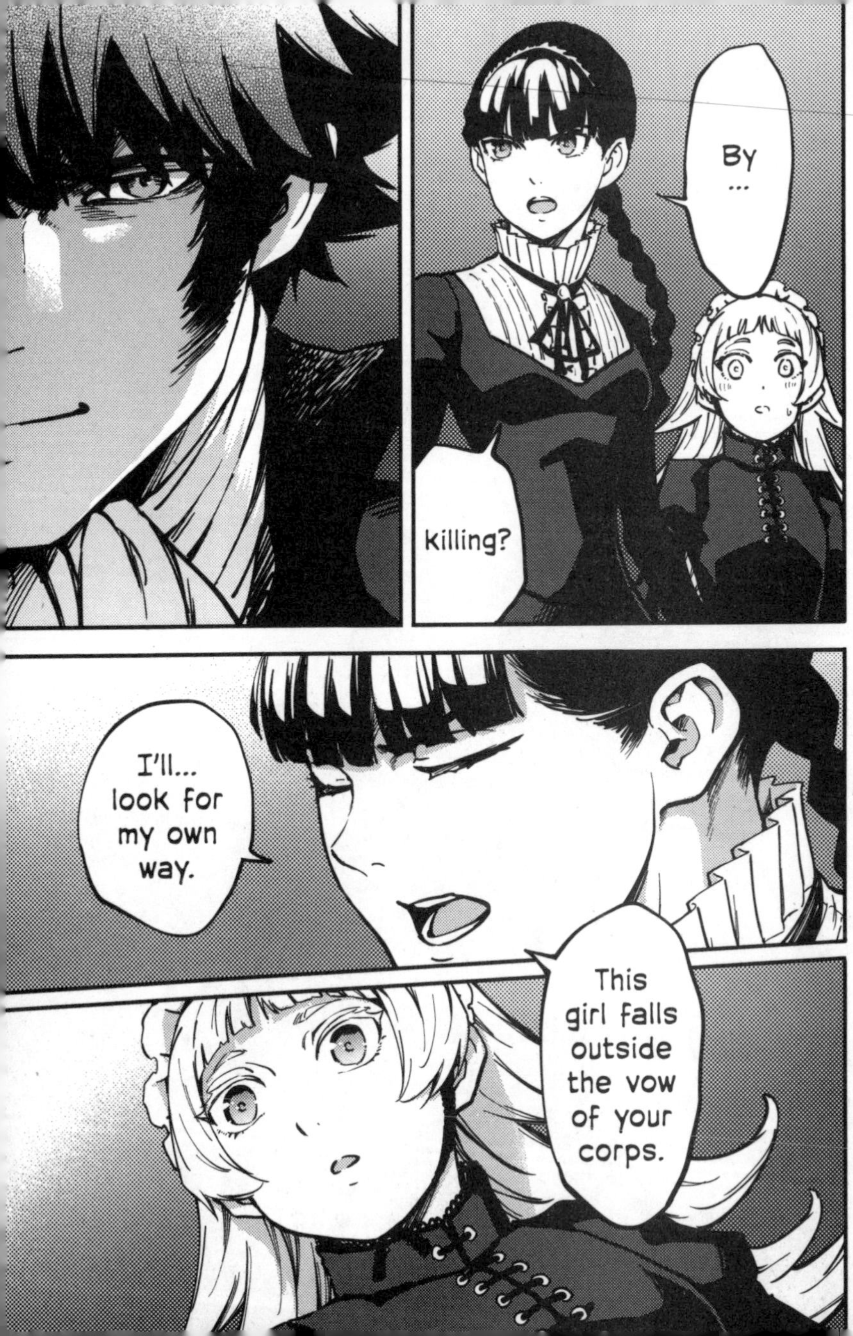
By ...
killing?
I'll... look for my own way.
This girl falls outside the vow of your corps.

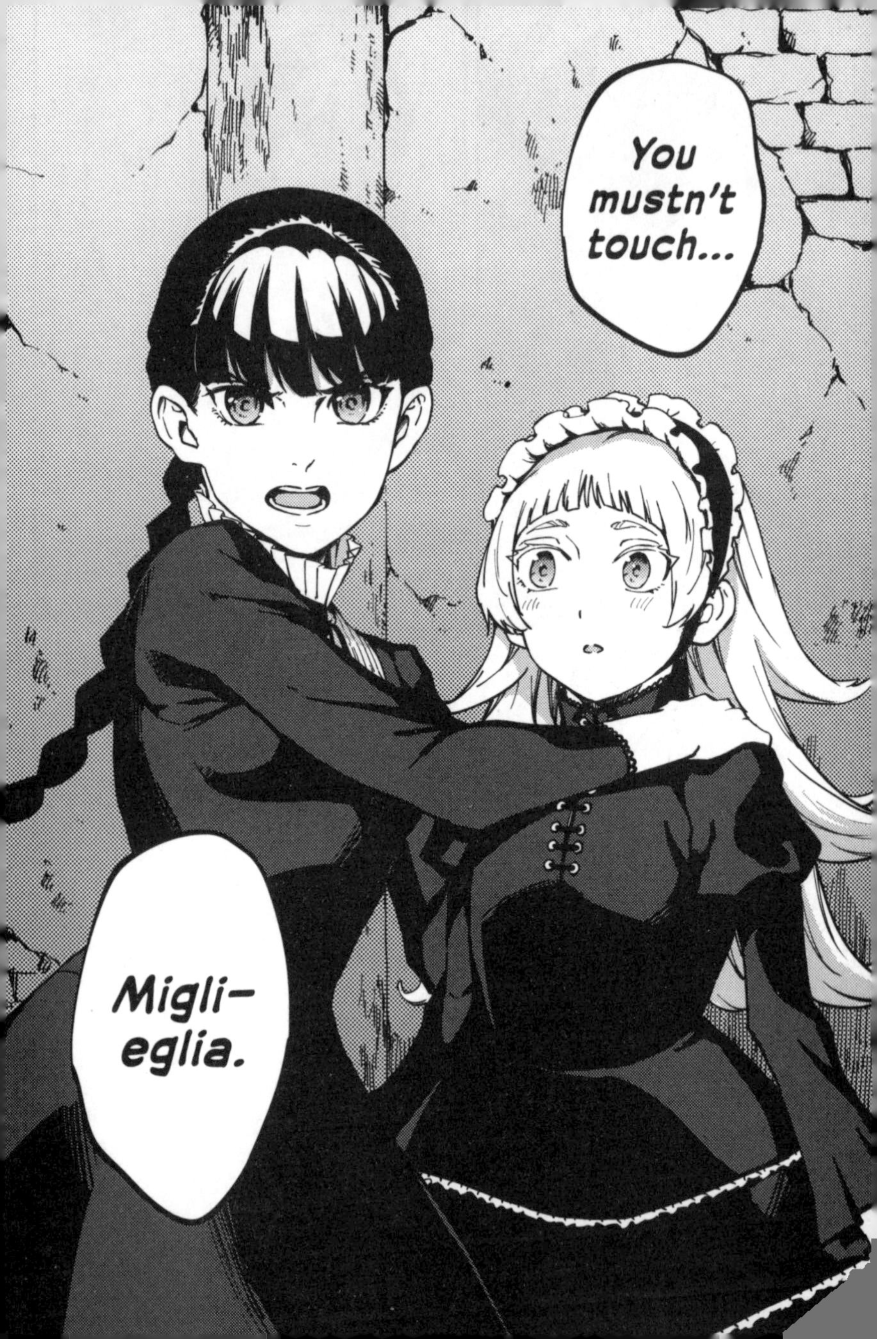
You mustn't touch...
Migli-eglia.

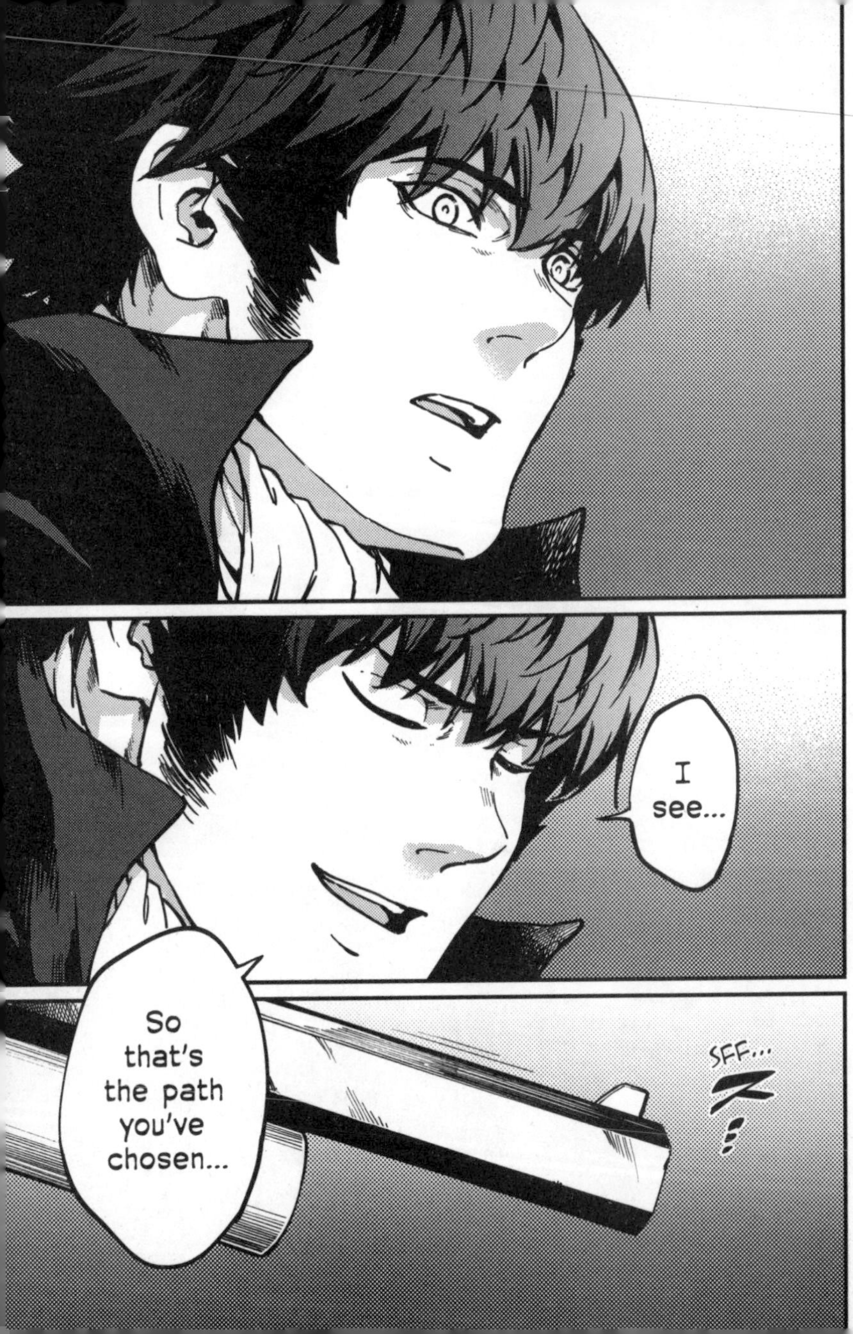
I see...
So that's the path you've chosen...
SFF...

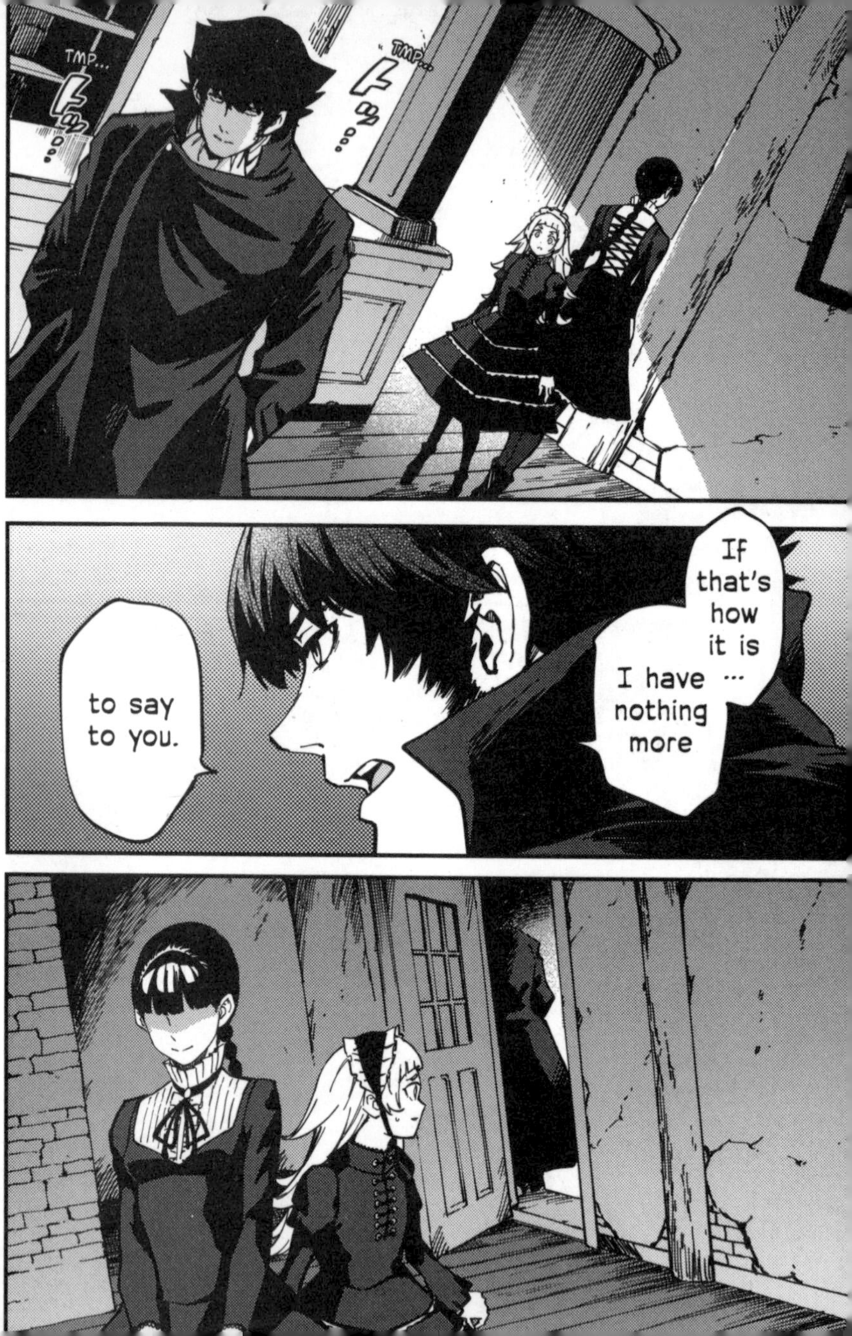
TMP...
TMP...
If that's how it is ... I have nothing more
to say to you.

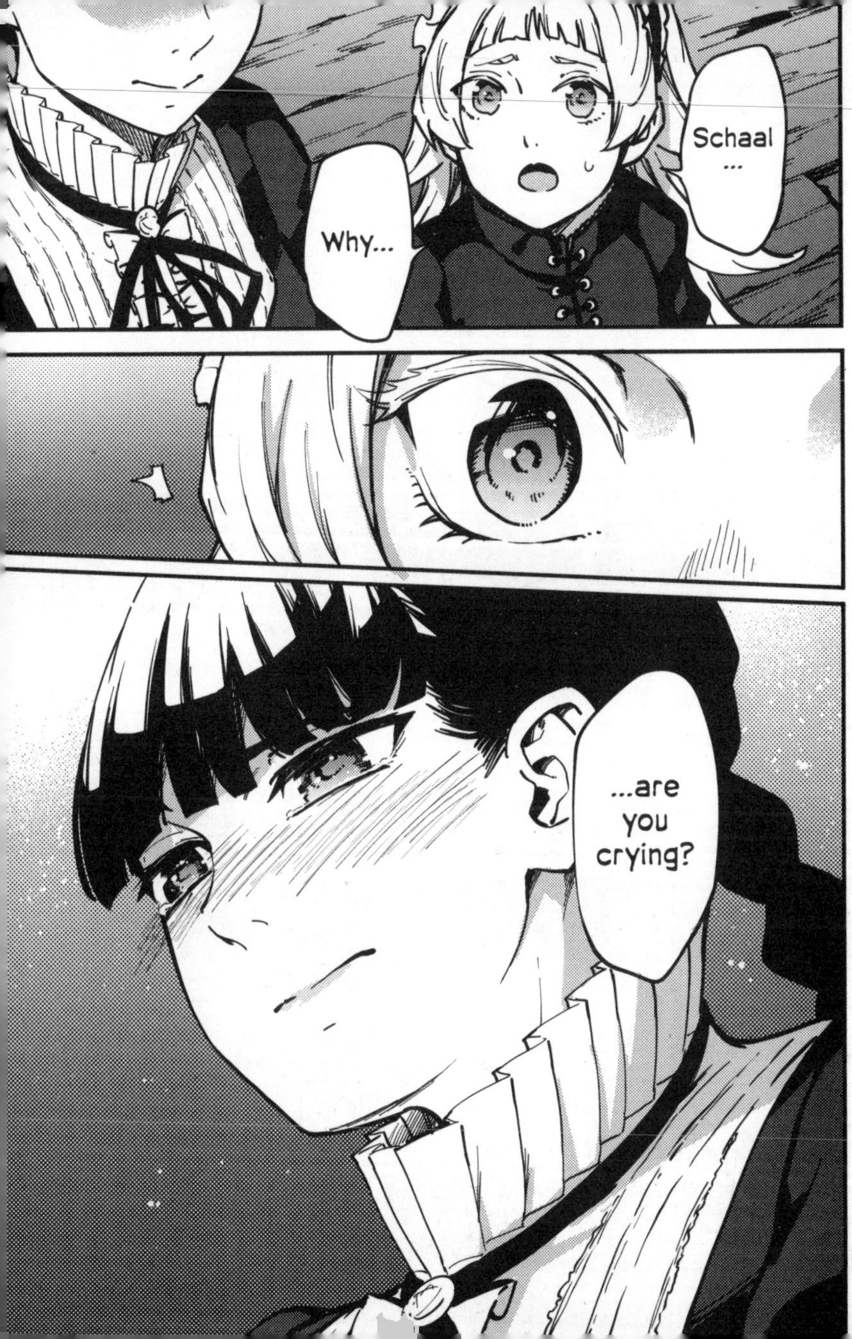
Schaal ...
Why...
...are you crying?

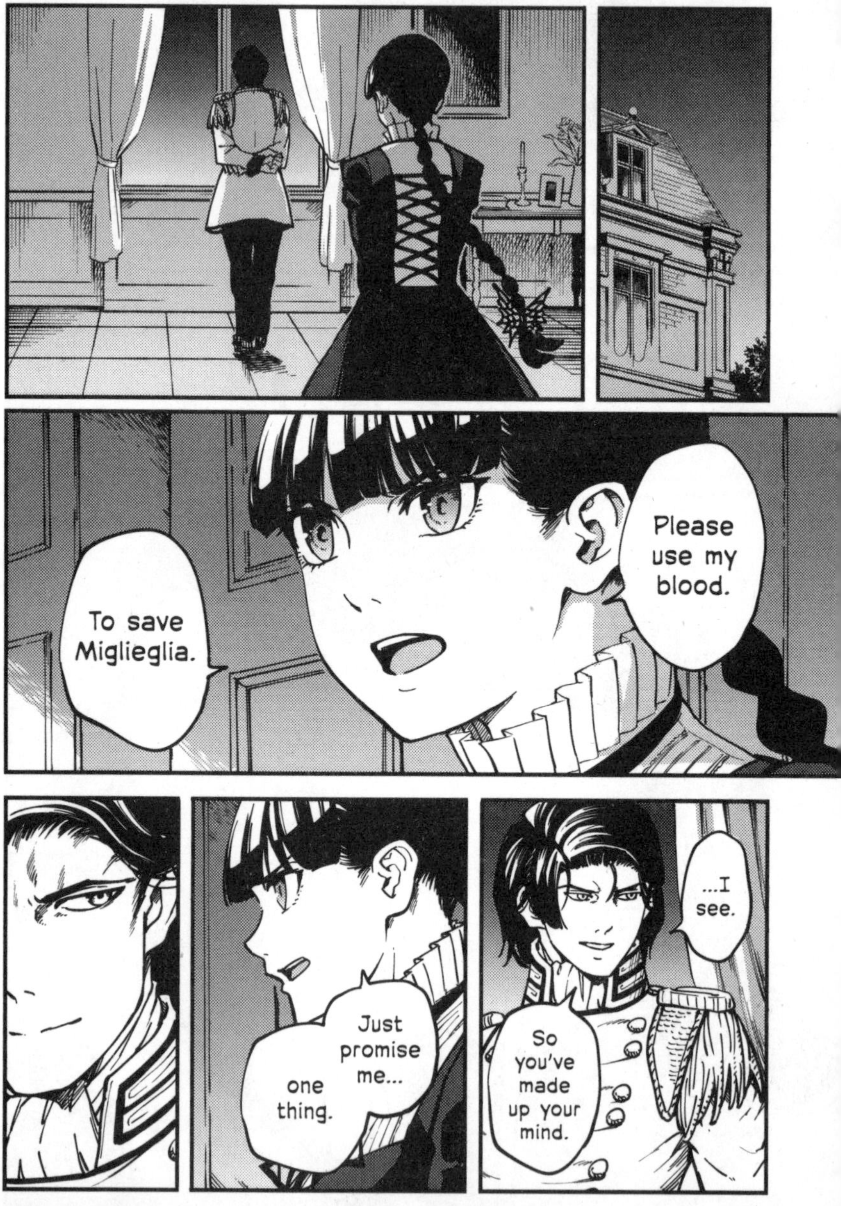
Please use my blood.
To save Miglieglia.
...I see.
So you've made up your mind.
Just promise me...
one thing.

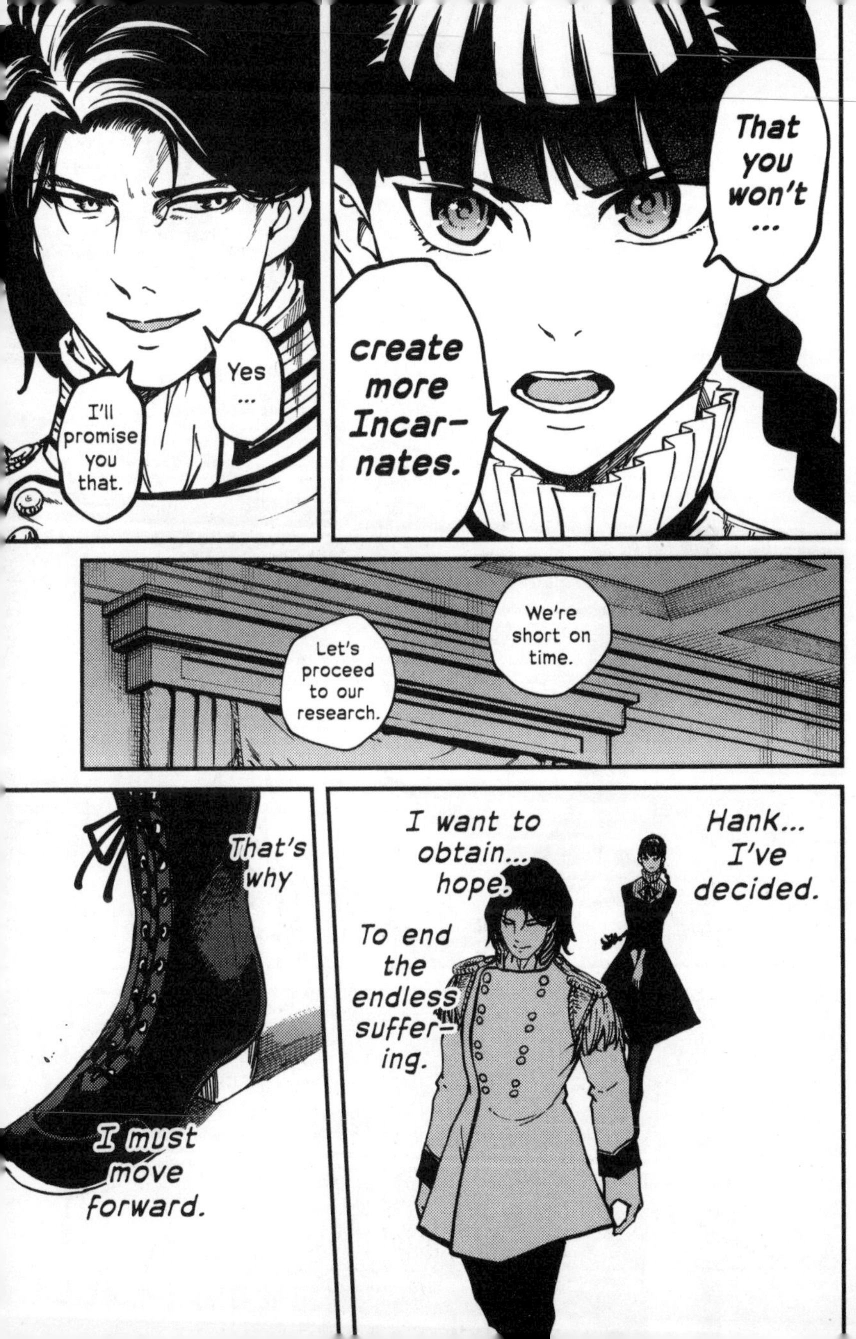
That you won't ...
create more Incar-nates.
Yes ...
I'll promise you that.
We're short on time.
Let's proceed to our research.
Hank... I've decided.
I want to obtain... hope.
To end the endless suffer-ing.
That's why
I must move forward.

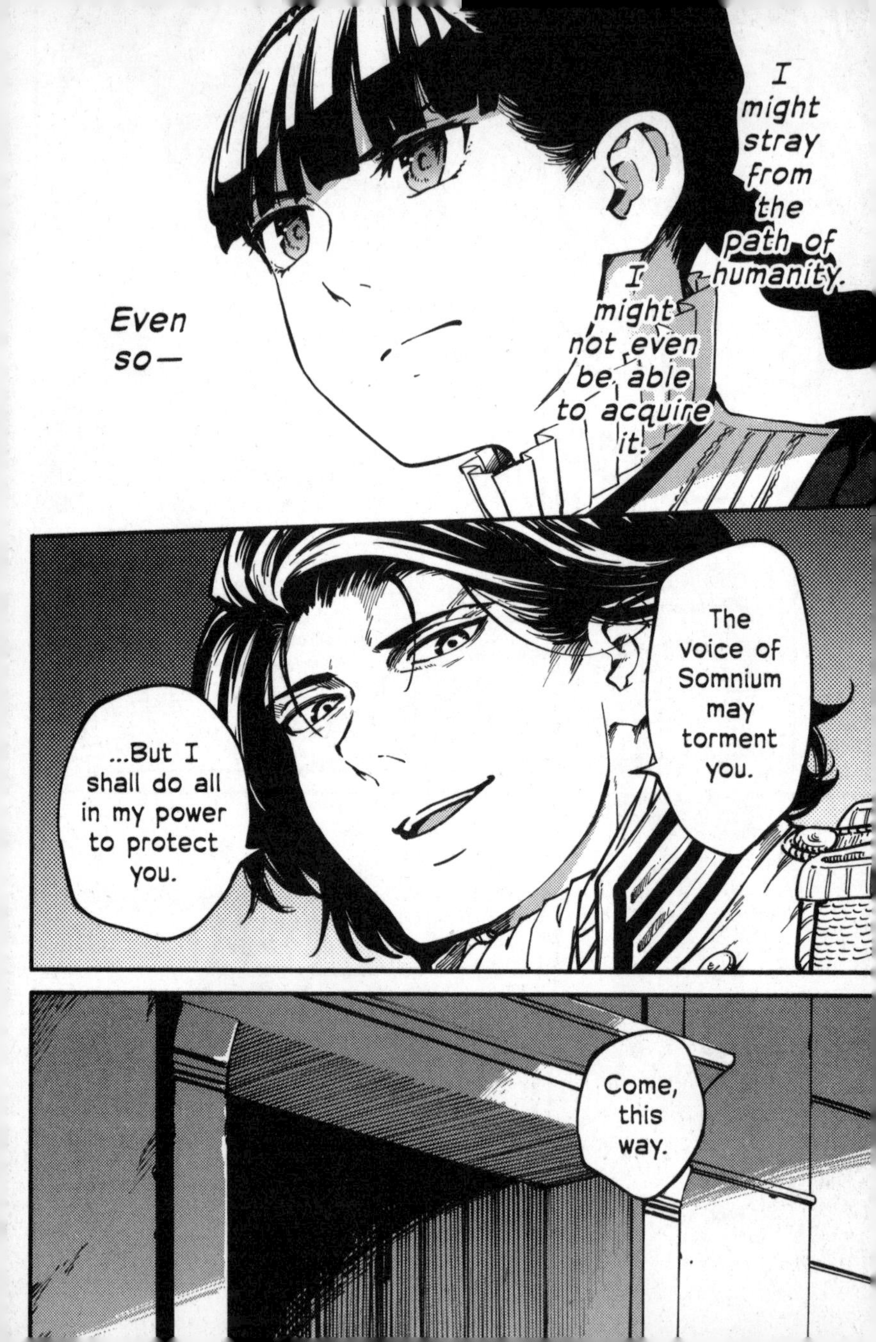
I might stray from the path of humanity.
I might not even be able to acquire it.
Even so—
The voice of Somnium may torment you.
...But I shall do all in my power to protect you.
Come, this way.

To the Abandoned
Sacred Beasts

To the Abandoned
Sacred Beasts

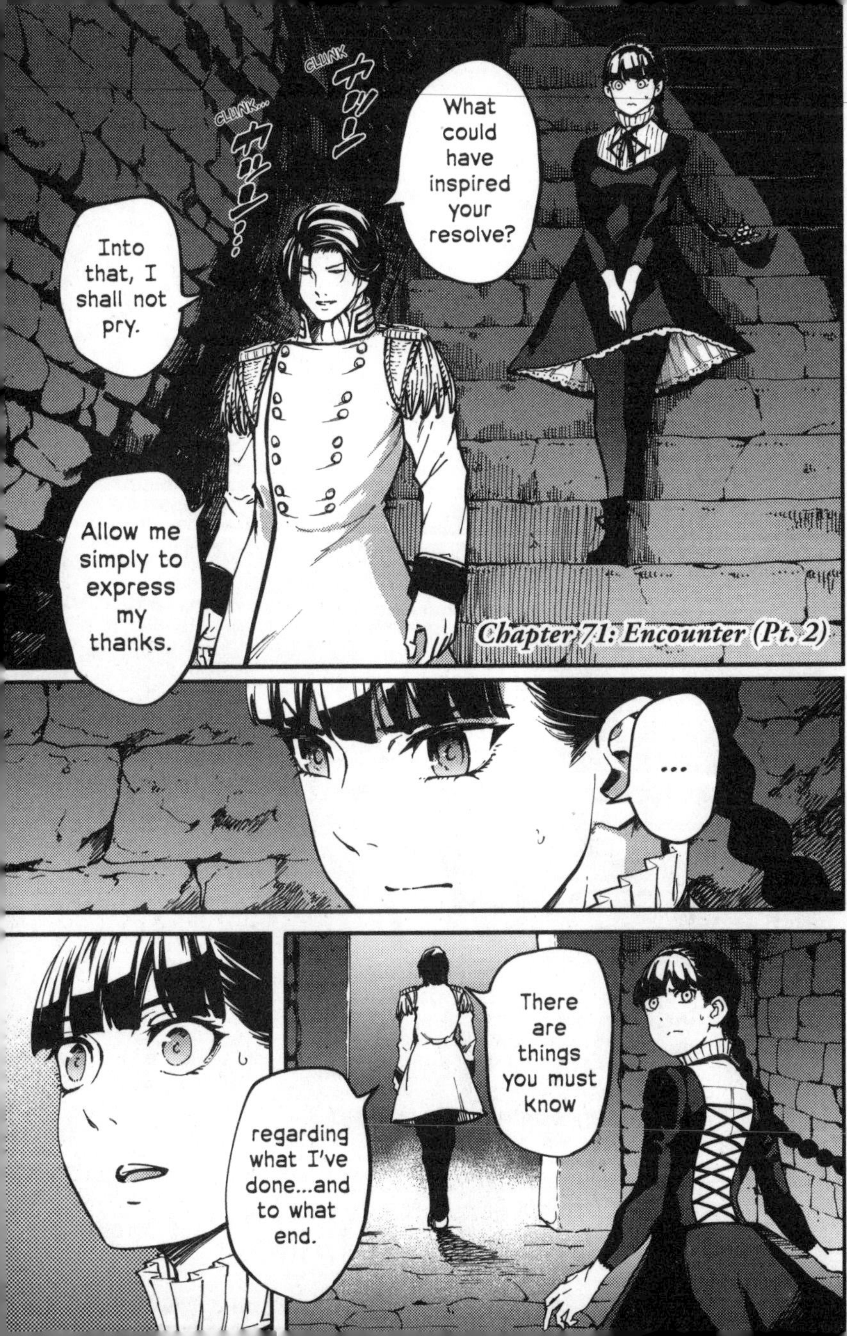
What could have inspired your resolve?
CLINK
CLINK...
Into that, I shall not pry.
Allow me simply to express my thanks.
Chapter 71: Encounter (Pt. 2)
...
There are things you must know
regarding what I've done...and to what end.

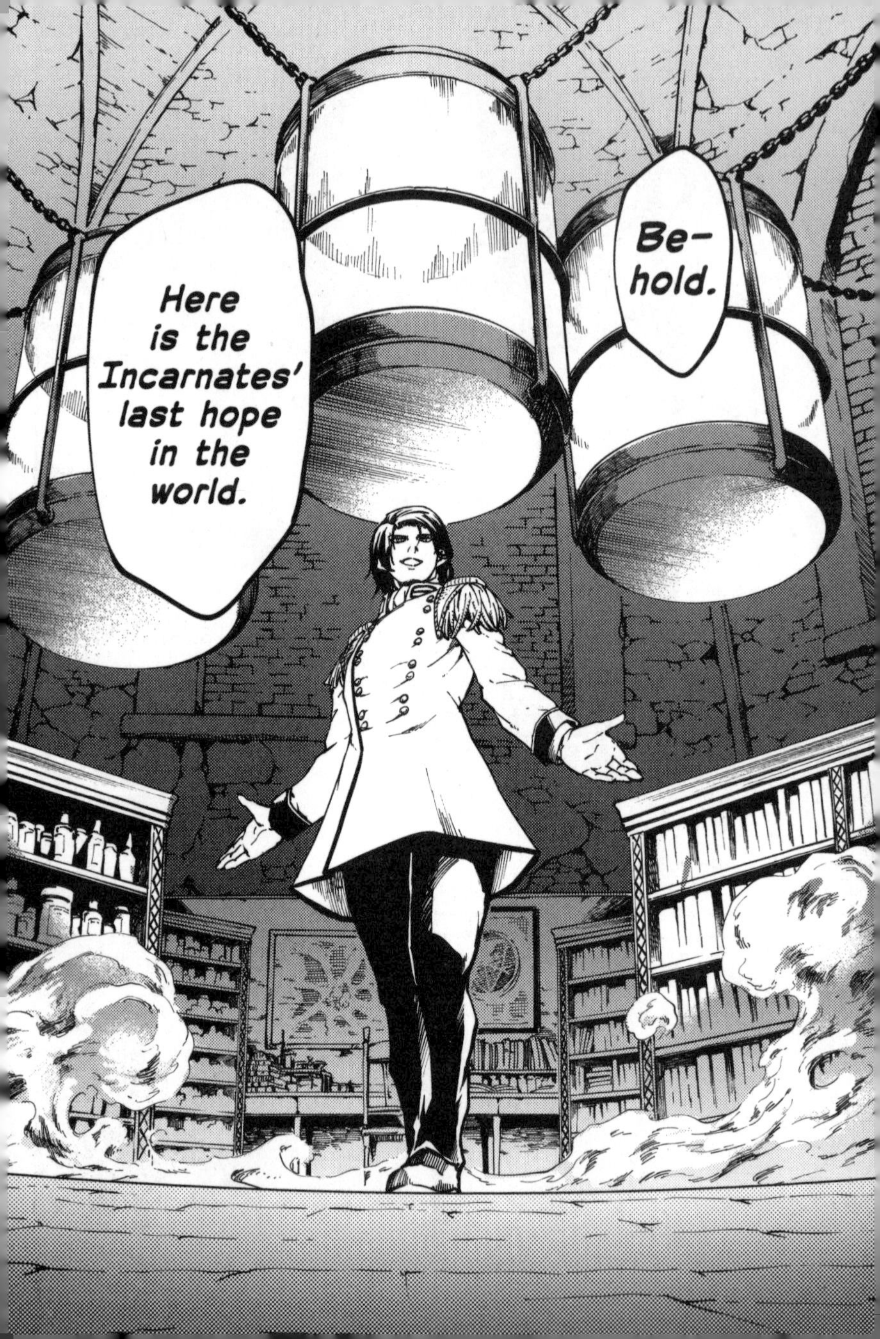
Be-hold.
Here is the Incarnates' last hope in the world.

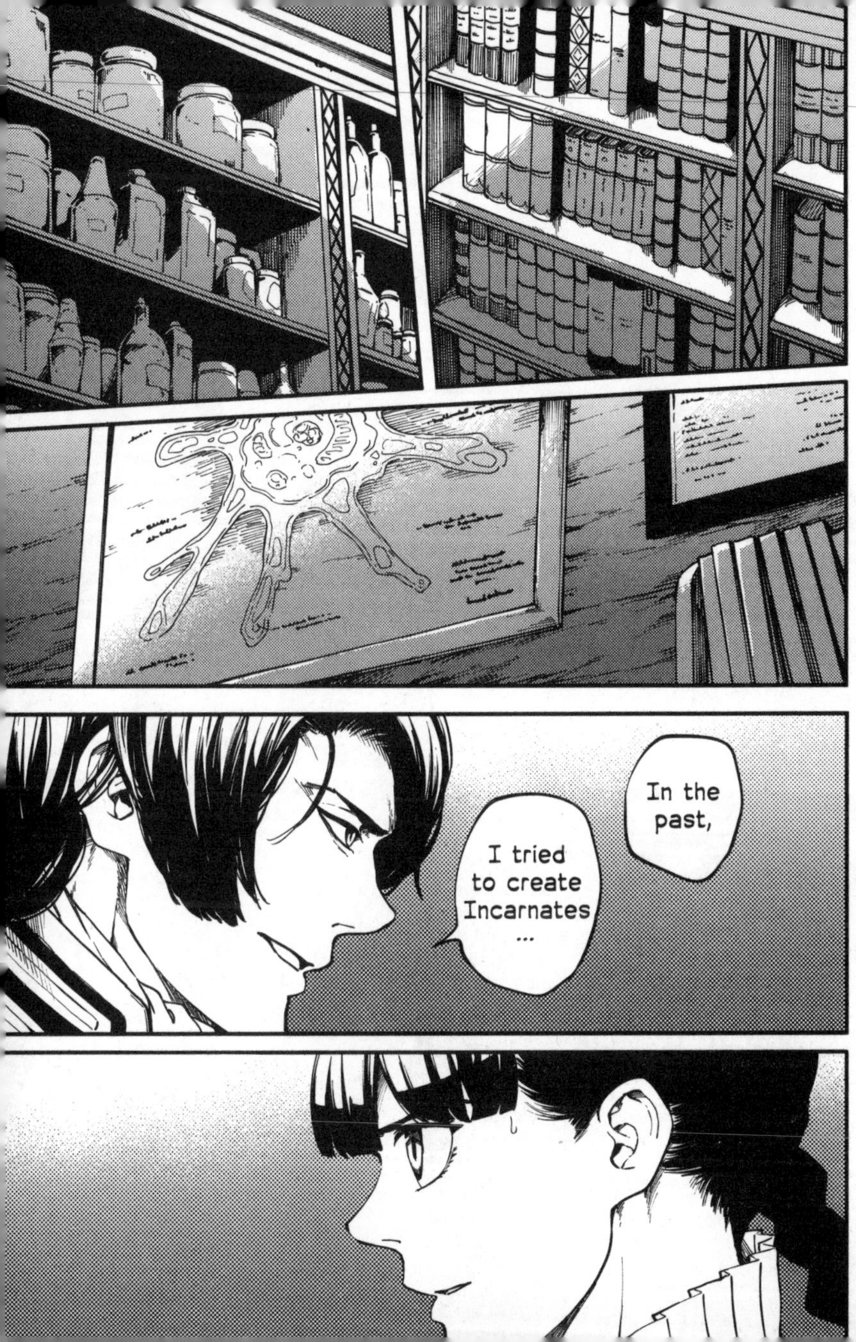
In the past,
I tried to create Incarnates ...

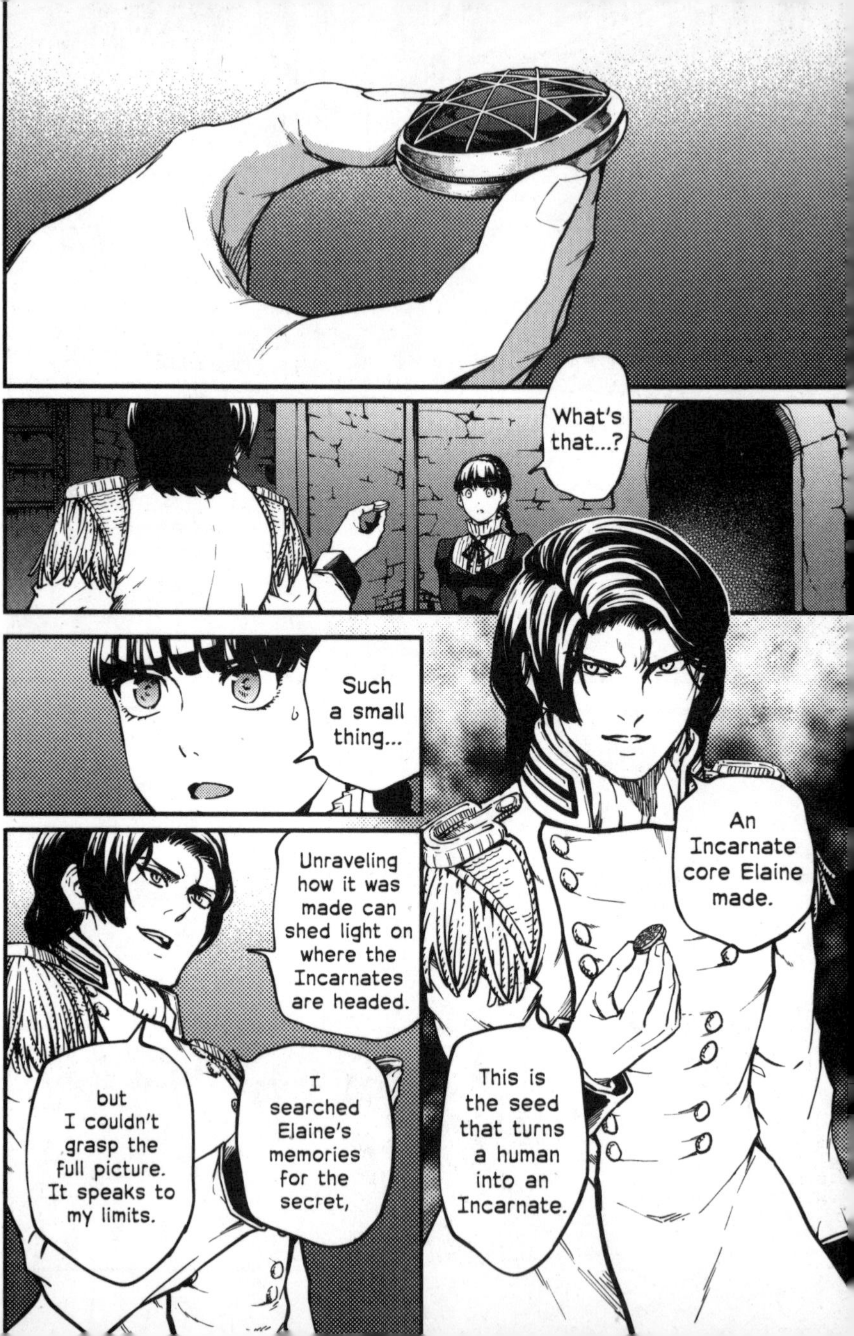
What's that...?
An Incarnate core Elaine made.
This is the seed that turns a human into an Incarnate.
Such a small thing...
Unraveling how it was made can shed light on where the Incarnates are headed.
I searched Elaine's memories for the secret,
but I couldn't grasp the full picture. It speaks to my limits.

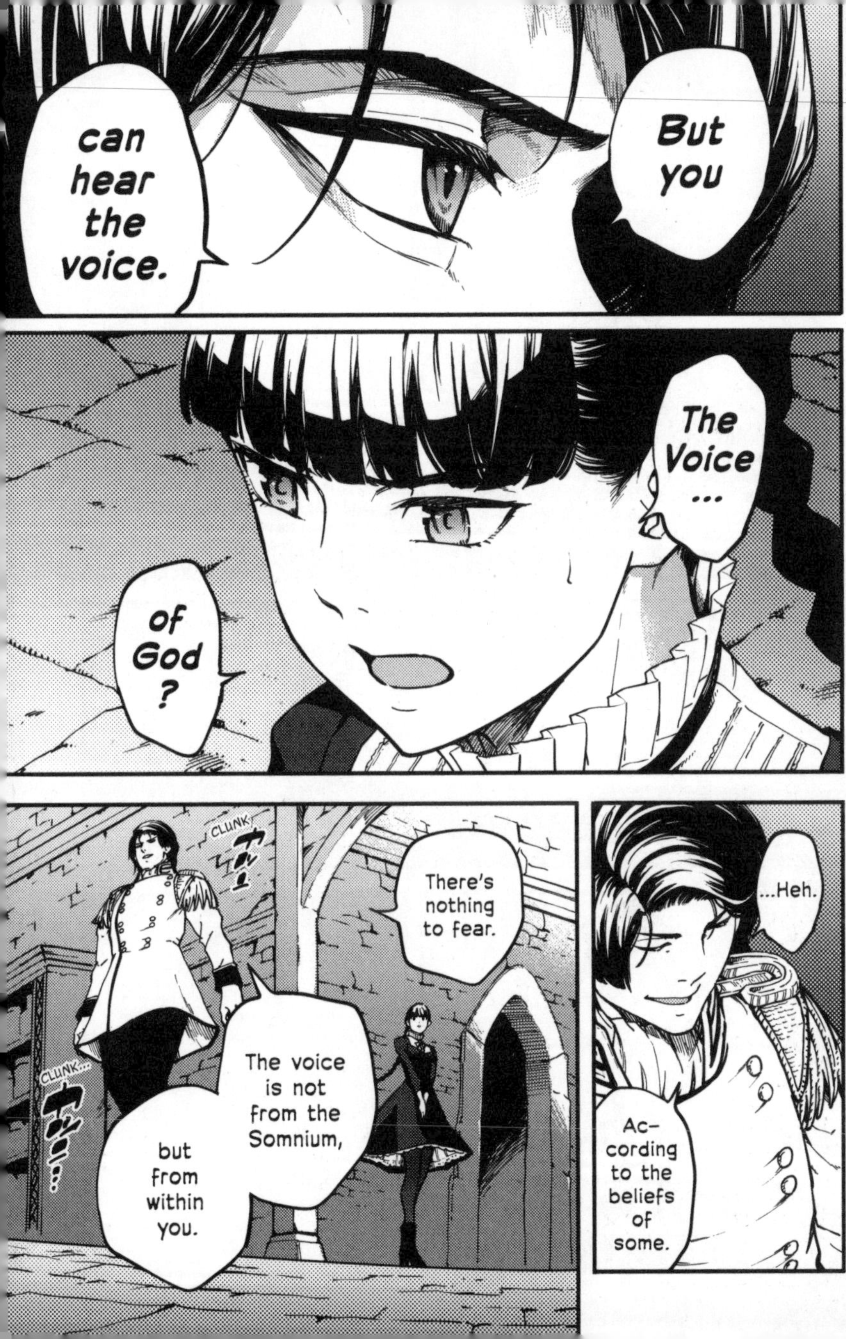

But you
can hear the voice.
The Voice...
of God?
...Heh.
Ac-cording to the beliefs of some.
There's nothing to fear.
CLUNK
The voice is not from the Somnium,
CLUNK...
but from within you.

Sit.

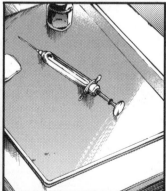

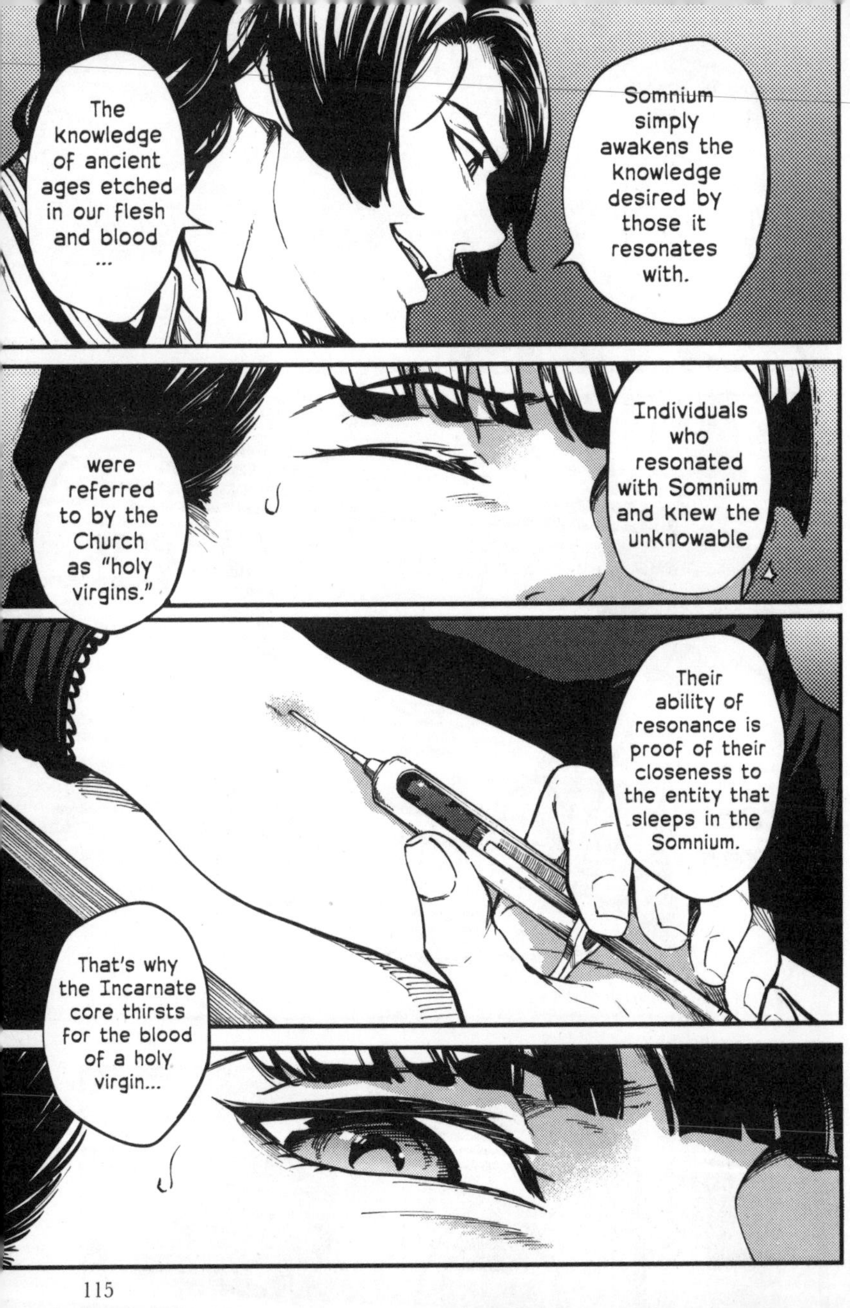
Somnium simply awakens the knowledge desired by those it resonates with.
The knowledge of ancient ages etched in our flesh and blood ...
Individuals who resonated with Somnium and knew the unknowable
were referred to by the Church as "holy virgins."
Their ability of resonance is proof of their closeness to the entity that sleeps in the Somnium.
That's why the Incarnate core thirsts for the blood of a holy virgin...

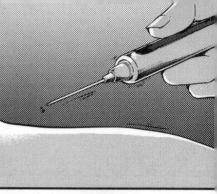

I pray that your wish

is real- ized.

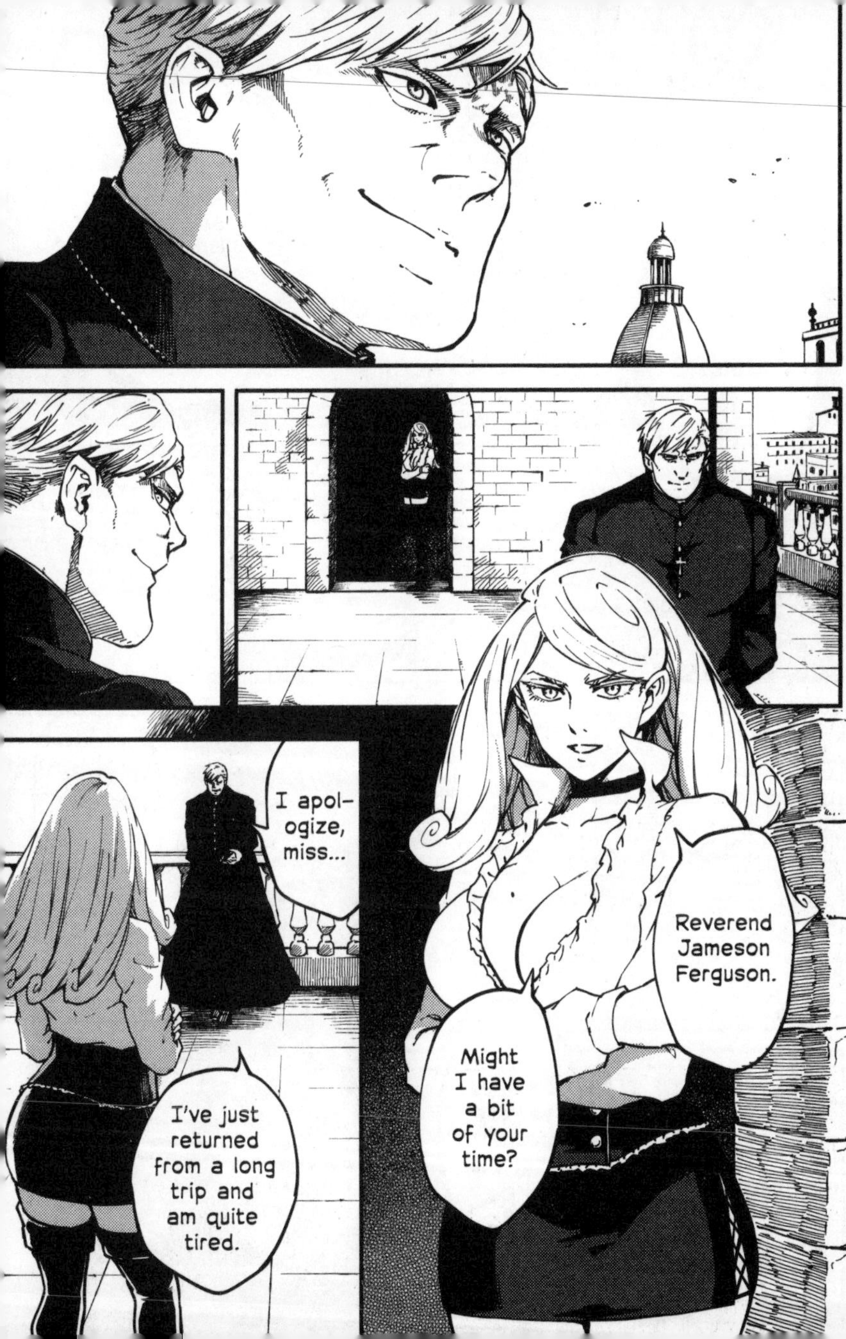
Reverend Jameson Ferguson.
Might I have a bit of your time?
I apologize, miss...
I've just returned from a long trip and am quite tired.

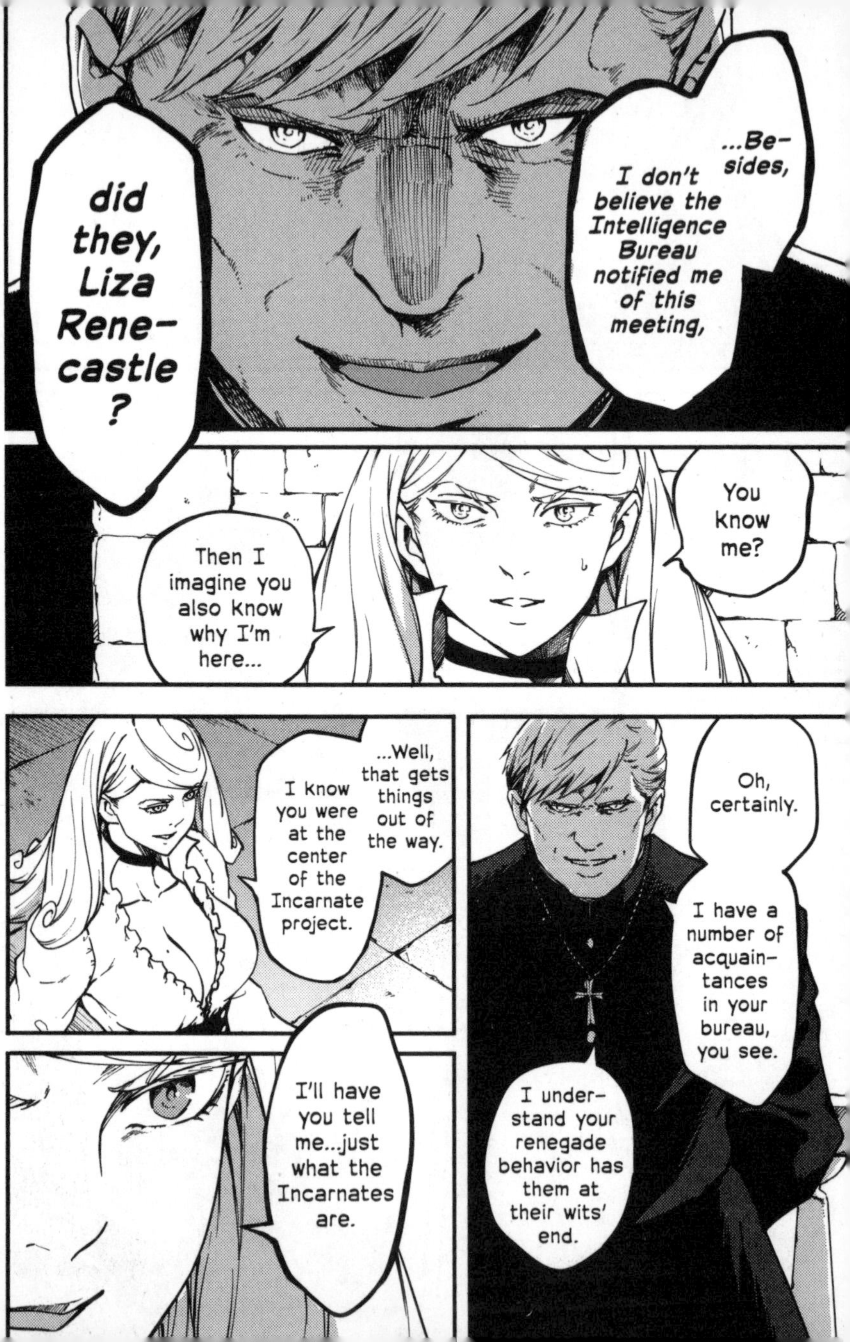
...Besides,
I don't believe the Intelligence Bureau notified me of this meeting,
did they, Liza Renecastle?
You know me?
Then I imagine you also know why I'm here...
Oh, certainly.
I have a number of acquaintances in your bureau, you see.
I understand your renegade behavior has them at their wits' end.
...Well, that gets things out of the way.
I know you were at the center of the Incarnate project.
I'll have you tell me...just what the Incarnates are.

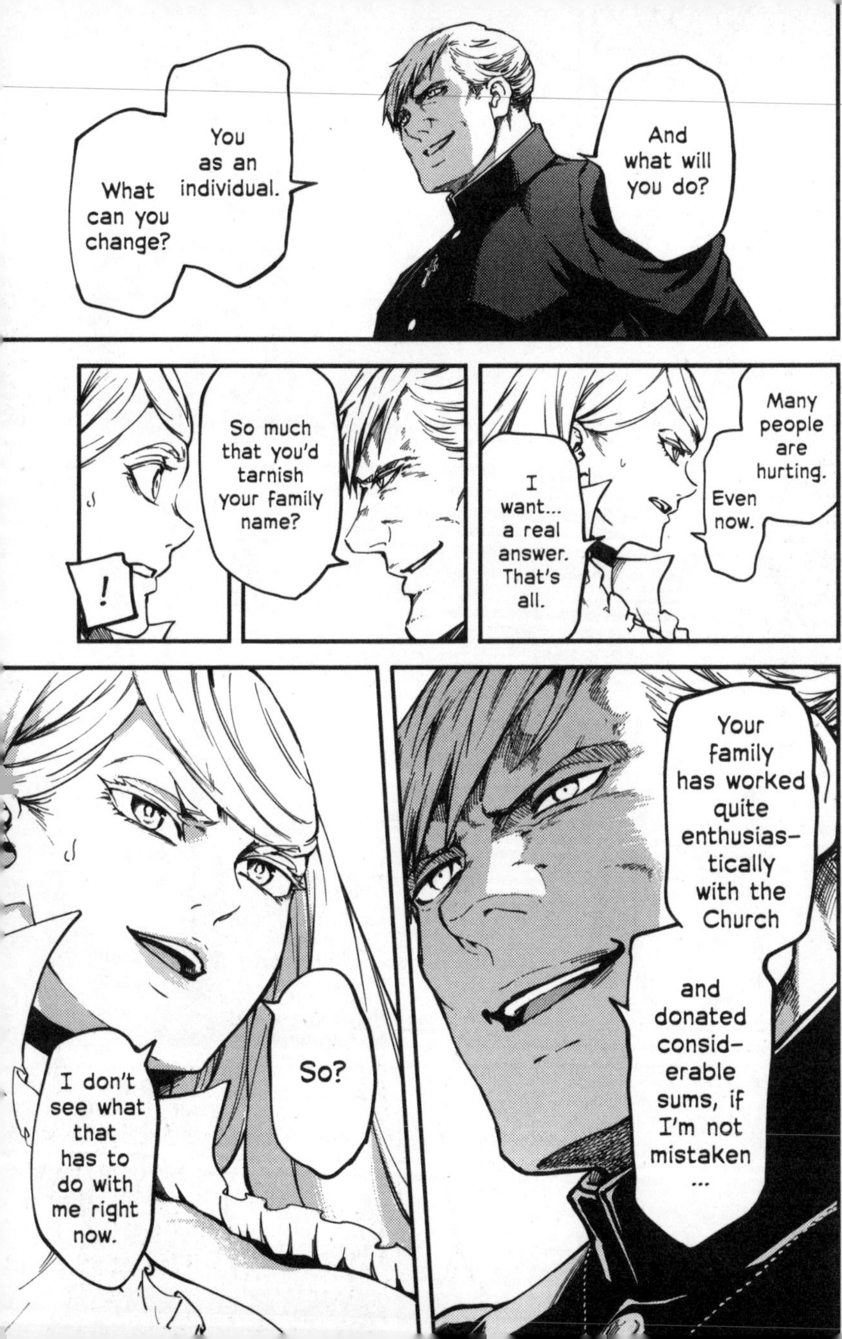
And what will you do?
You as an individual.
What can you change?
Many people are hurting.
Even now.
I want... a real answer. That's all.
So much that you'd tarnish your family name?
!
Your family has worked quite enthusias-tically with the Church
and donated consid-erable sums, if I'm not mistaken ...
So?
I don't see what that has to do with me right now.

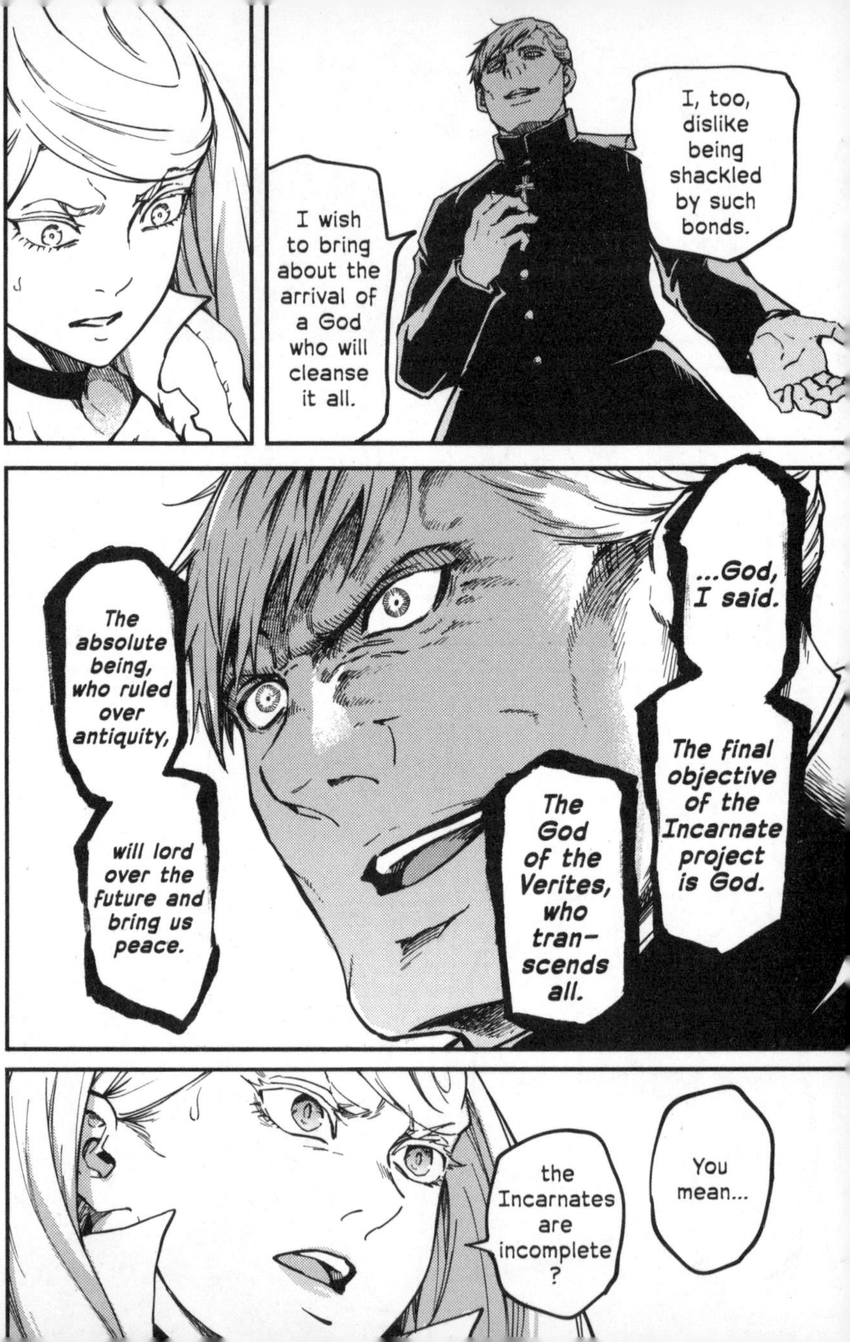
I, too, dislike being shackled by such bonds.
I wish to bring about the arrival of a God who will cleanse it all.
...God, I said.
The final objective of the Incarnate project is God.
The God of the Verites, who tran-scends all.
The absolute being, who ruled over antiquity,
will lord over the future and bring us peace.
You mean...
the Incarnates are incomplete ?

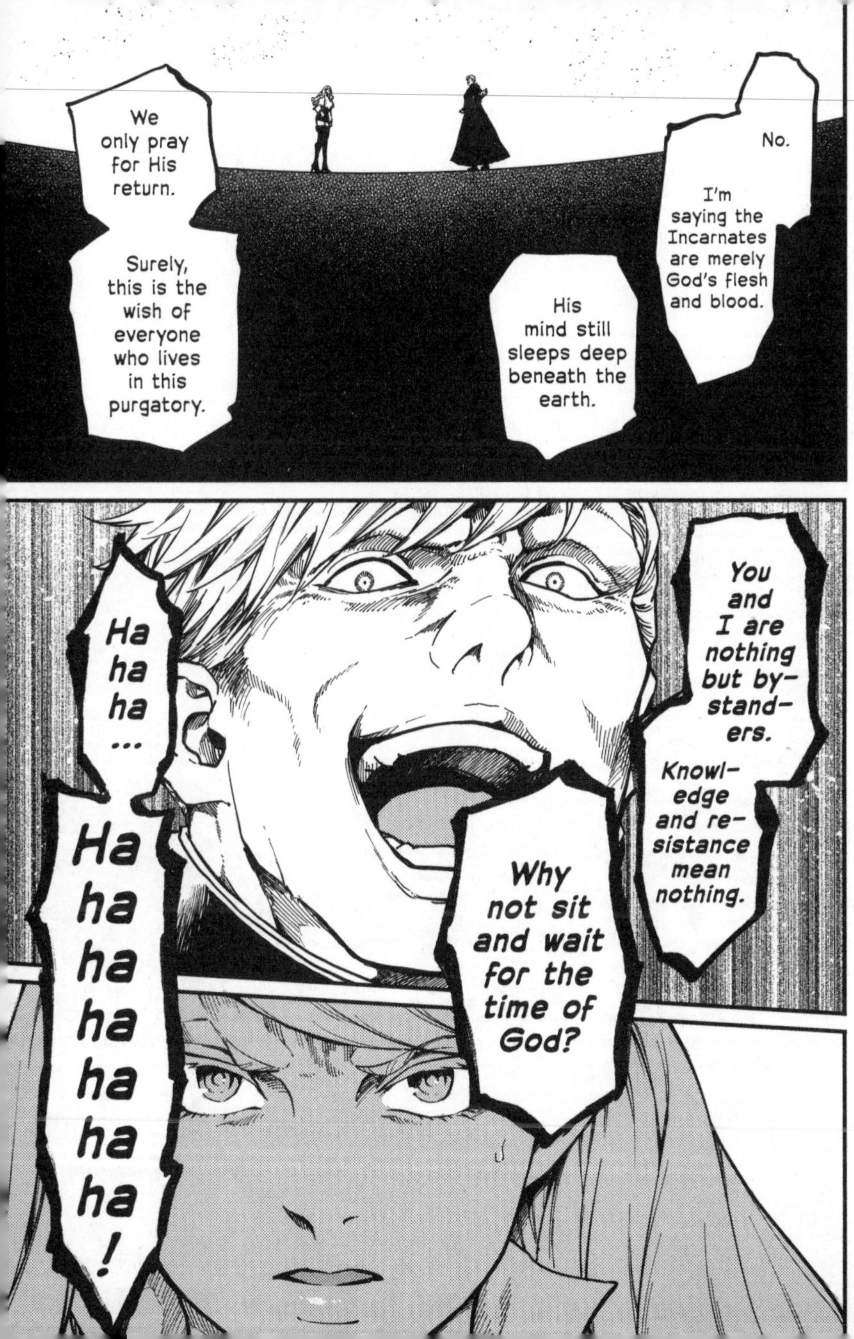
No.
I'm saying the Incarnates are merely God's flesh and blood.
His mind still sleeps deep beneath the earth.
We only pray for His return.
Surely, this is the wish of everyone who lives in this purgatory.
You and I are nothing but by-standers.
Knowledge and resistance mean nothing.
Why not sit and wait for the time of God?
Ha ha ha...
Ha ha ha ha ha ha ha ha ha!

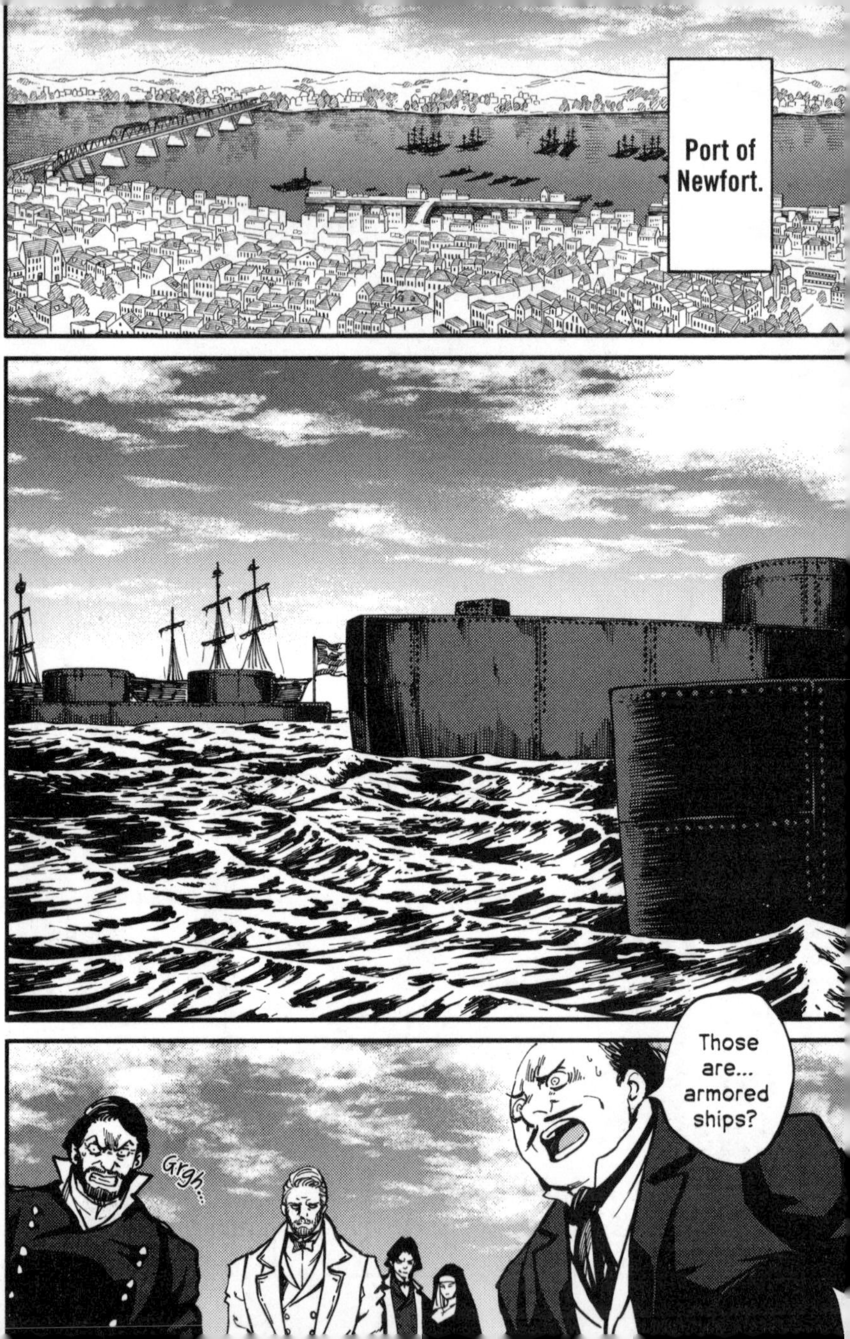
Port of Newfort.
Those are... armored ships?
Grgh...

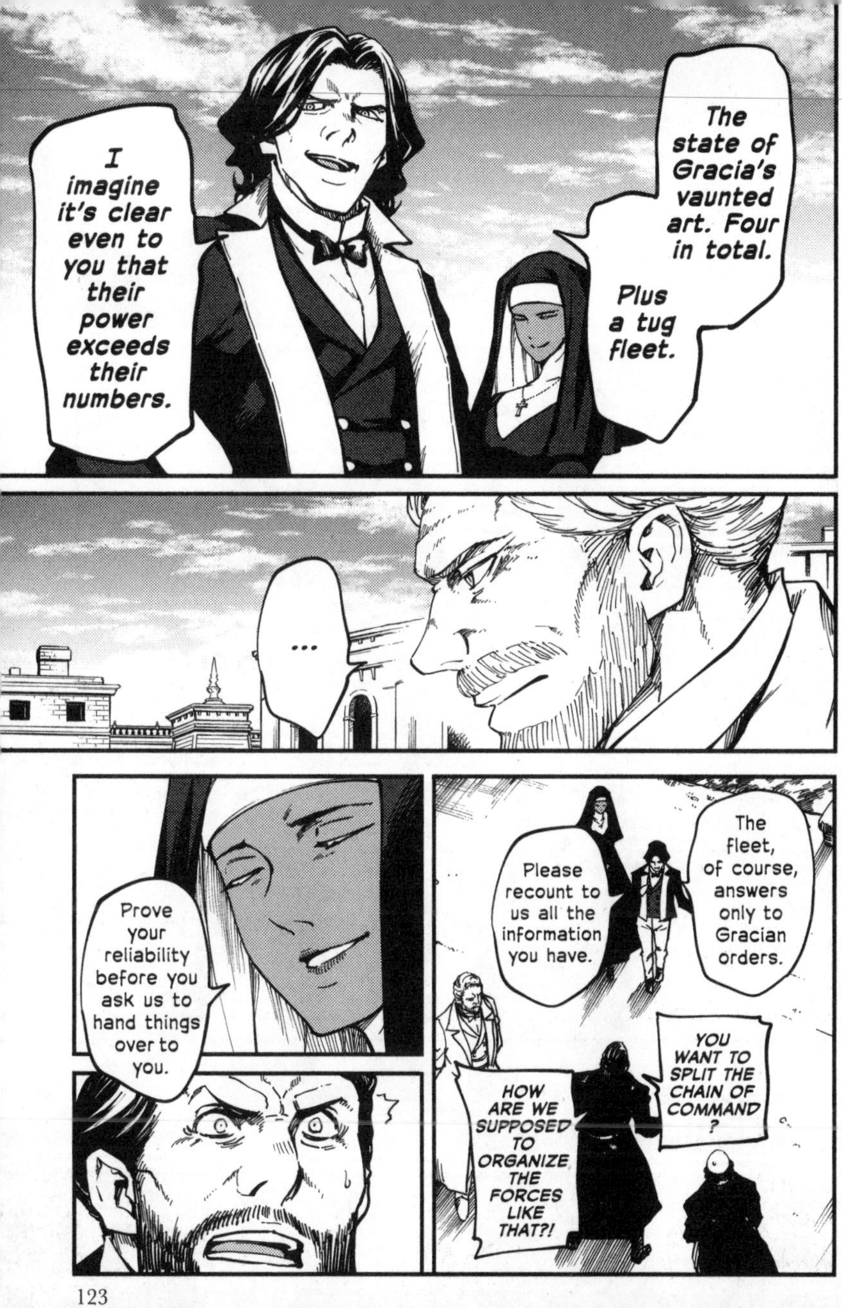

The state of Gracia's vaunted art. Four in total.
Plus a tug fleet.
I imagine it's clear even to you that their power exceeds their numbers.
...
The fleet, of course, answers only to Gracian orders.
Please recount to us all the information you have.
YOU WANT TO SPLIT THE CHAIN OF COMMAND?
HOW ARE WE SUPPOSED TO ORGANIZE THE FORCES LIKE THAT?!
Prove your reliability before you ask us to hand things over to you.

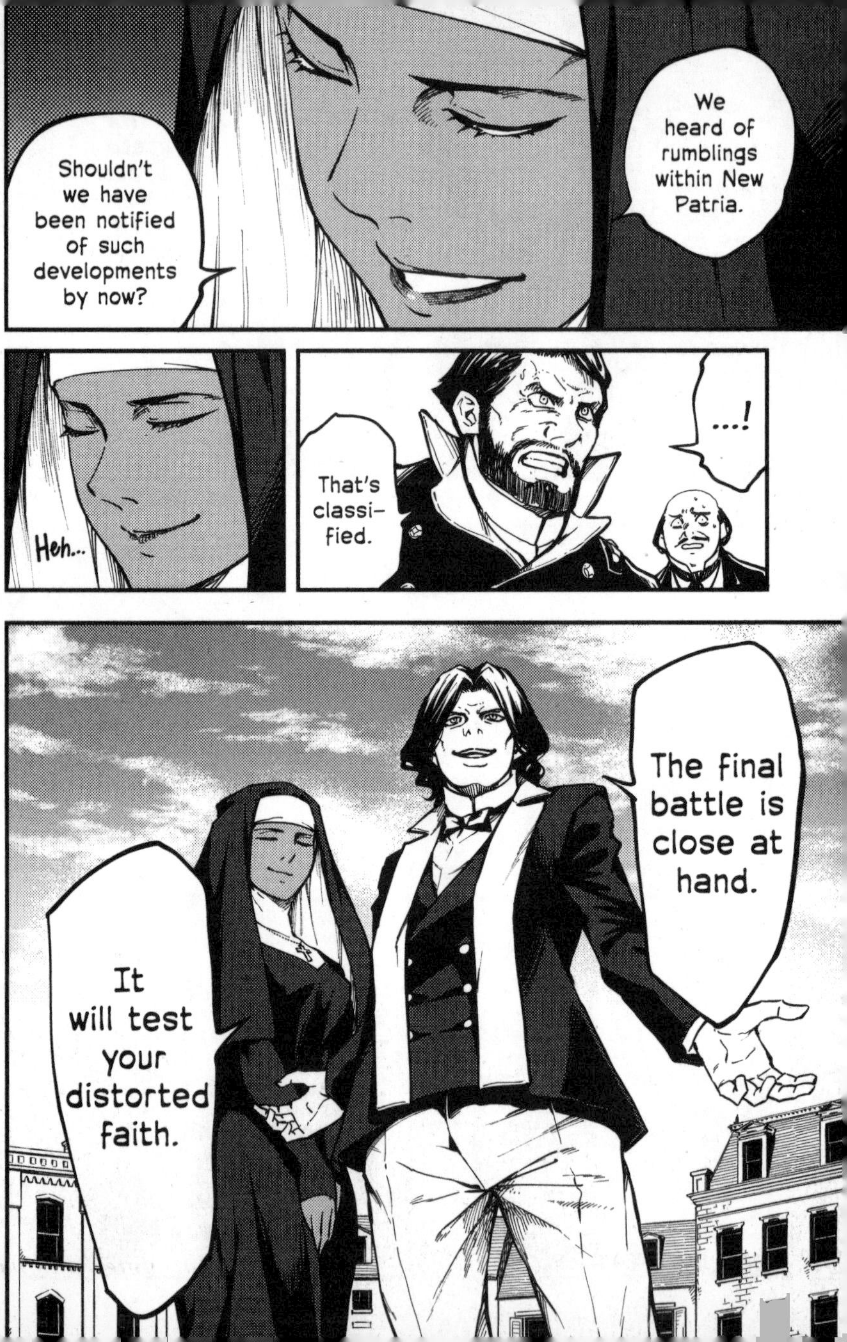
We heard of rumblings within New Patria.
Shouldn't we have been notified of such developments by now?
...!
That's classi-fied.
Heh...
The final battle is close at hand.
It will test your distorted faith.

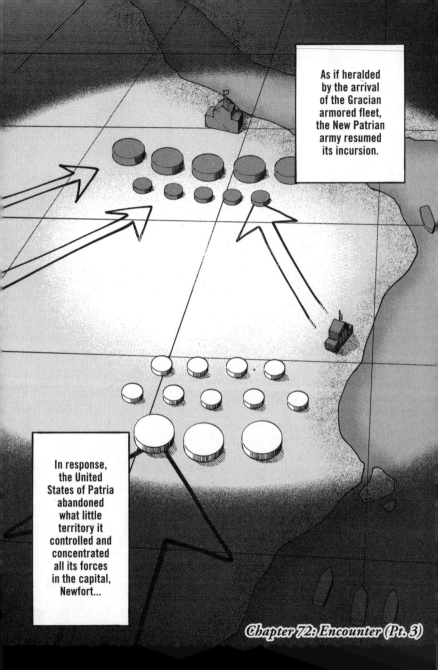

As if heralded by the arrival of the Gracian armored fleet, the New Patrian army resumed its incursion.

In response, the United States of Patria abandoned what little territory it controlled and concentrated all its forces in the capital, Newfort...

Chapter 72: Encounter (Pt. 3)

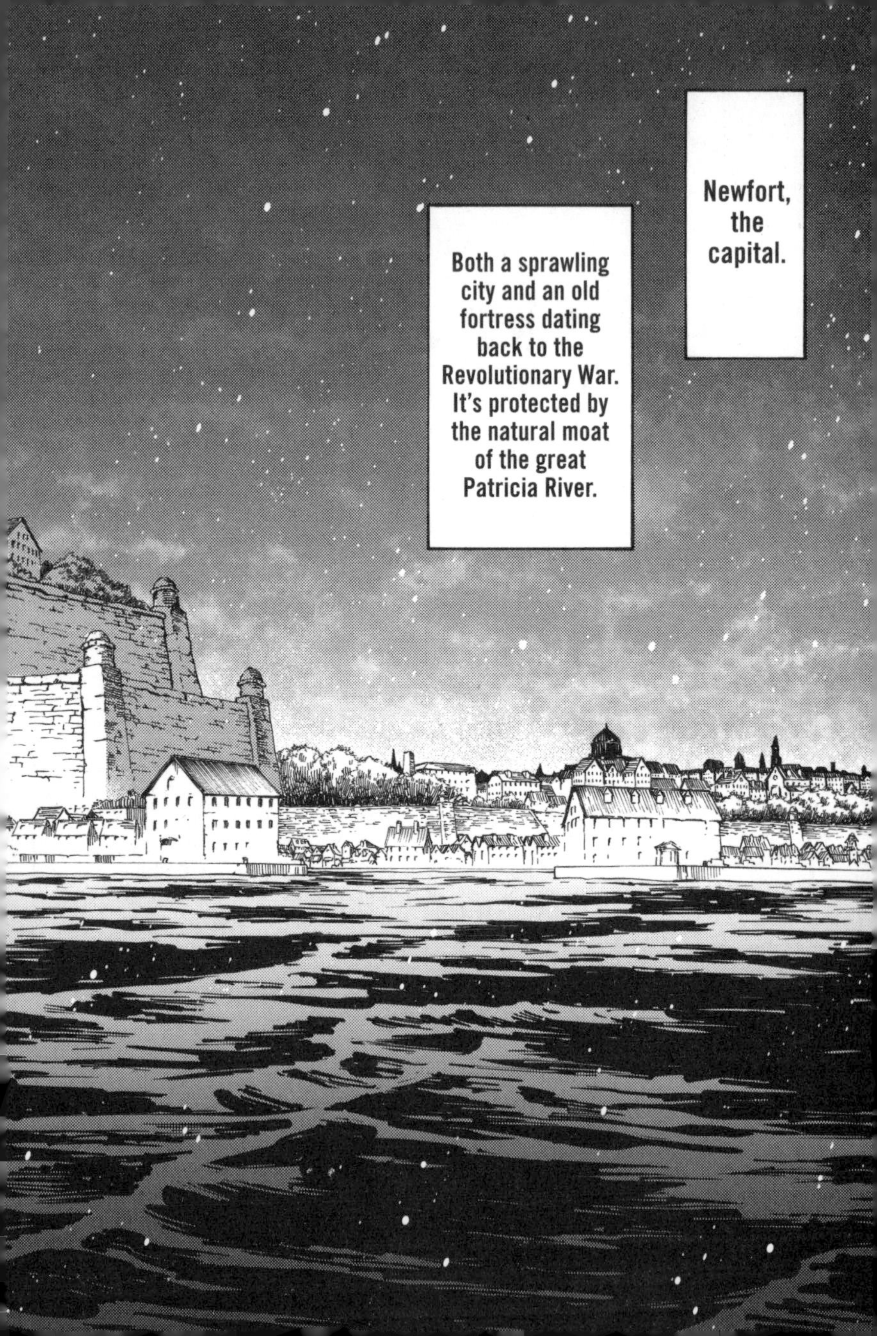
Newfort,
the
capital.
Both a sprawling
city and an old
fortress dating
back to the
Revolutionary War.
It's protected by
the natural moat
of the great
Patricia River.

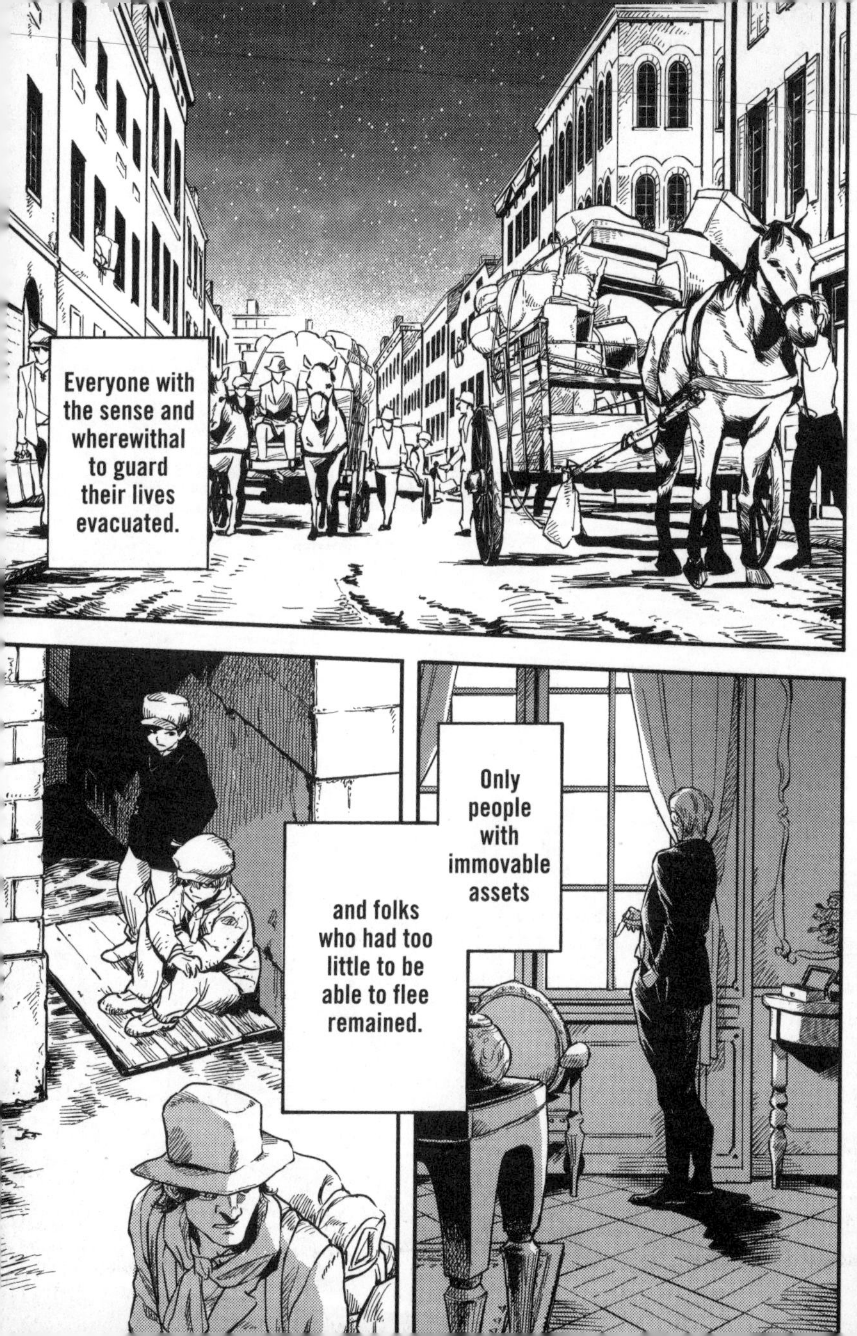
Everyone with the sense and wherewithal to guard their lives evacuated.
Only people with immovable assets
and folks who had too little to be able to flee remained.

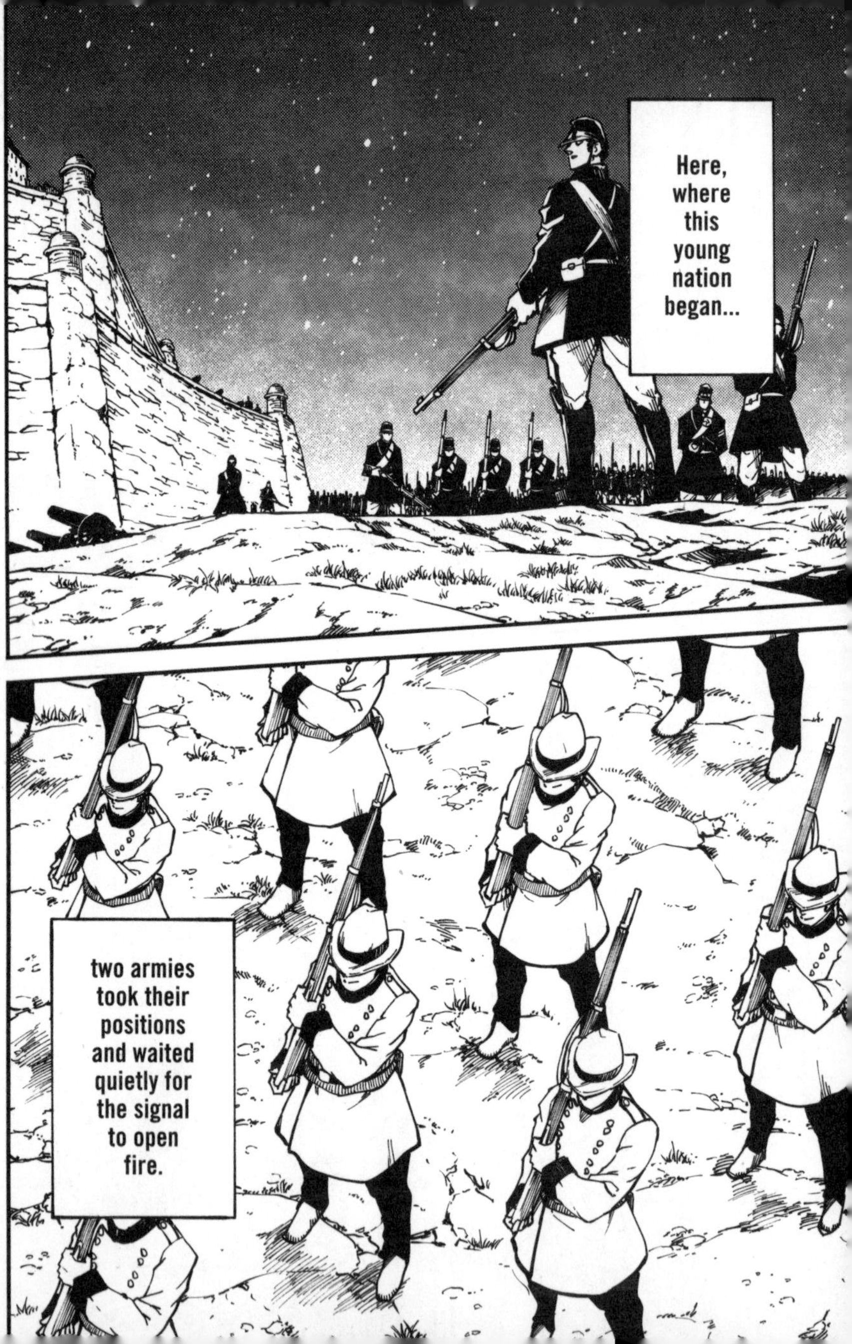
Here, where this young nation began...
two armies took their positions and waited quietly for the signal to open fire.

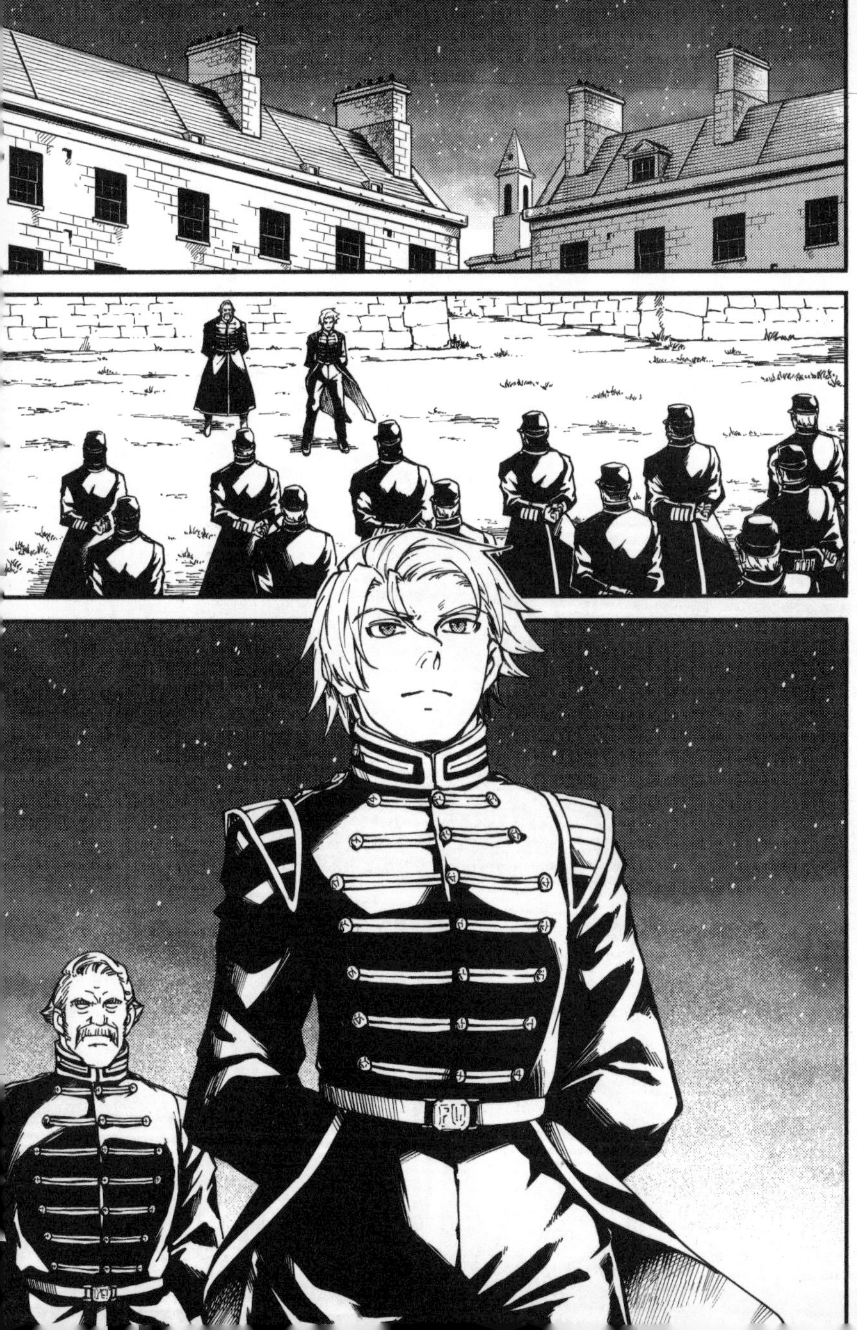

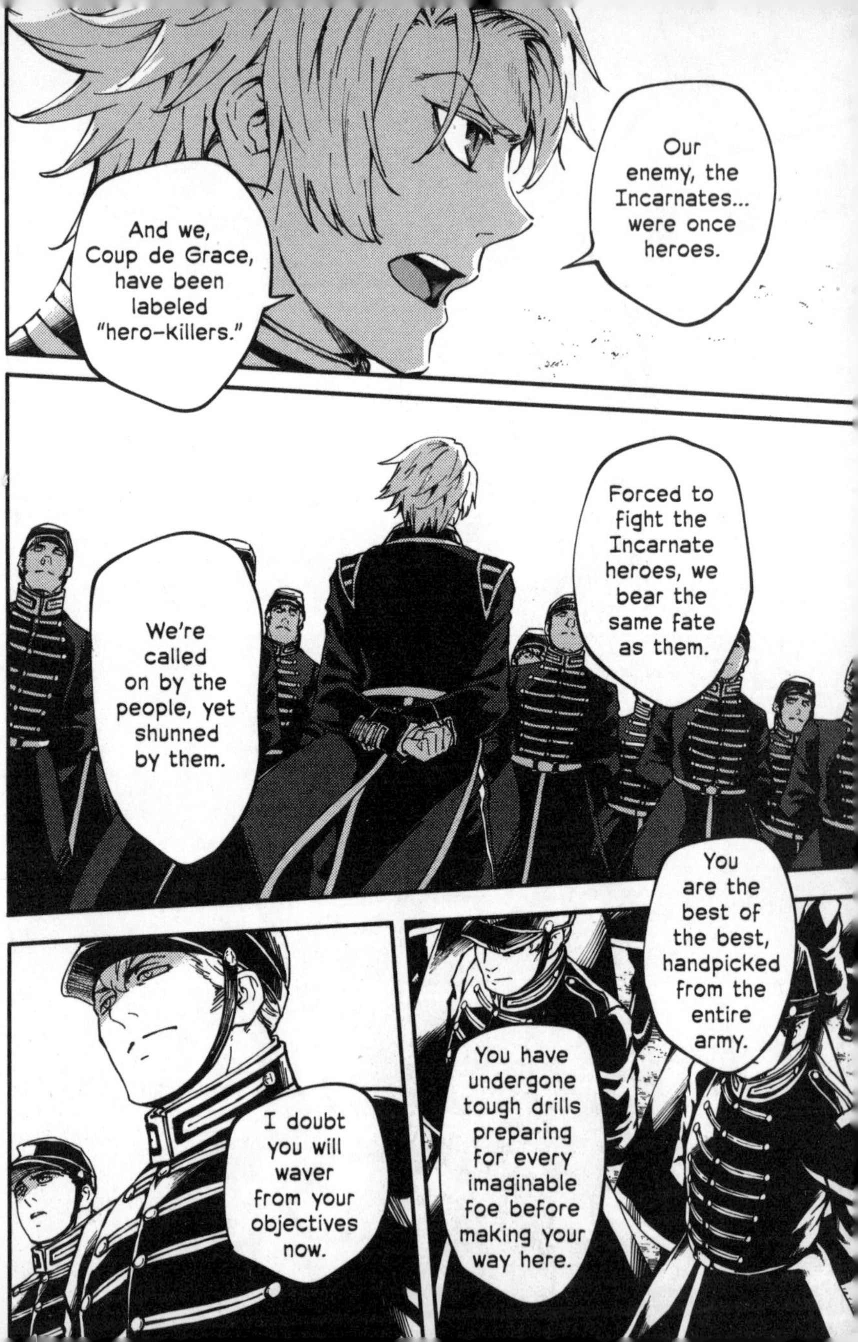
Our enemy, the Incarnates... were once heroes.
And we, Coup de Grace, have been labeled "hero-killers."
Forced to fight the Incarnate heroes, we bear the same fate as them.
We're called on by the people, yet shunned by them.
You are the best of the best, handpicked from the entire army.
You have undergone tough drills preparing for every imaginable foe before making your way here.
I doubt you will waver from your objectives now.

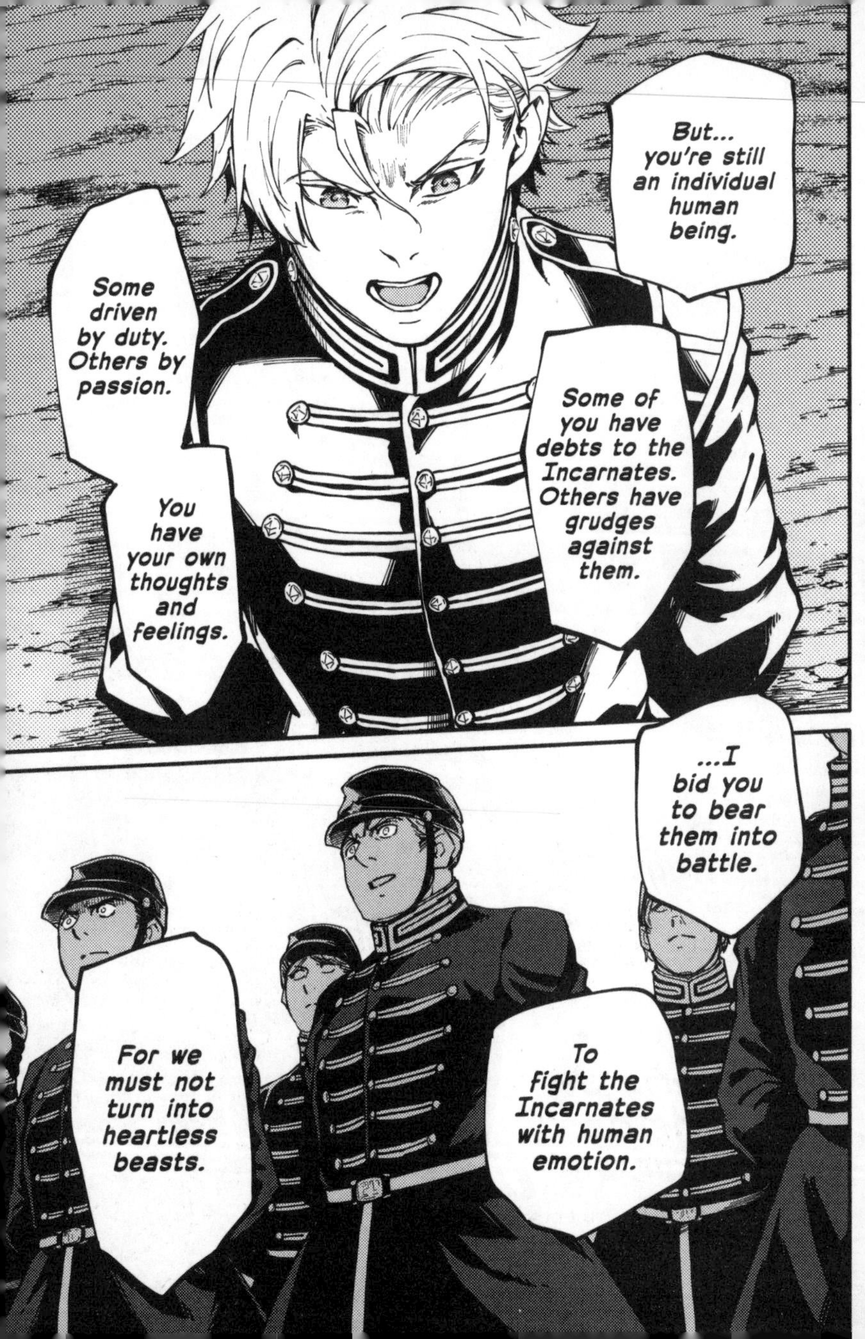
But... you're still an individual human being.
Some driven by duty. Others by passion.
Some of you have debts to the Incarnates. Others have grudges against them.
You have your own thoughts and feelings.
...I bid you to bear them into battle.
To fight the Incarnates with human emotion.
For we must not turn into heartless beasts.

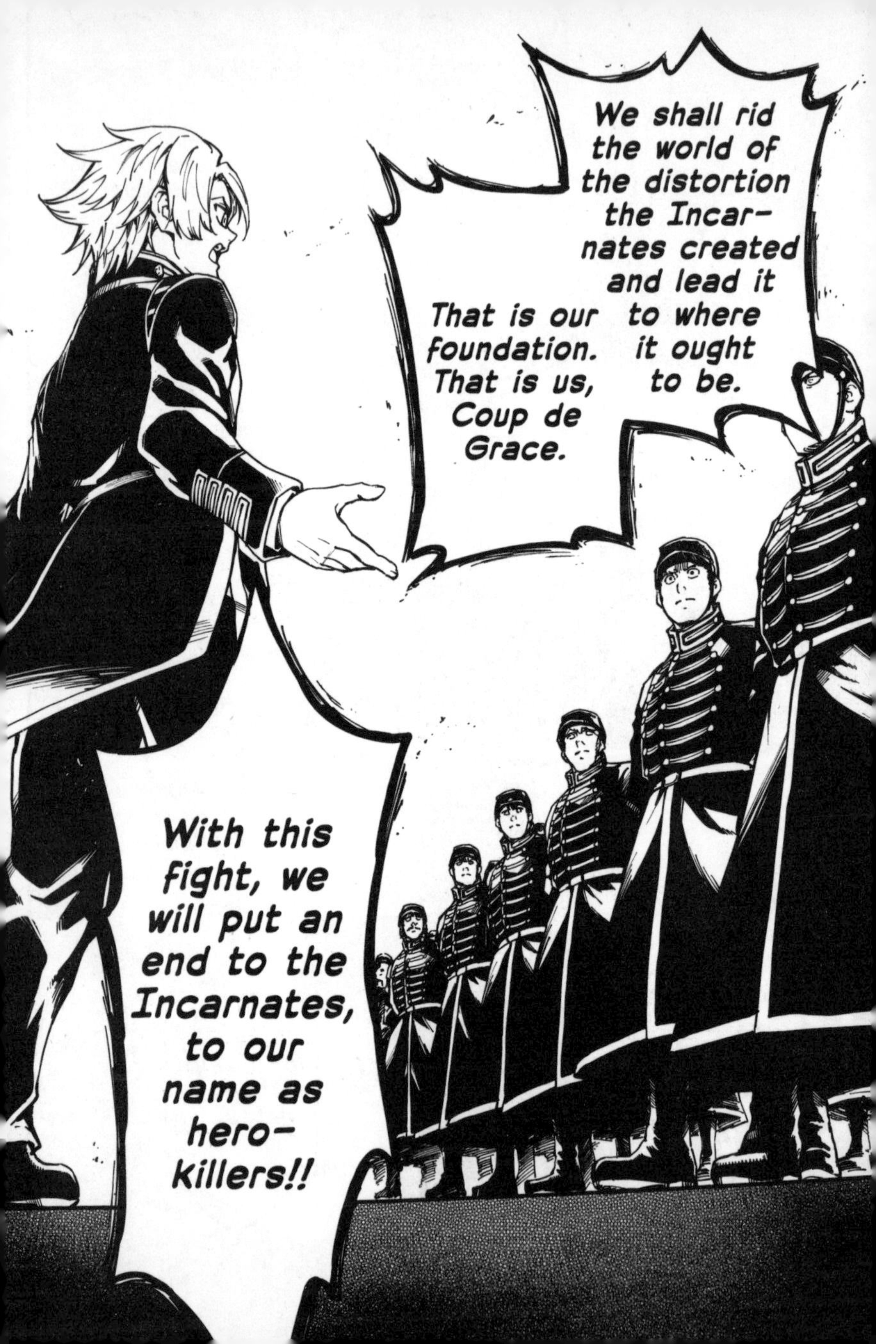
We shall rid the world of the distortion the Incar- nates created and lead it to where it ought to be.
That is our foundation. That is us, Coup de Grace.
With this fight, we will put an end to the Incarnates, to our name as hero- killers!!

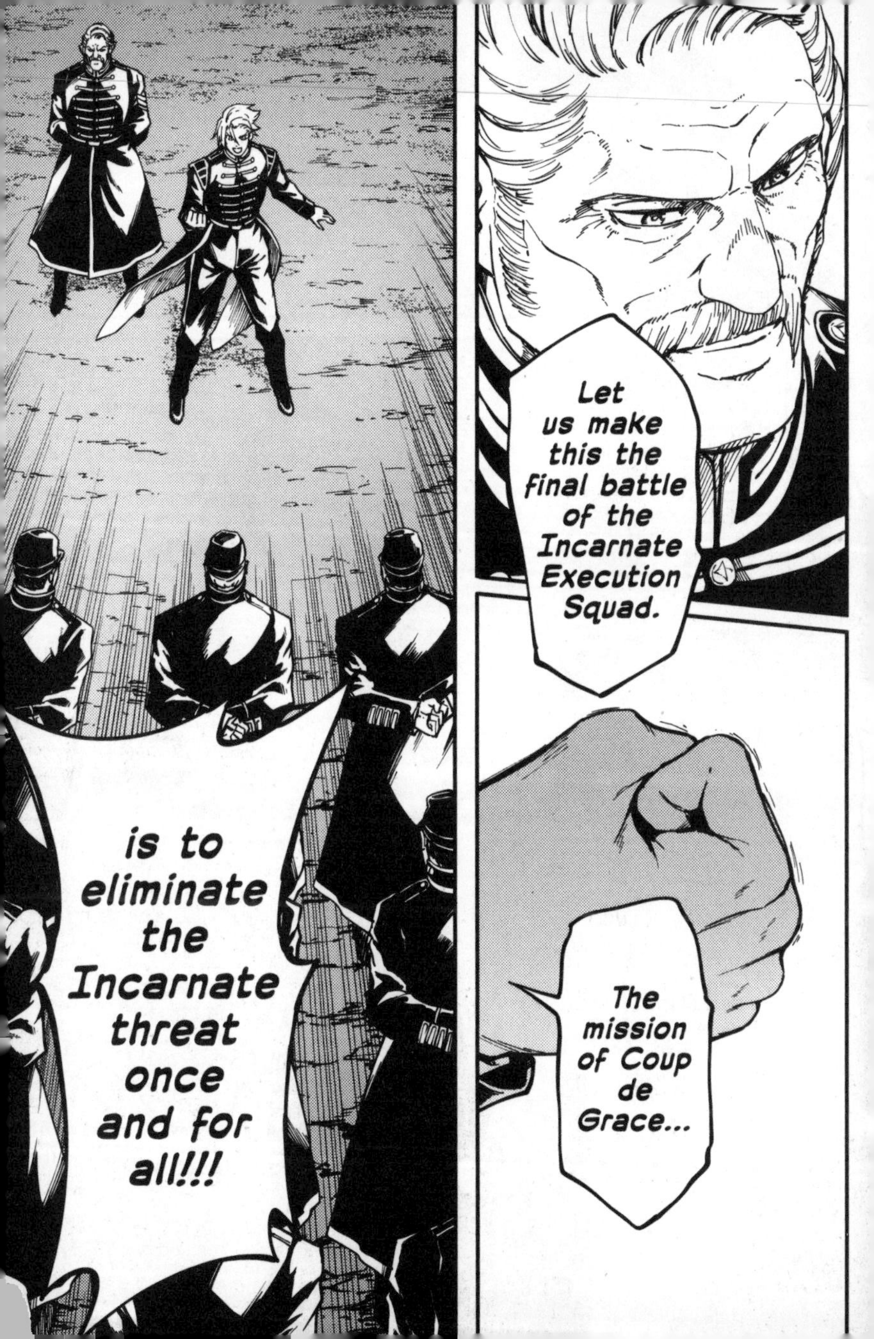
Let us make this the final battle of the Incarnate Execution Squad.
The mission of Coup de Grace...
is to eliminate the Incarnate threat once and for all!!!

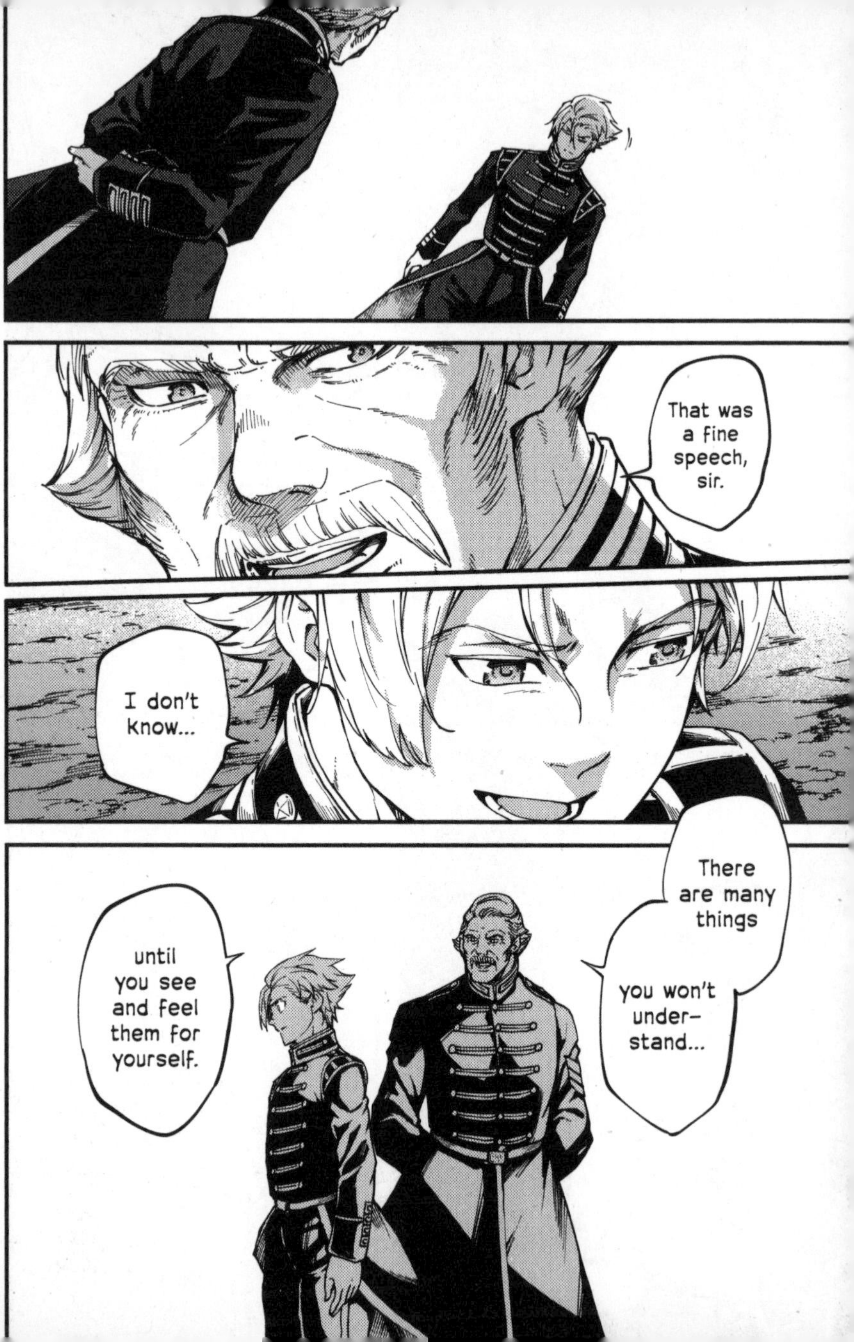
That was a fine speech, sir.
I don't know...
There are many things
you won't under-stand...
until you see and feel them for yourself.

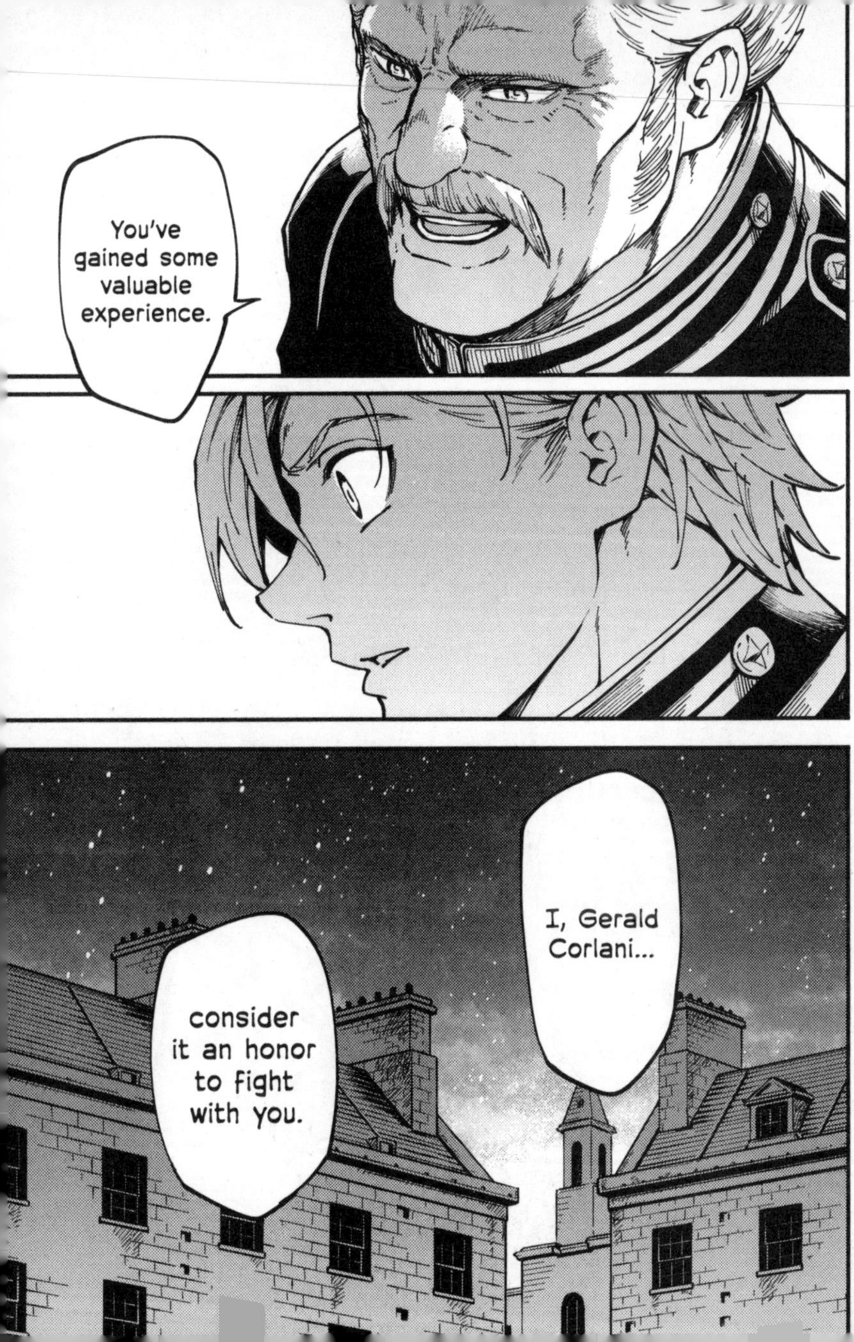
You've gained some valuable experience.
I, Gerald Corlani...
consider it an honor to fight with you.

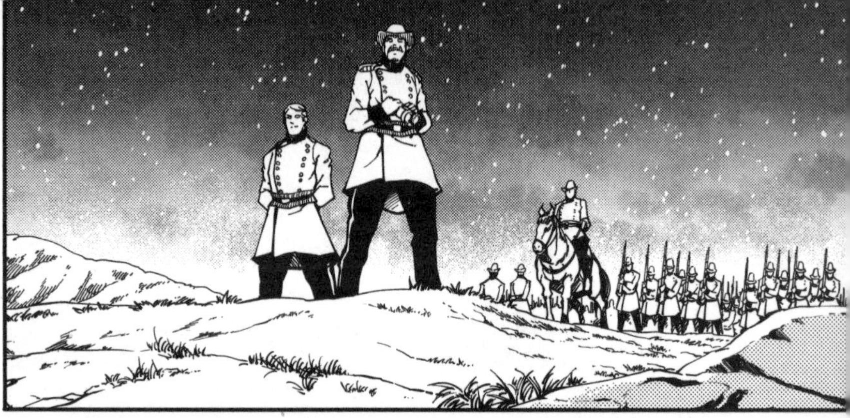
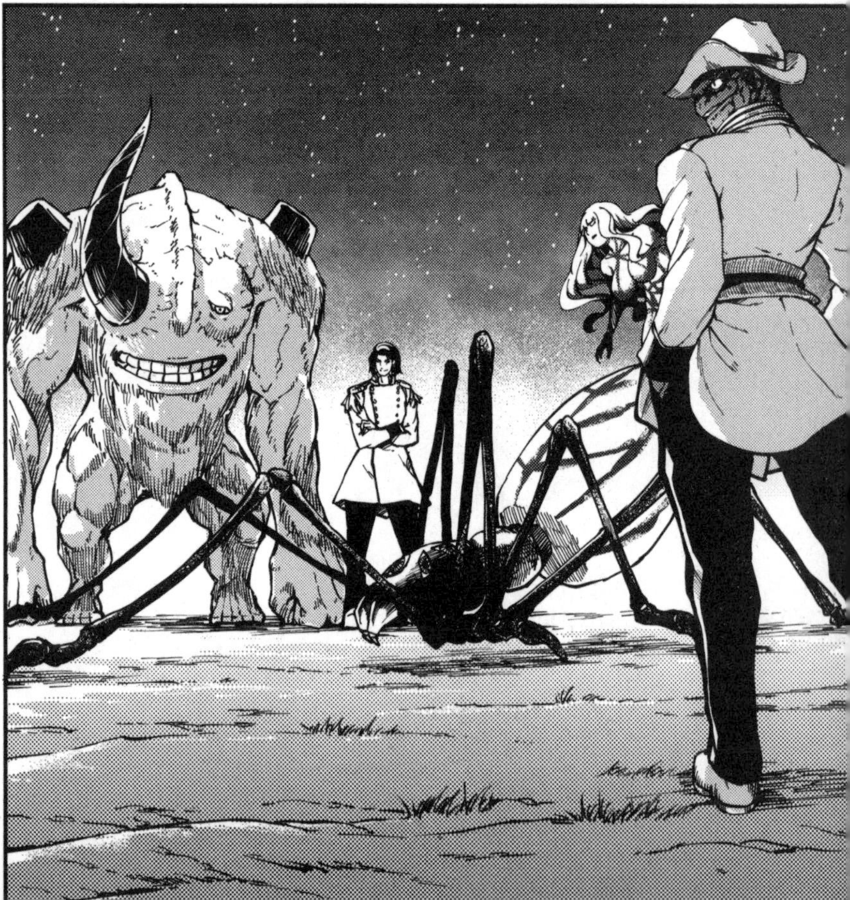

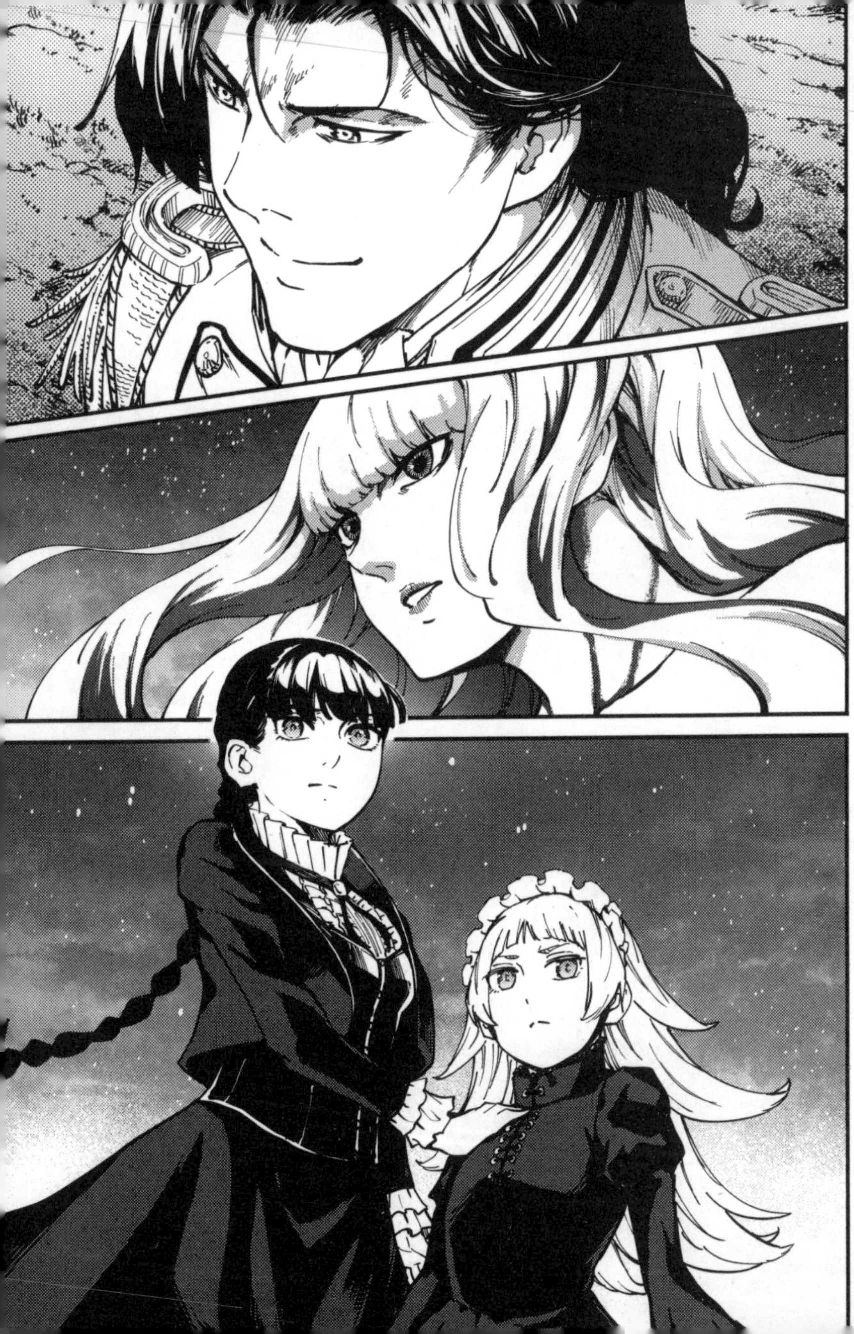

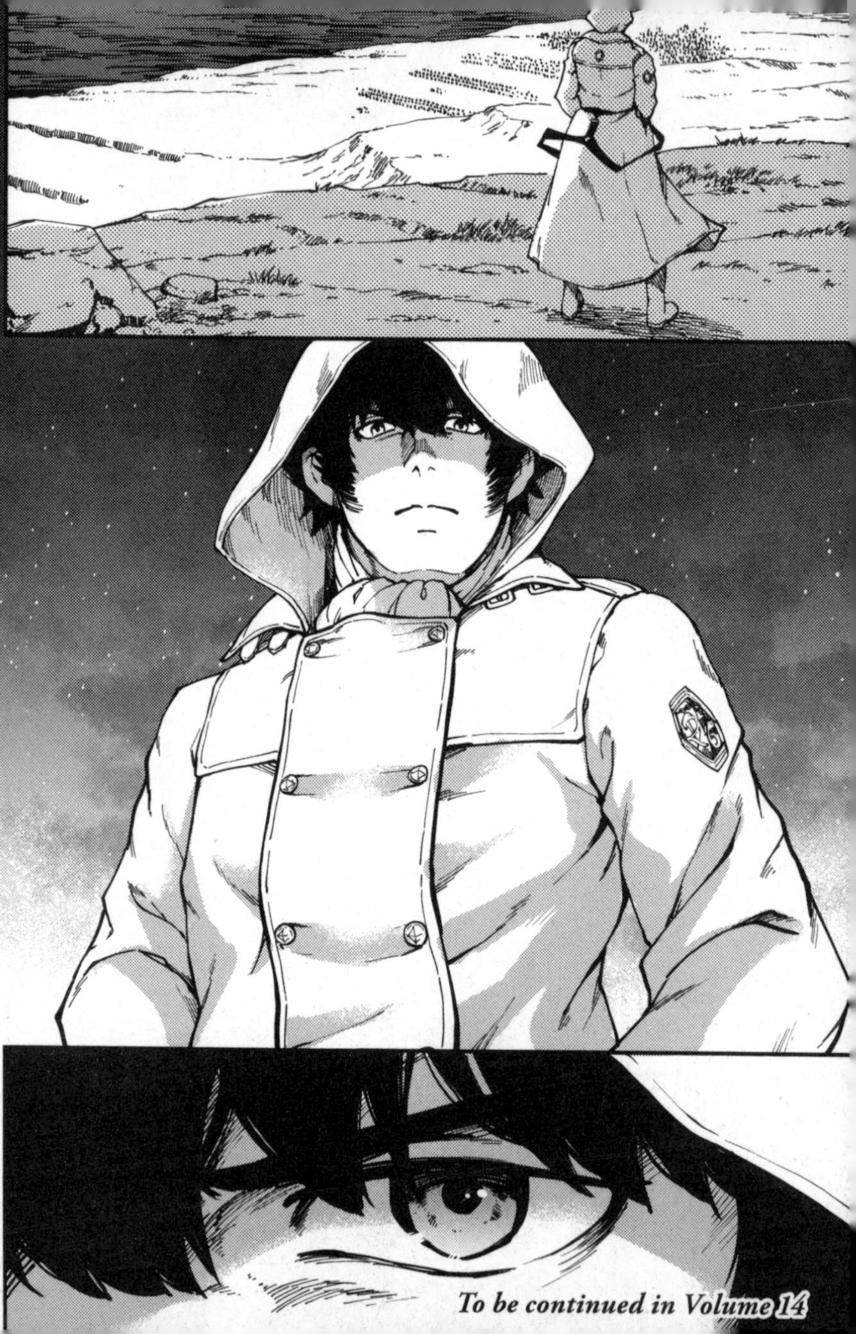
To be continued in Volume 14

To the Abandoned
Sacred Beasts

To the Abandoned
Sacred Beasts

Side Story: The Incarnate Is Coming!

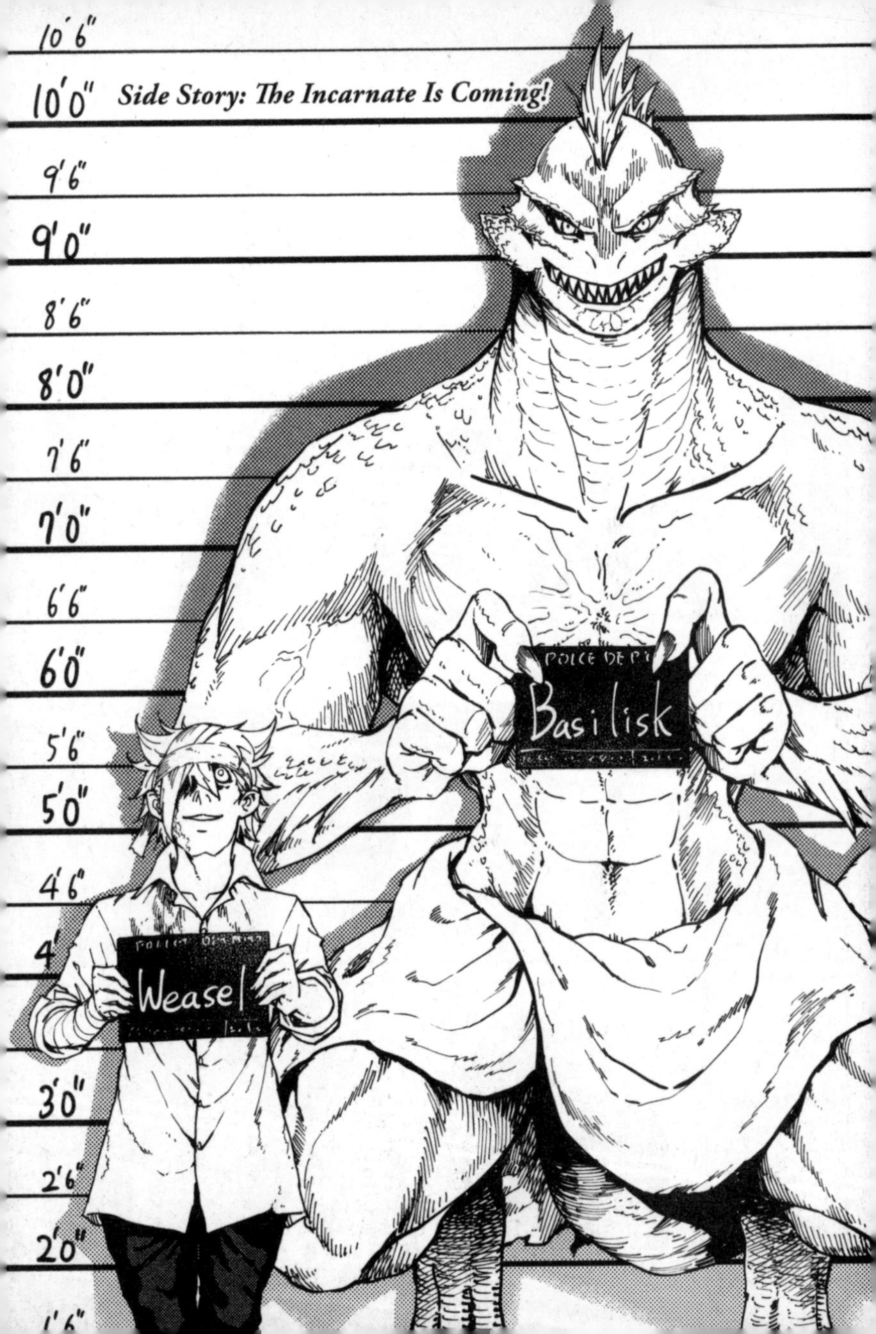
10'6"
10'0"
9'6"
9'0"
8'6"
8'0"
7'6"
7'0"
6'6"
6'0"
5'6"
5'0"
4'6"
4'
3'0"
2'6"
2'0"
POLICE DEPT
Basilisk
Weasel

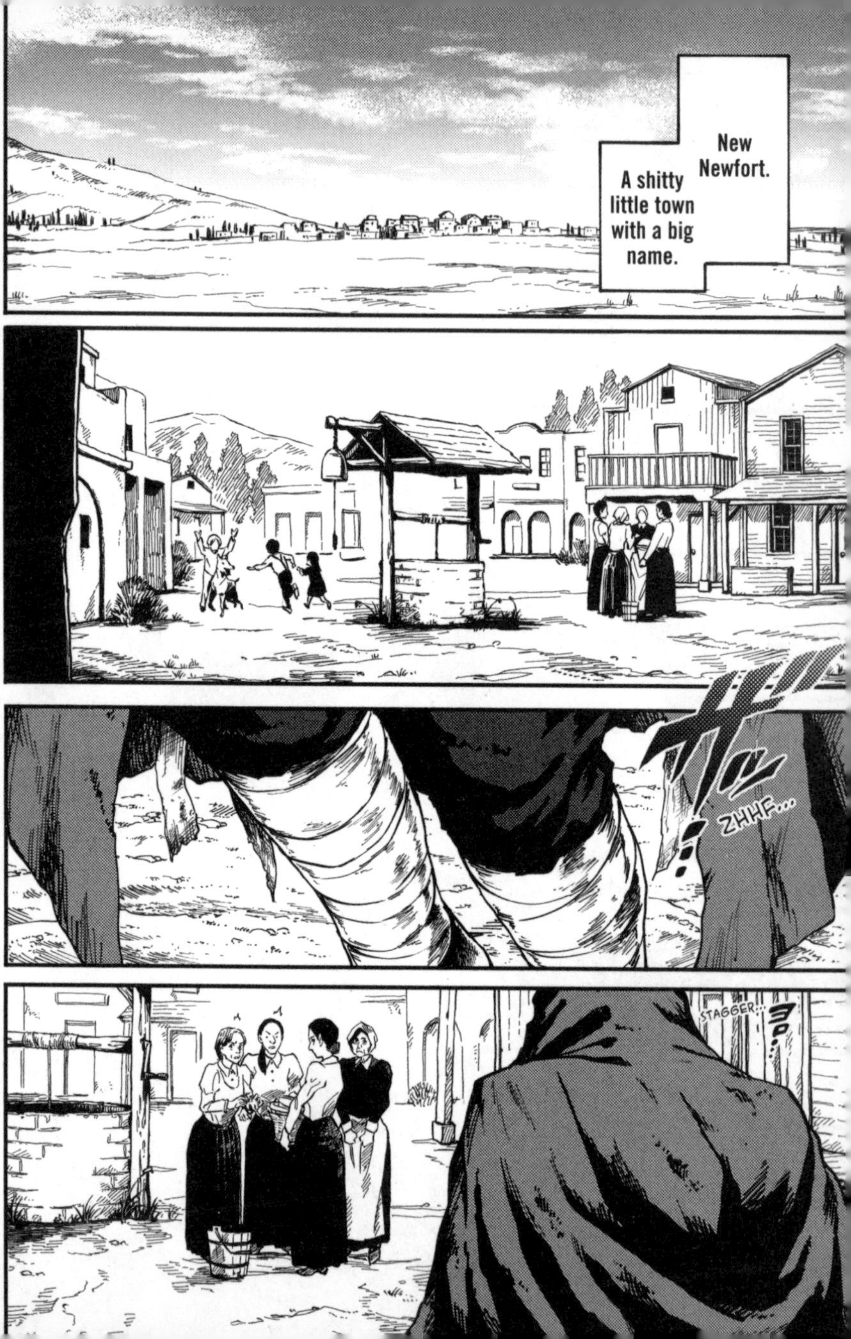
New Newfort.
A shitty little town with a big name.
ZHHF...
STAGGER...

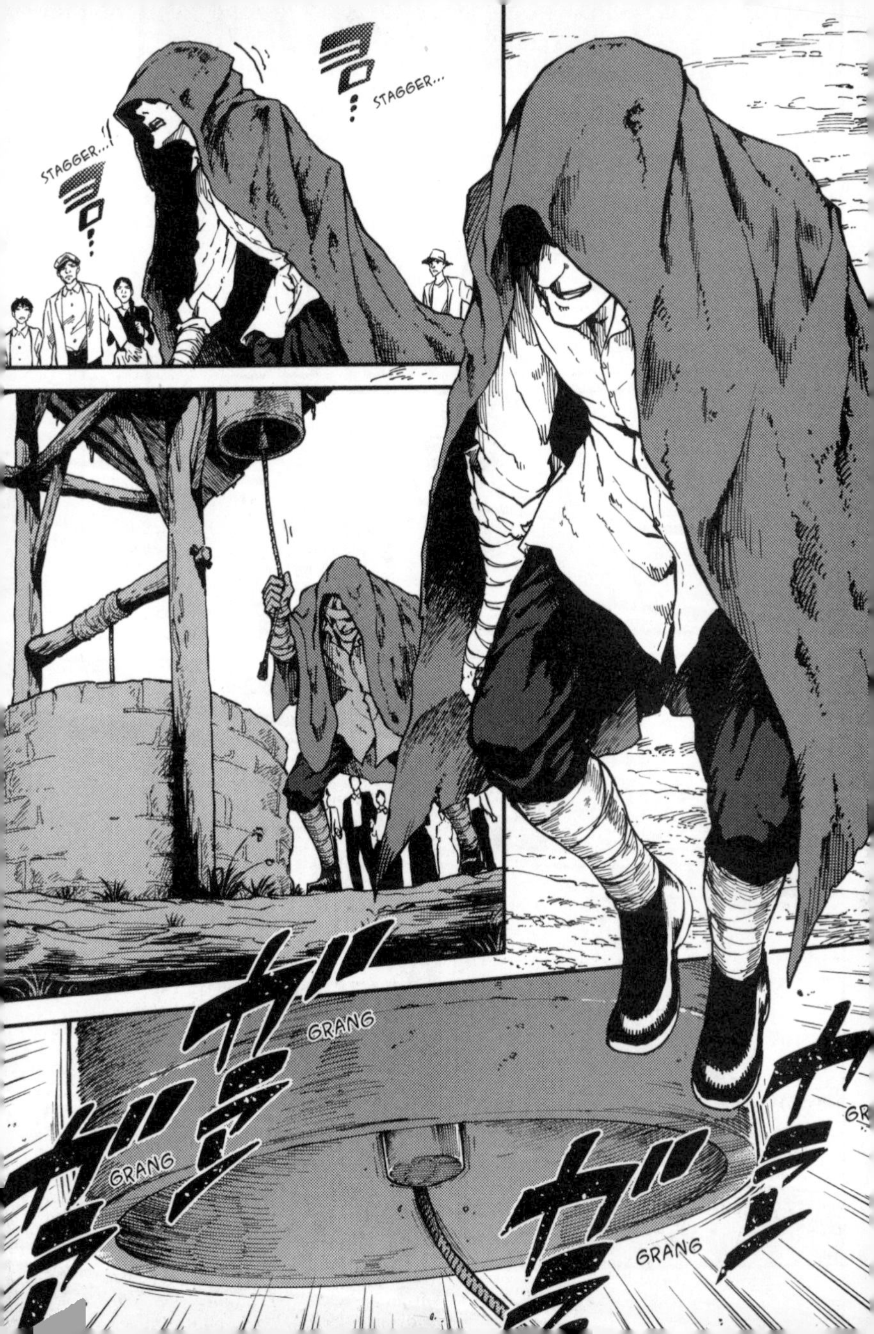
ヨロ…
STAGGER...
STAGGER...!!
ヨロ…
GRANG
GRANG
GRANG

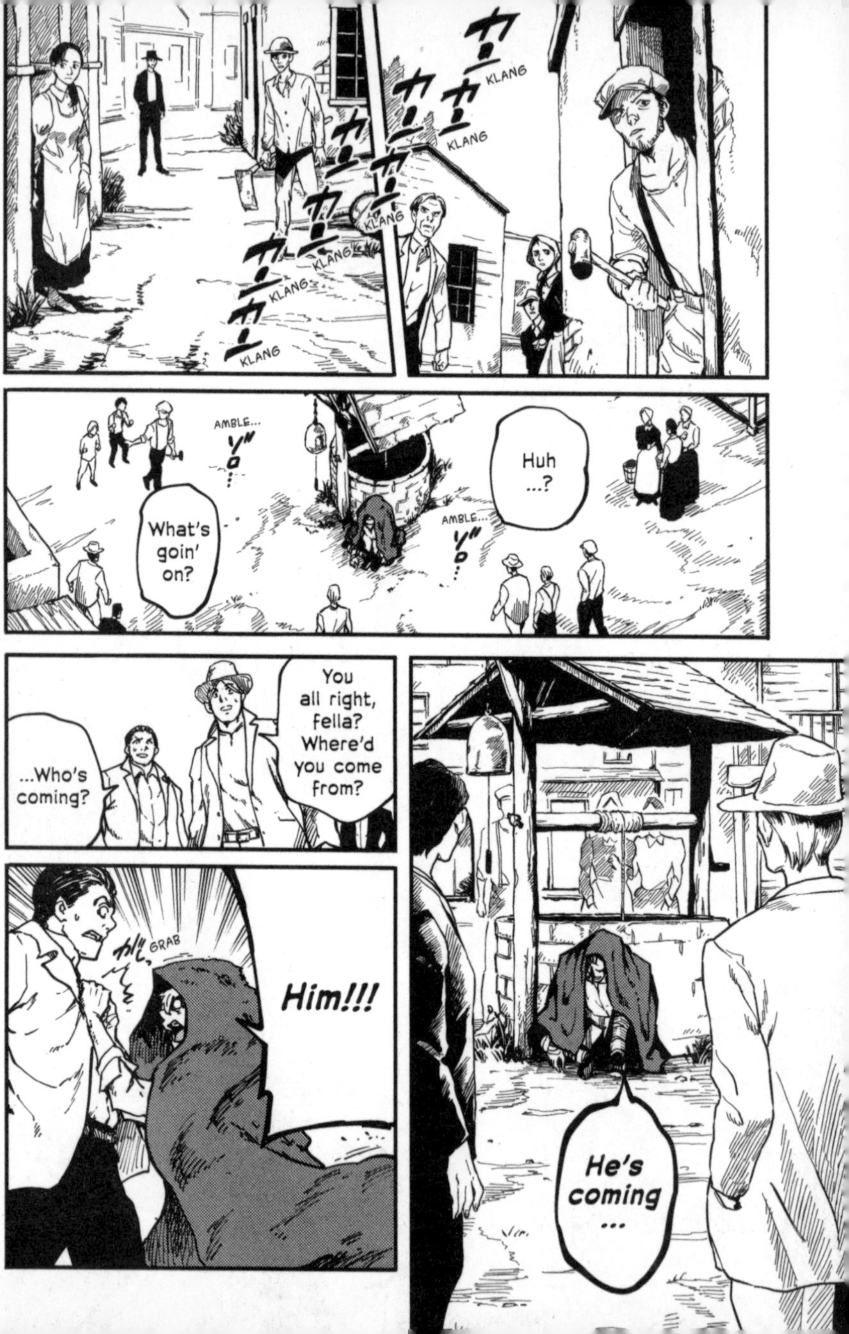
KLANG
KLANG
KLANG
KLANG
KLANG
KLANG
Huh ...?
AMBLE...
AMBLE...
What's goin' on?
He's coming ...
You all right, fella? Where'd you come from?
...Who's coming?
GRAB
Him!!!

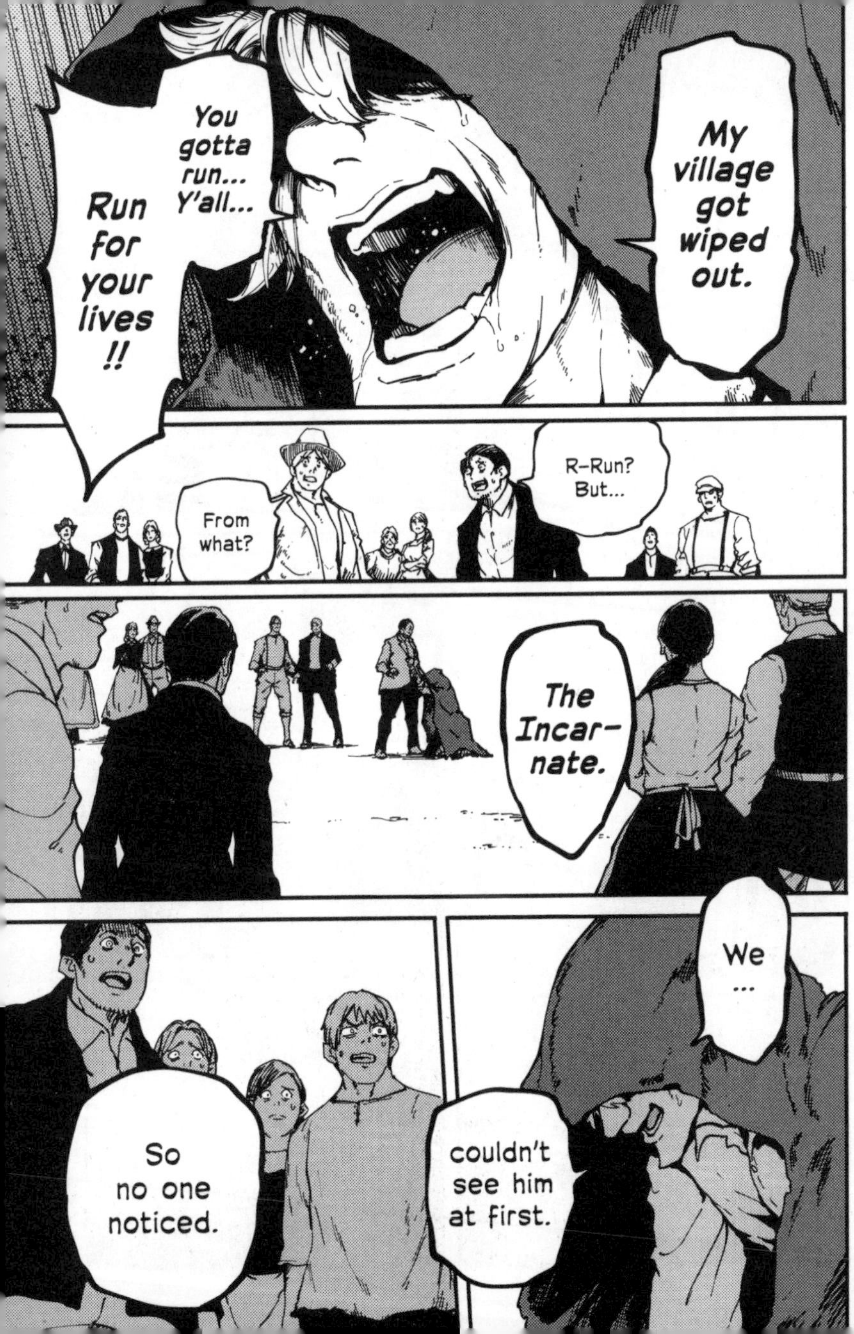
My village got wiped out.
You gotta run... Y'all...
Run for your lives!!
R-Run? But...
From what?
The Incarnate.
We ...
couldn't see him at first.
So no one noticed.

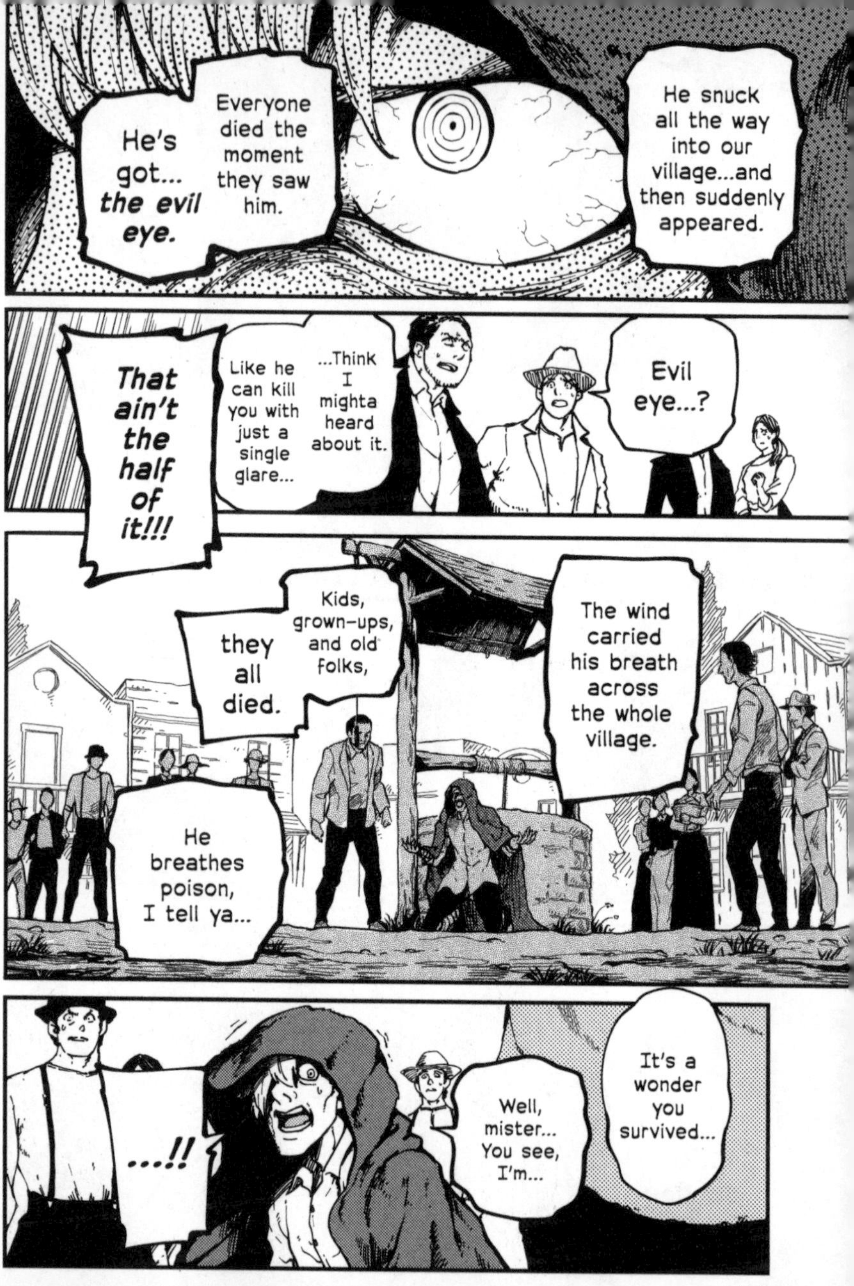
He snuck all the way into our village...and then suddenly appeared.
Everyone died the moment they saw him.
He's got... *the evil eye.*
Evil eye...?
...Think I mighta heard about it.
Like he can kill you with just a single glare...
That ain't the half of it!!!
The wind carried his breath across the whole village.
Kids, grown-ups, and old folks,
they all died.
He breathes poison, I tell ya...
It's a wonder you survived...
Well, mister... You see, I'm...
...!!

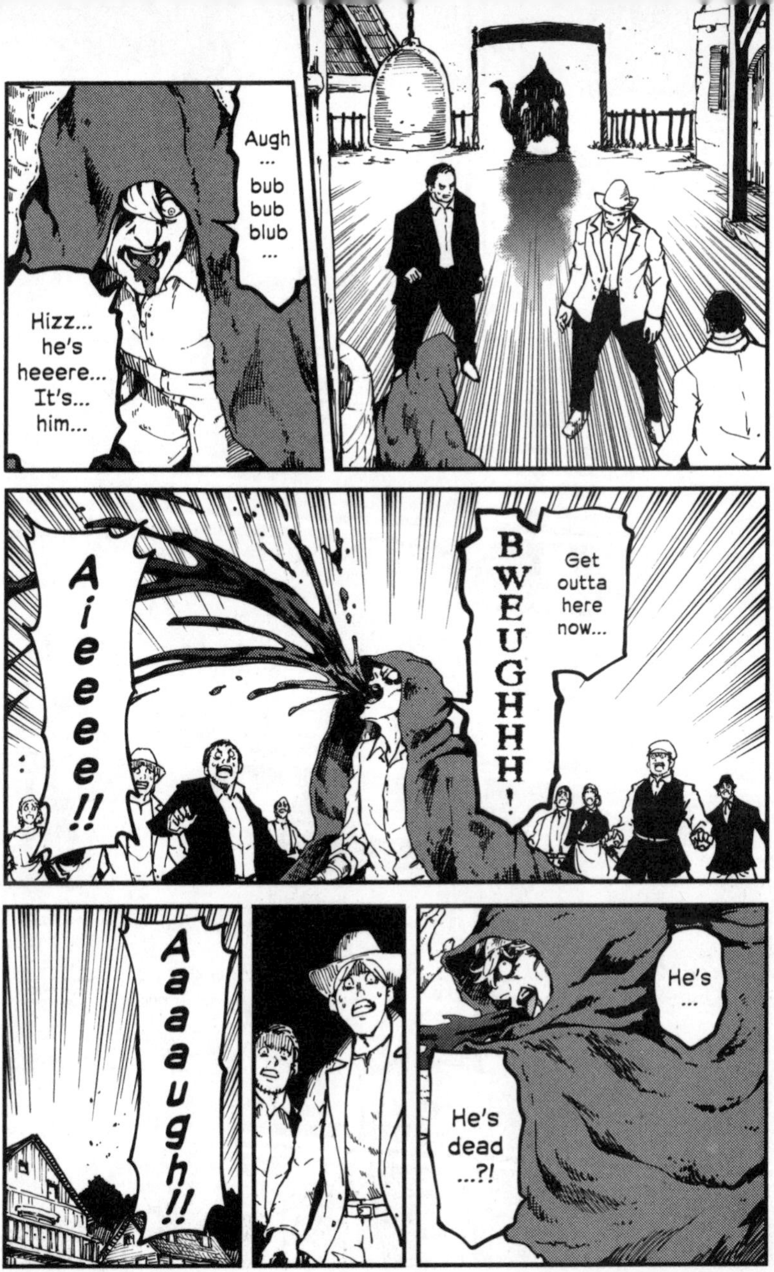
Augh ... bub bub blub ...
Hizz... he's heeere... It's... him...
Get outta here now...
BWEUGHHH!
Aieeeee!!
He's ...
He's dead ...?!
Aaaaugh!!

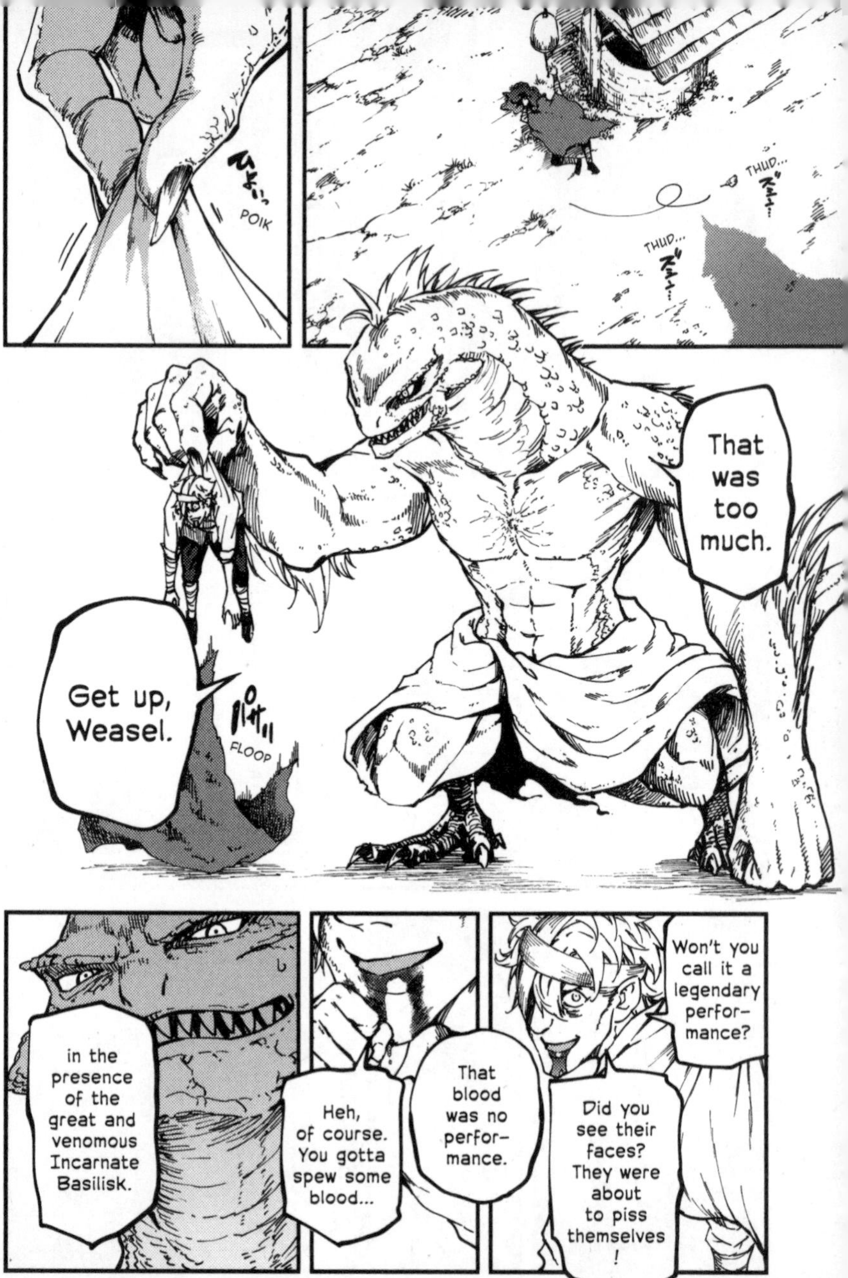
THUD...
THUD...
POIK
That was too much.
Get up, Weasel.
FLOOP
Won't you call it a legendary perfor-mance?
Did you see their faces? They were about to piss themselves!
That blood was no perfor-mance.
Heh, of course. You gotta spew some blood...
in the presence of the great and venomous Incarnate Basilisk.

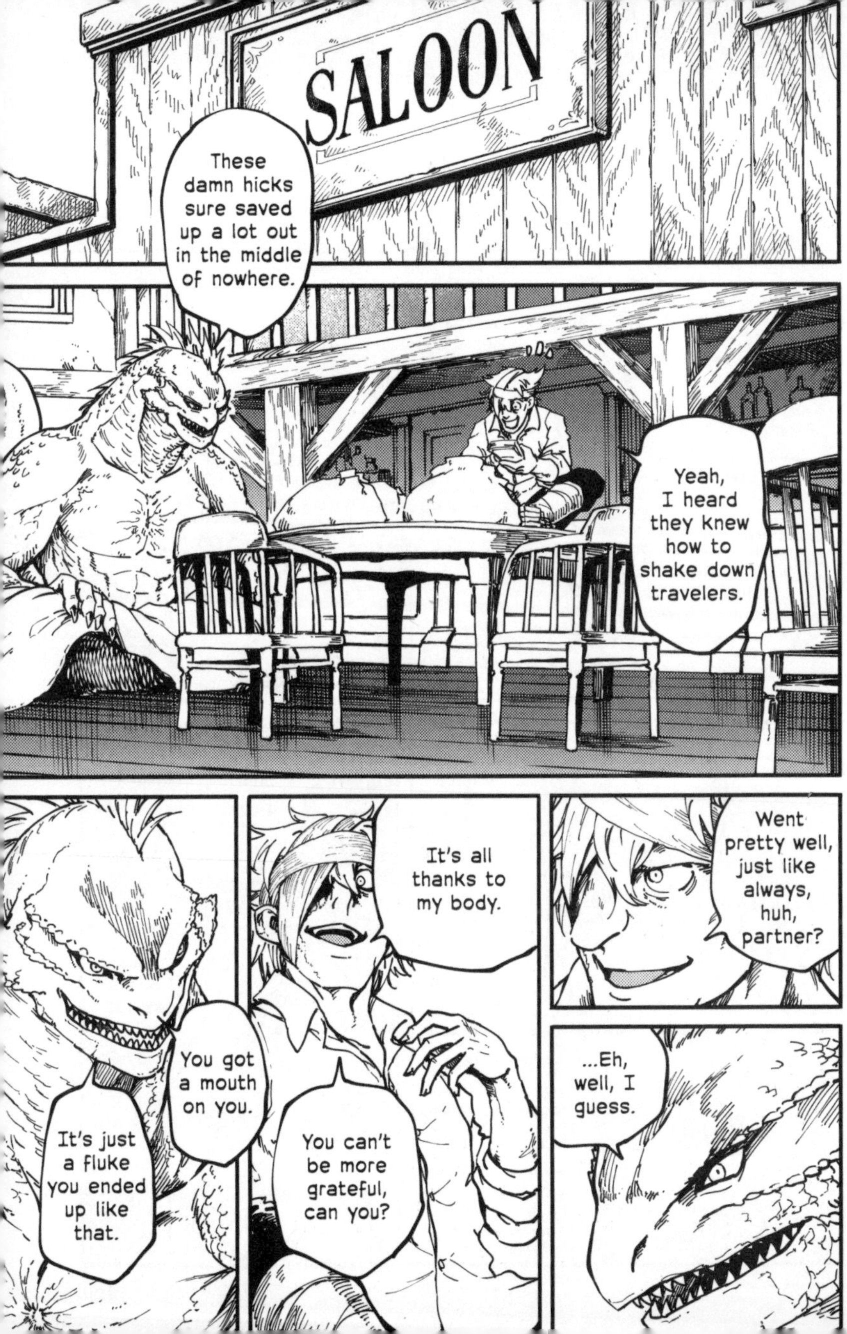
SALOON
These damn hicks sure saved up a lot out in the middle of nowhere.
Yeah, I heard they knew how to shake down travelers.
Went pretty well, just like always, huh, partner?
...Eh, well, I guess.
It's all thanks to my body.
You can't be more grateful, can you?
You got a mouth on you.
It's just a fluke you ended up like that.

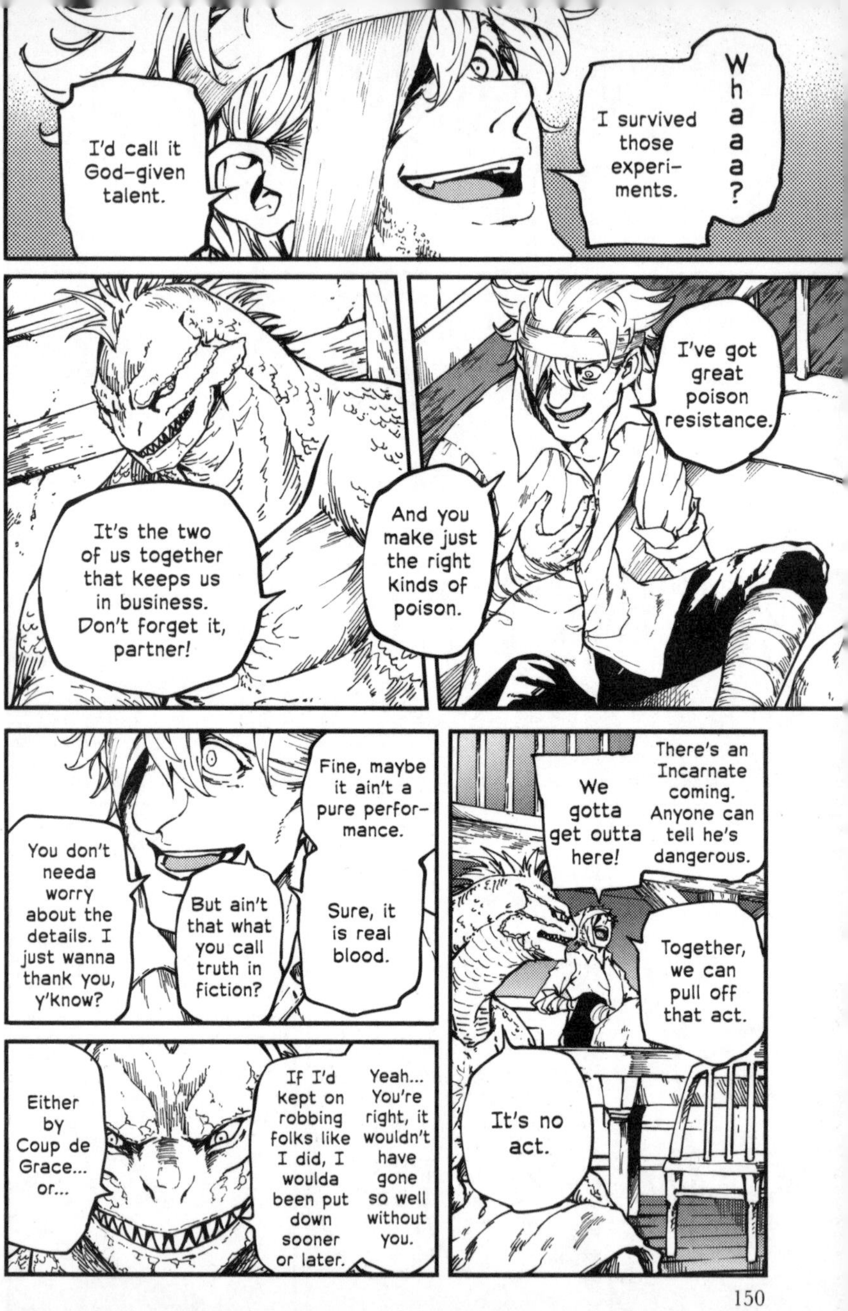
Whaaa?
I survived those experiments.
I'd call it God-given talent.
I've got great poison resistance.
And you make just the right kinds of poison.
It's the two of us together that keeps us in business. Don't forget it, partner!
There's an Incarnate coming. Anyone can tell he's dangerous.
We gotta get outta here!
Together, we can pull off that act.
It's no act.
Fine, maybe it ain't a pure performance.
Sure, it is real blood.
But ain't that what you call truth in fiction?
You don't needa worry about the details. I just wanna thank you, y'know?
Yeah... You're right, it wouldn't have gone so well without you.
If I'd kept on robbing folks like I did, I woulda been put down sooner or later.
Either by Coup de Grace... or...

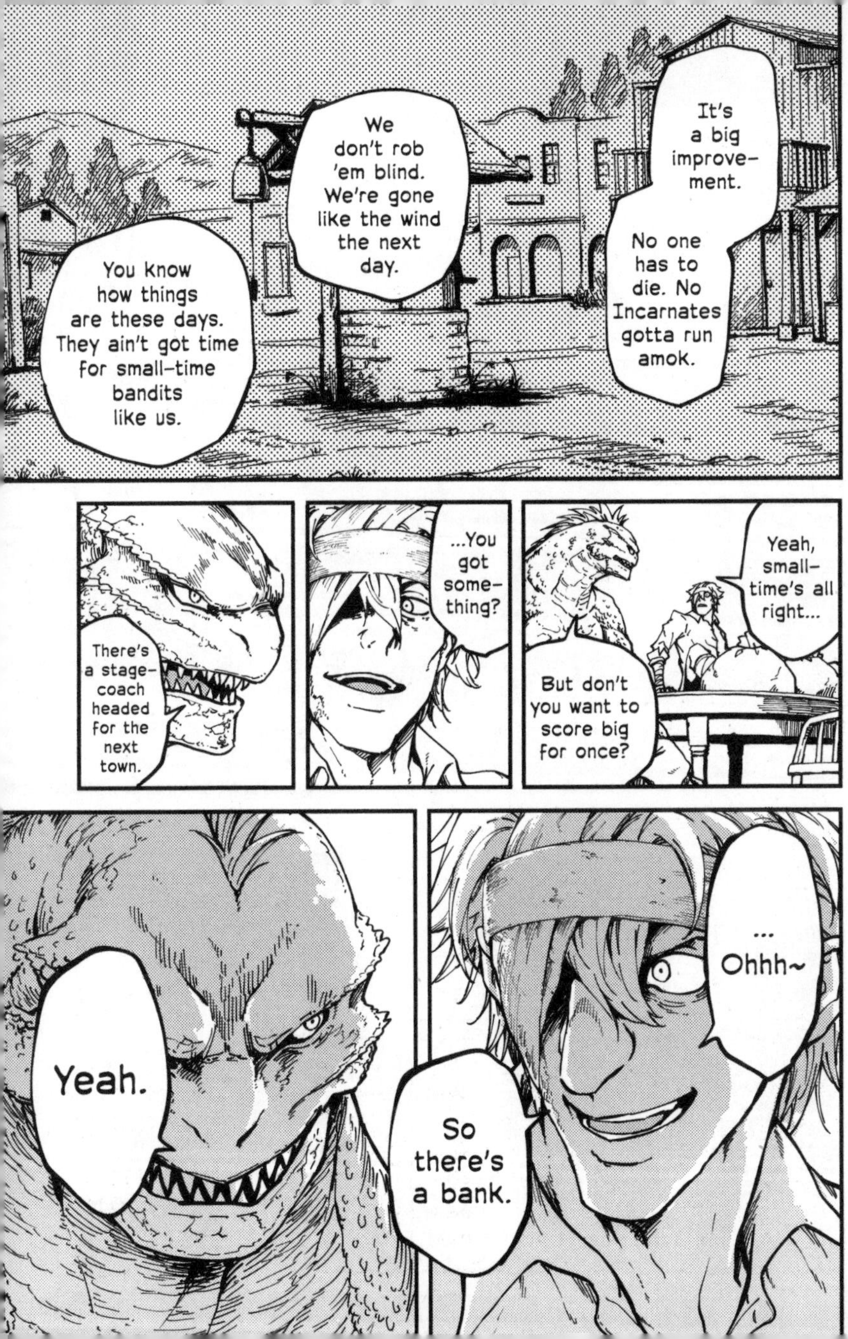
It's a big improvement.
No one has to die. No Incarnates gotta run amok.
We don't rob 'em blind. We're gone like the wind the next day.
You know how things are these days. They ain't got time for small-time bandits like us.
Yeah, small-time's all right...
But don't you want to score big for once?
...You got something?
There's a stagecoach headed for the next town.
... Ohhh~
So there's a bank.
Yeah.

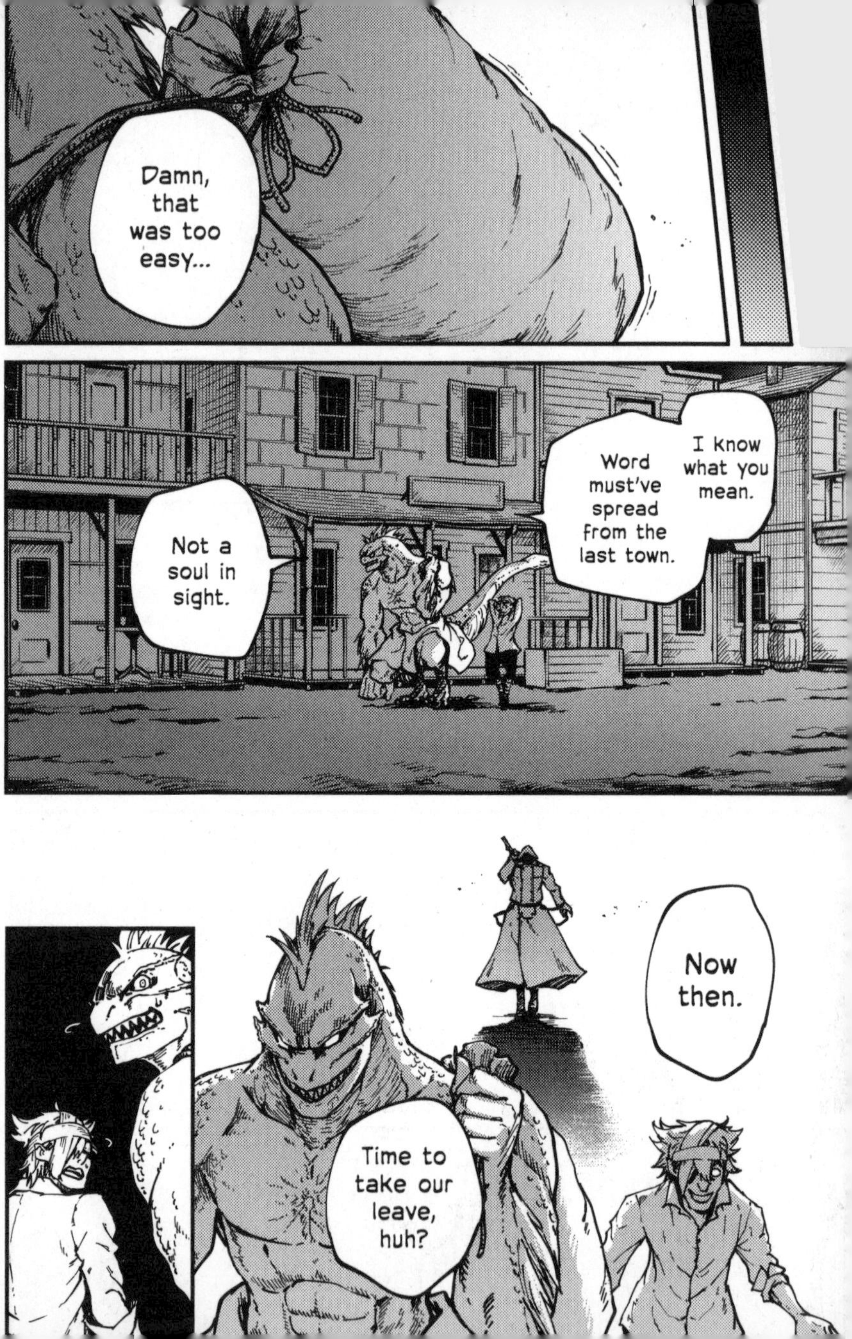
Damn, that was too easy...
I know what you mean.
Word must've spread from the last town.
Not a soul in sight.
Now then.
Time to take our leave, huh?

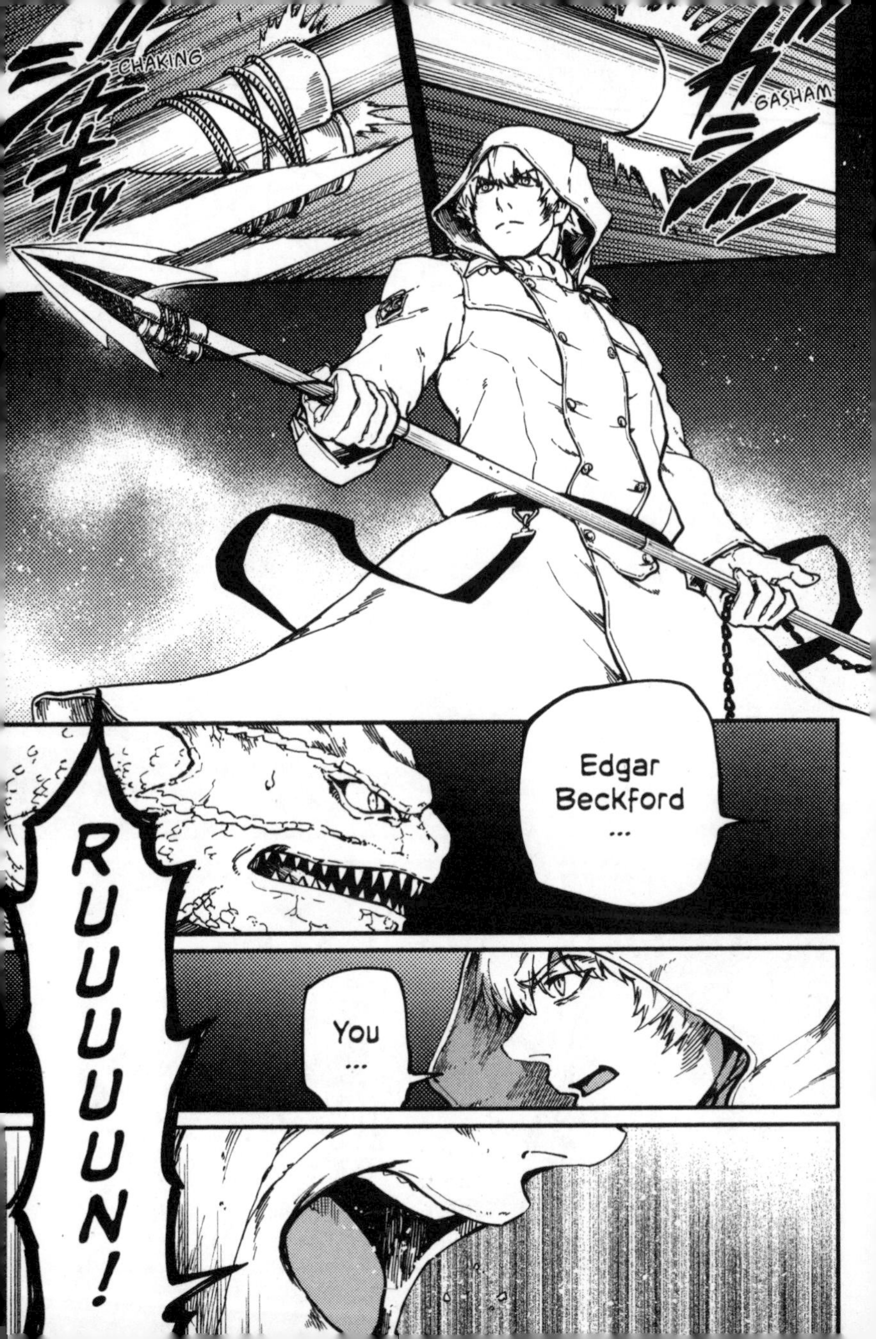
GASHAM
CHAKING
Edgar Beckford ...
You ...
RUUUUUN!

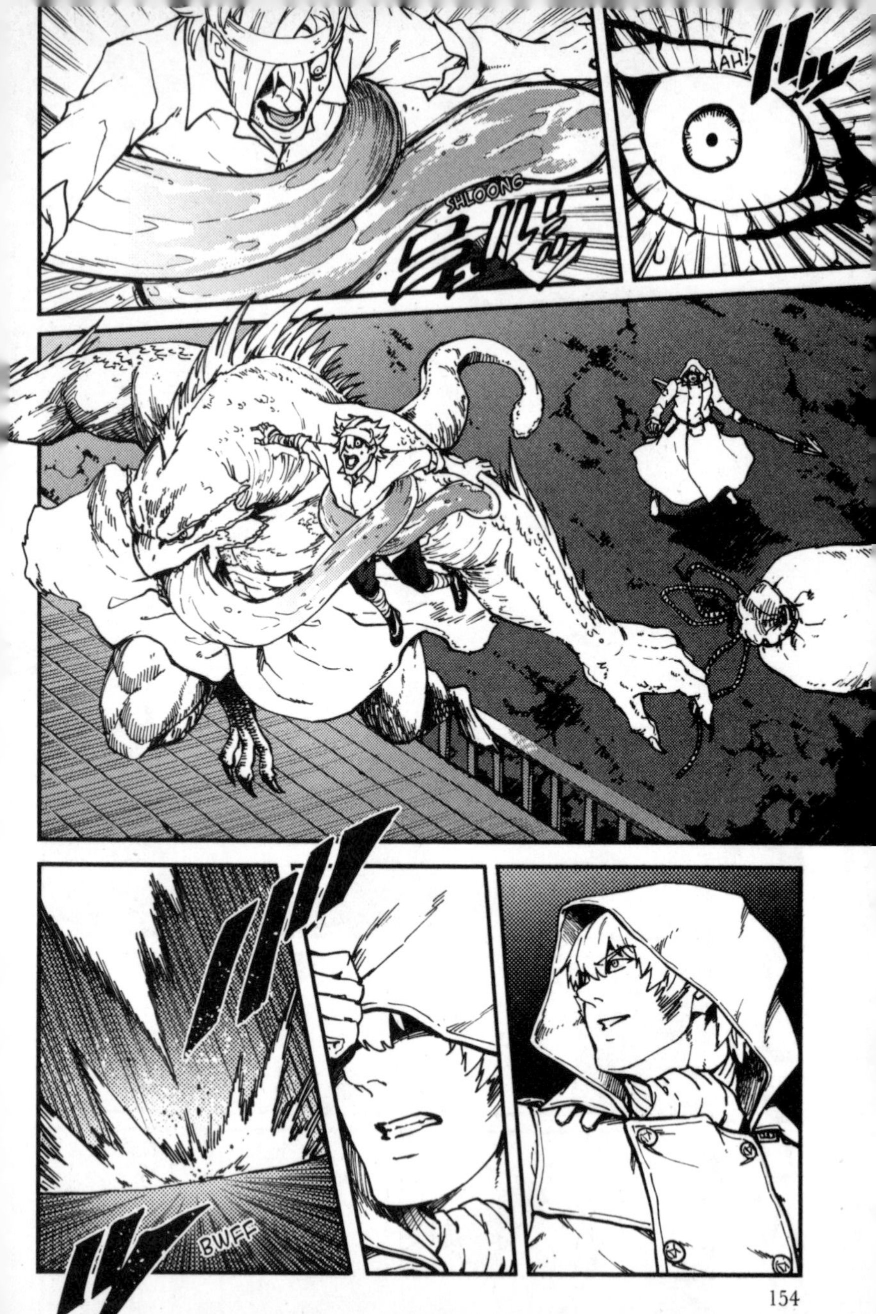
AH!
SHLOONG
BWFF

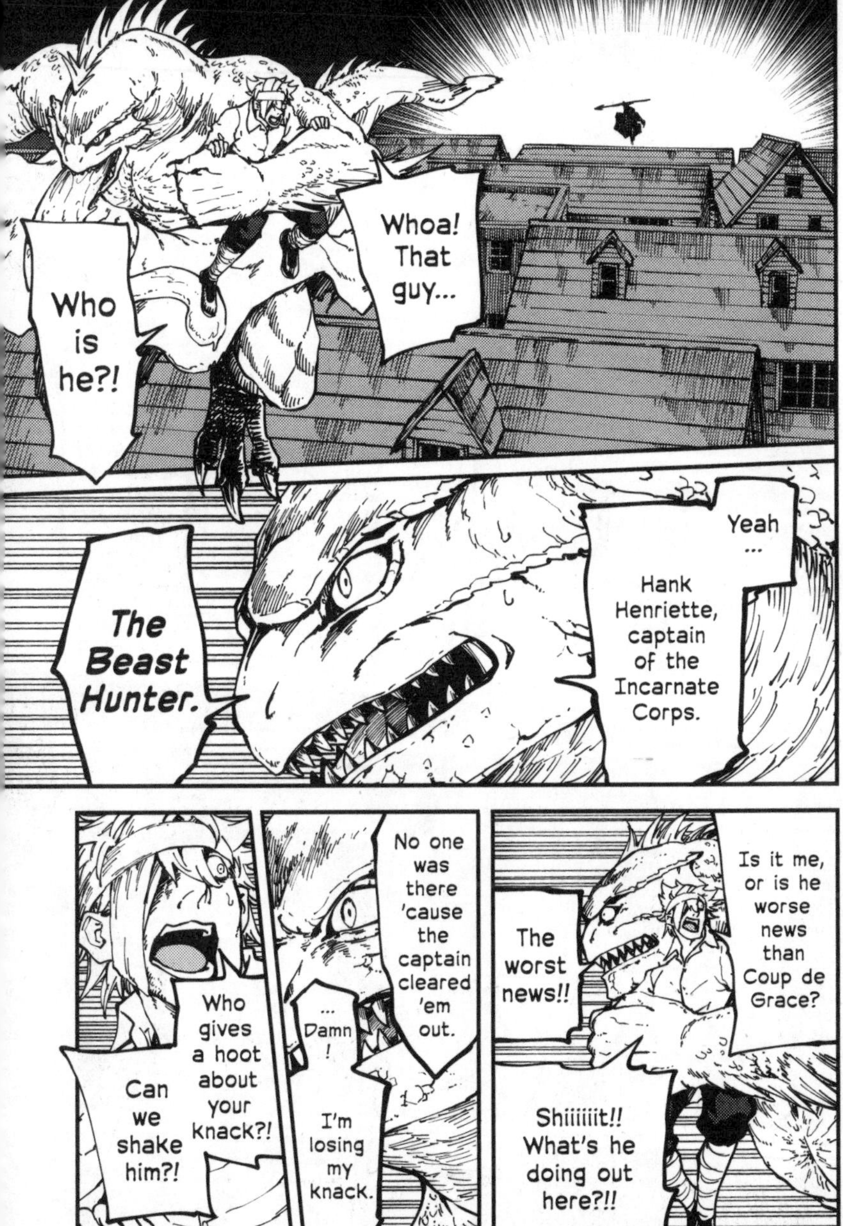
Whoa! That guy...
Who is he?!
Yeah... Hank Henriette, captain of the Incarnate Corps.
The Beast Hunter.
Is it me, or is he worse news than Coup de Grace?
The worst news!!
Shiiiiiit!! What's he doing out here?!!
No one was there 'cause the captain cleared 'em out.
...Damn!
I'm losing my knack.
Who gives a hoot about your knack?!
Can we shake him?!

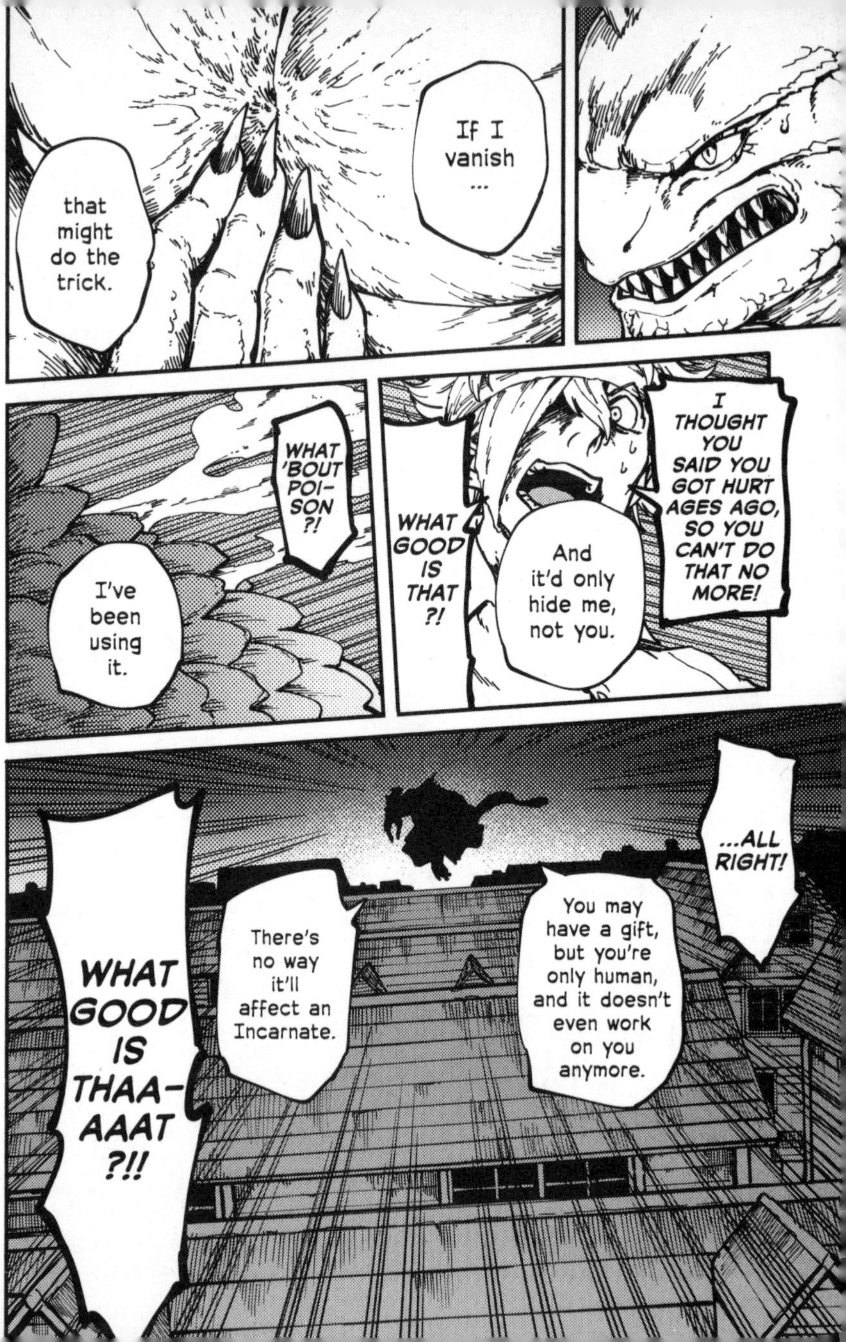
If I vanish ...
that might do the trick.
I THOUGHT YOU SAID YOU GOT HURT AGES AGO, SO YOU CAN'T DO THAT NO MORE!
And it'd only hide me, not you.
WHAT GOOD IS THAT ?!
WHAT 'BOUT POI-SON ?!
I've been using it.
...ALL RIGHT!
You may have a gift, but you're only human, and it doesn't even work on you anymore.
There's no way it'll affect an Incarnate.
WHAT GOOD IS THAA-AAAT ?!!

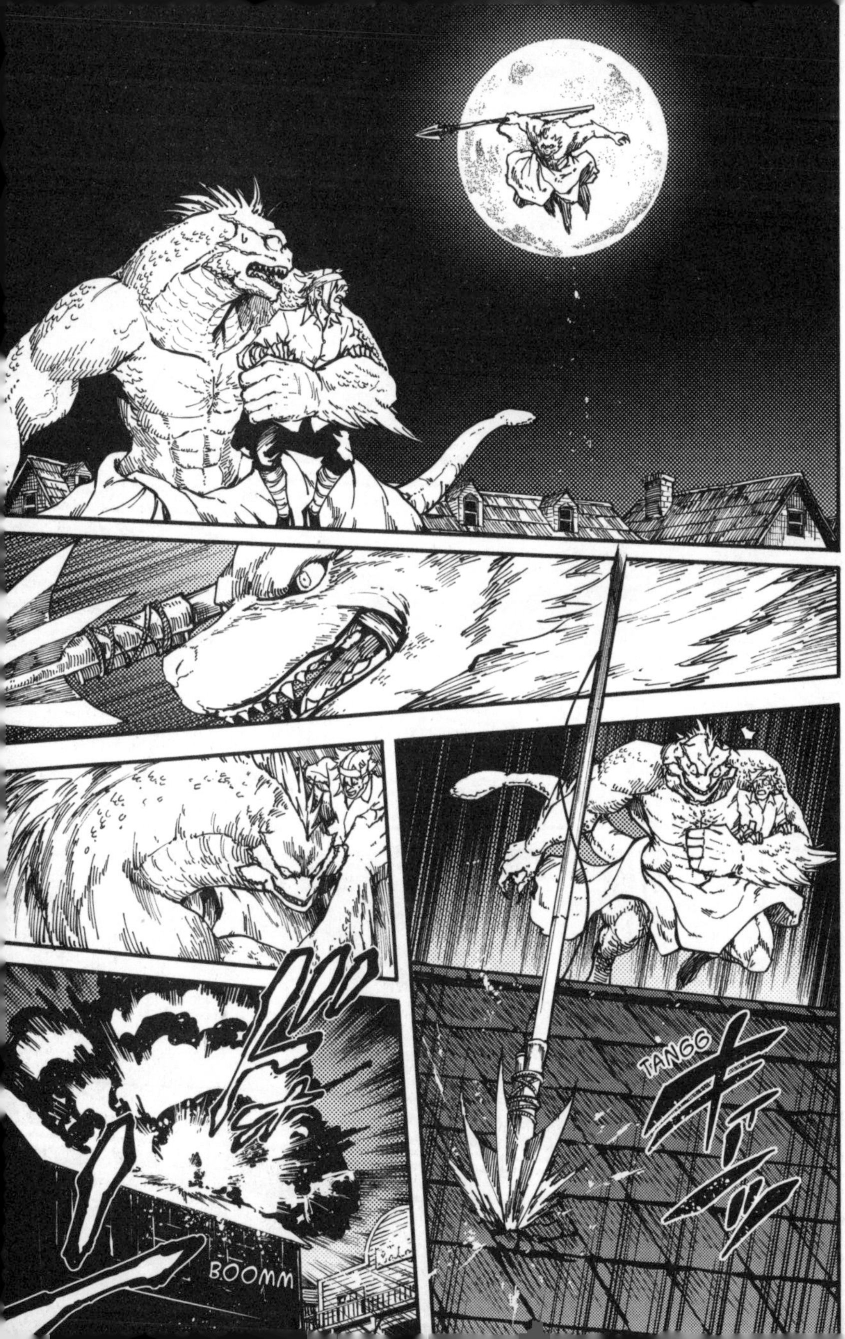
TANGG
BOOMM

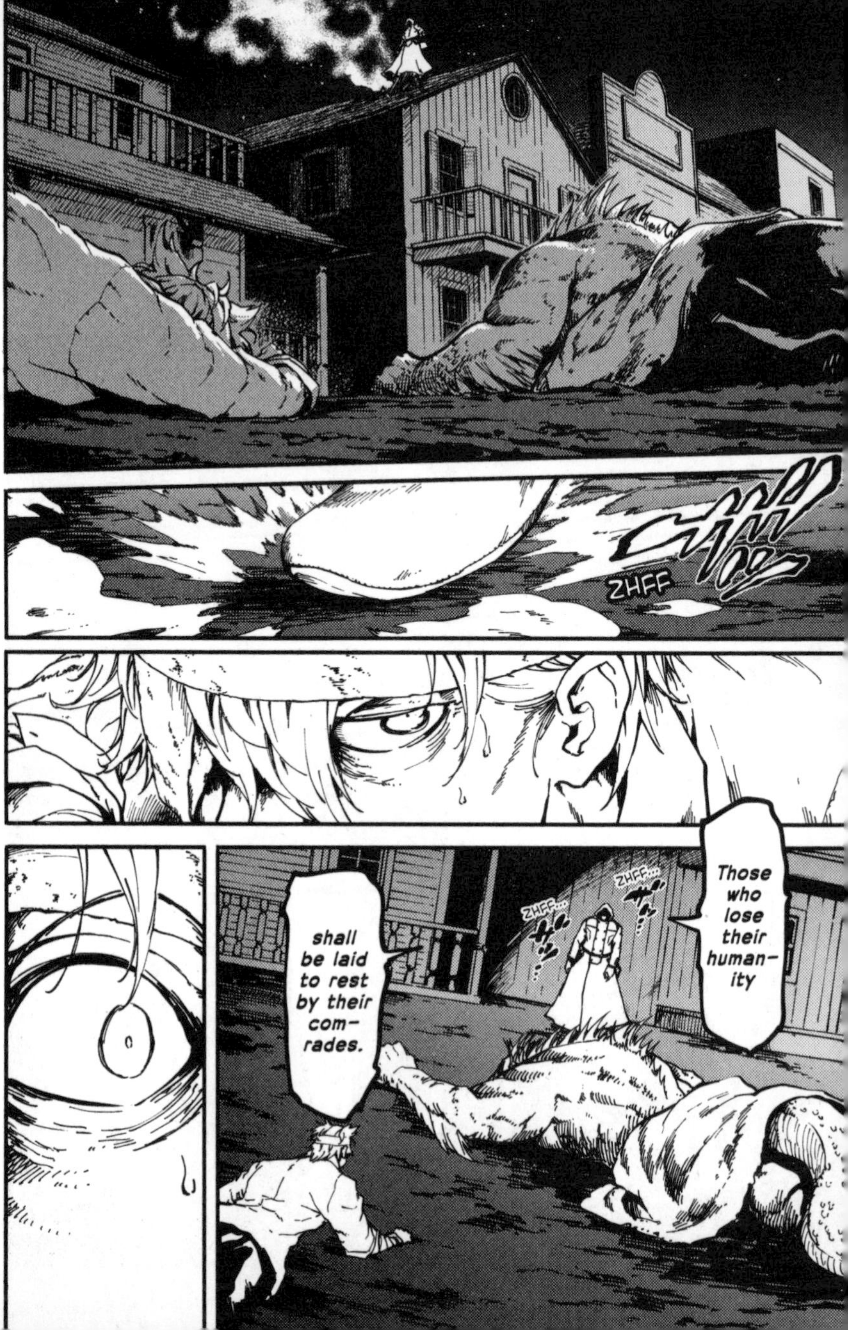
ZHFF
Those who lose their human-ity
ZHFF...
ZHFF...
shall be laid to rest by their com-rades.

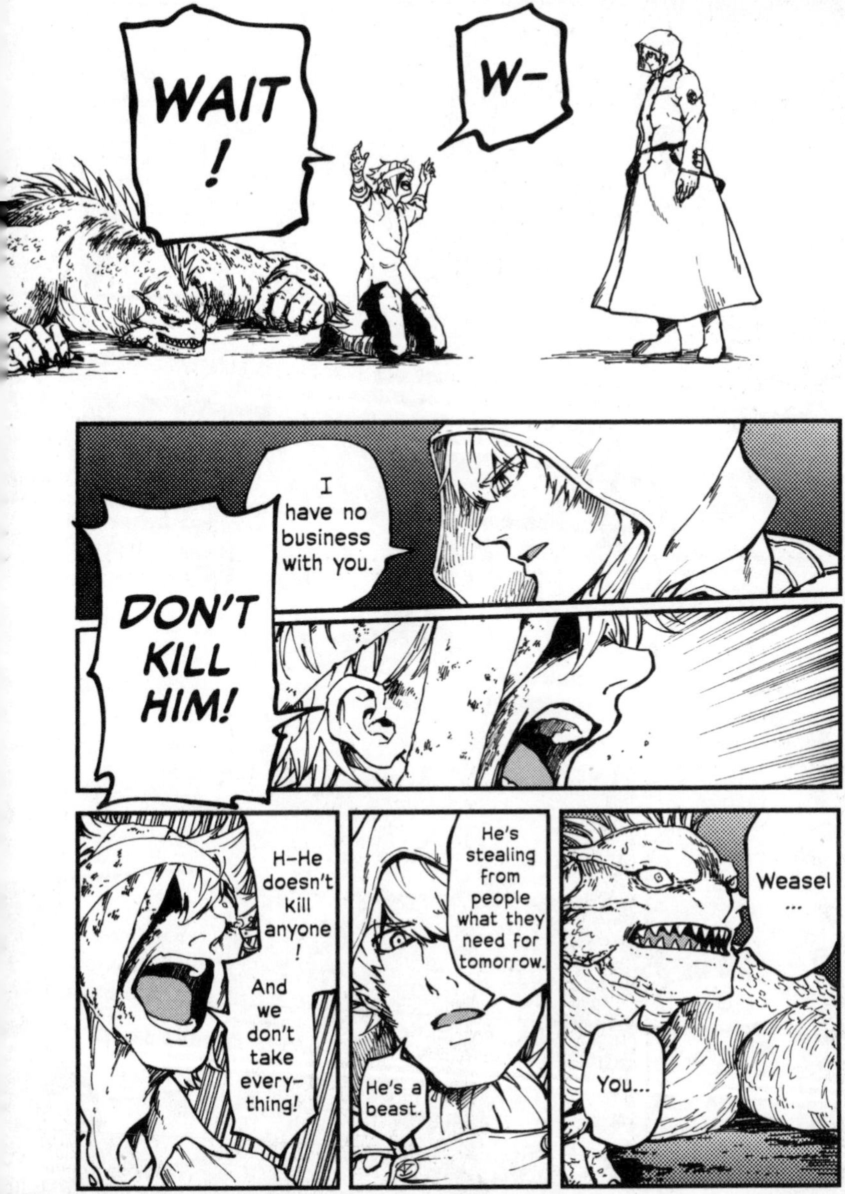
W-
WAIT!
I have no business with you.
DON'T KILL HIM!
Weasel...
You...
He's stealing from people what they need for tomorrow.
He's a beast.
H-He doesn't kill anyone!
And we don't take everything!

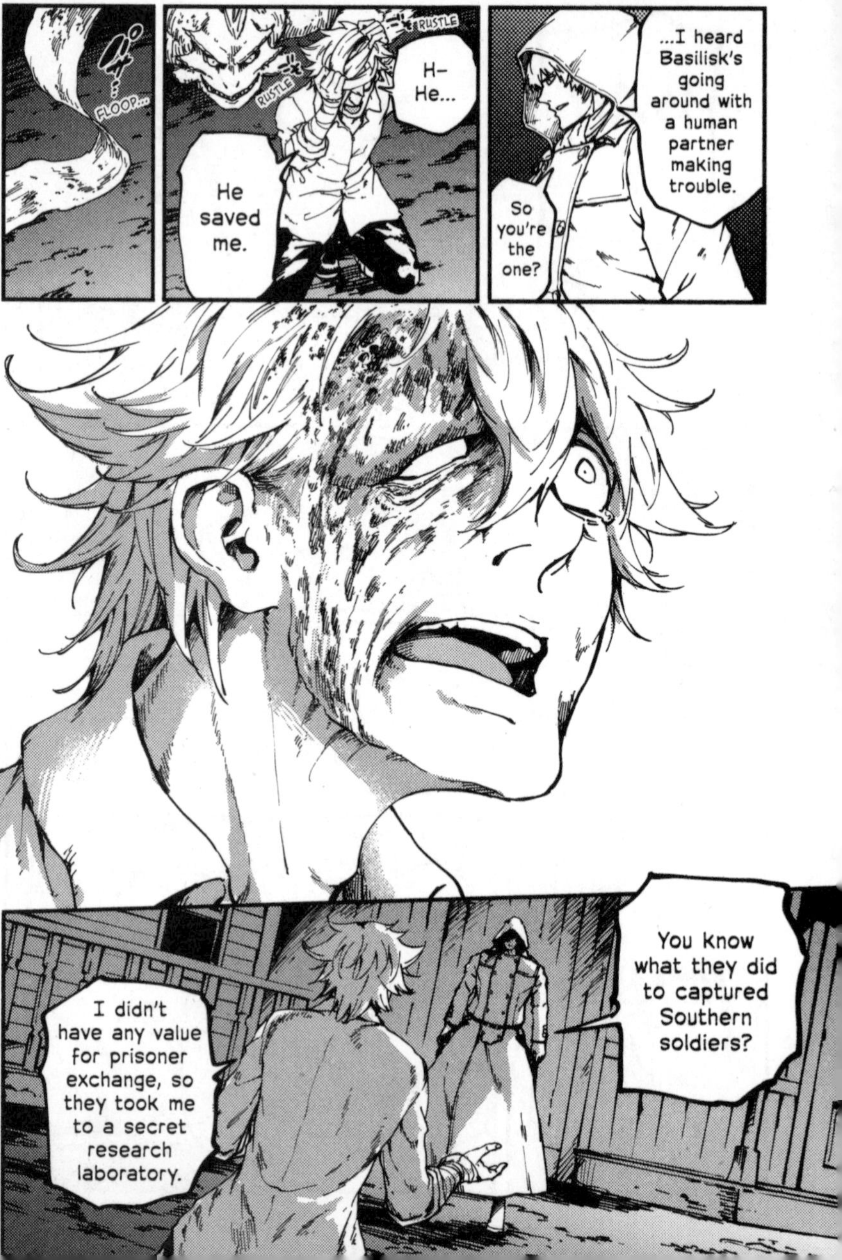
...I heard Basilisk's going around with a human partner making trouble.
So you're the one?
RUSTLE
RUSTLE
H– He...
He saved me.
FLOOP...
You know what they did to captured Southern soldiers?
I didn't have any value for prisoner exchange, so they took me to a secret research laboratory.

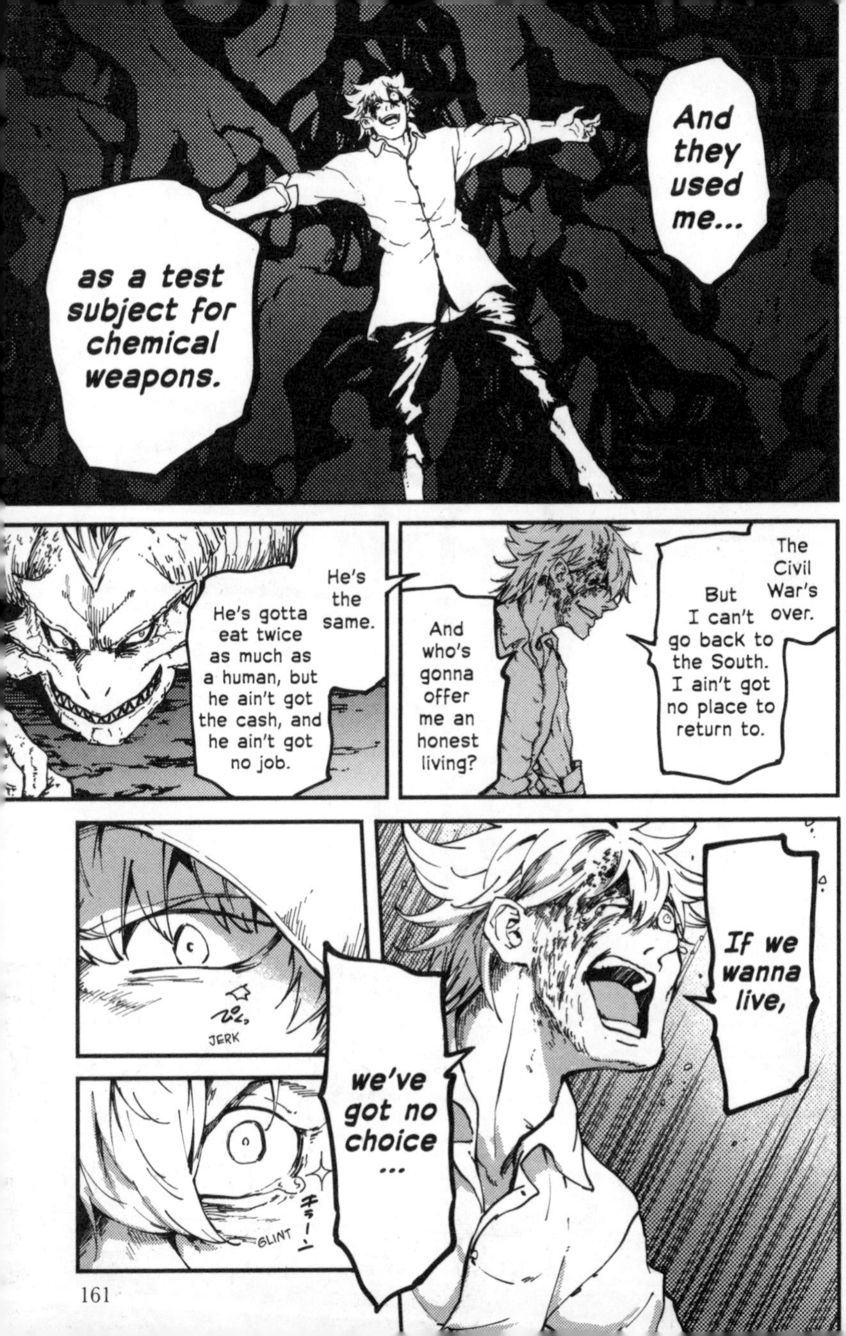
And they used me...
as a test subject for chemical weapons.
The Civil War's over.
But I can't go back to the South. I ain't got no place to return to.
And who's gonna offer me an honest living?
He's the same.
He's gotta eat twice as much as a human, but he ain't got the cash, and he ain't got no job.
If we wanna live,
we've got no choice ...
JERK
GLINT

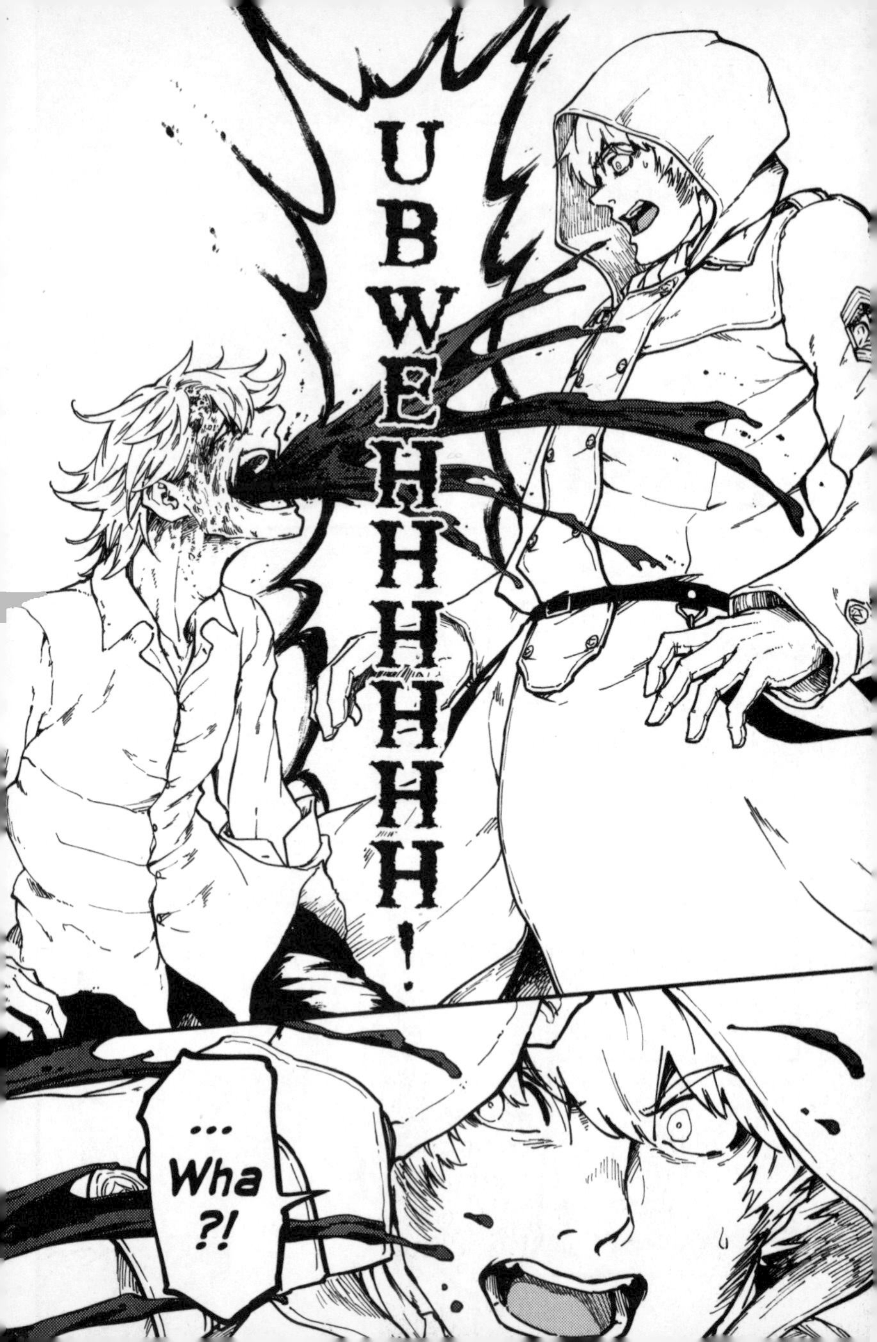
UBWEHHHHHH!
... Wha ?!

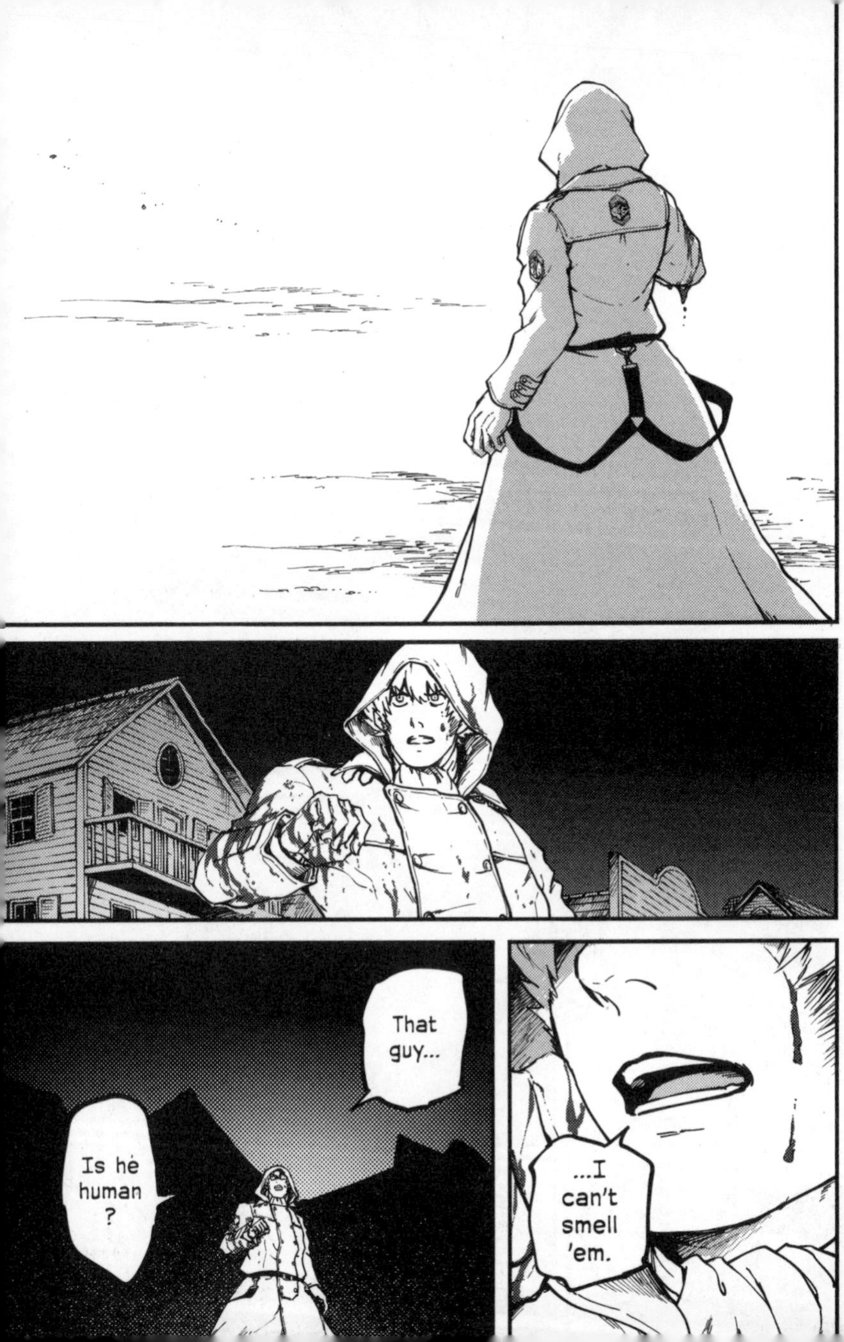
...I can't smell 'em.
That guy...
Is he human ?

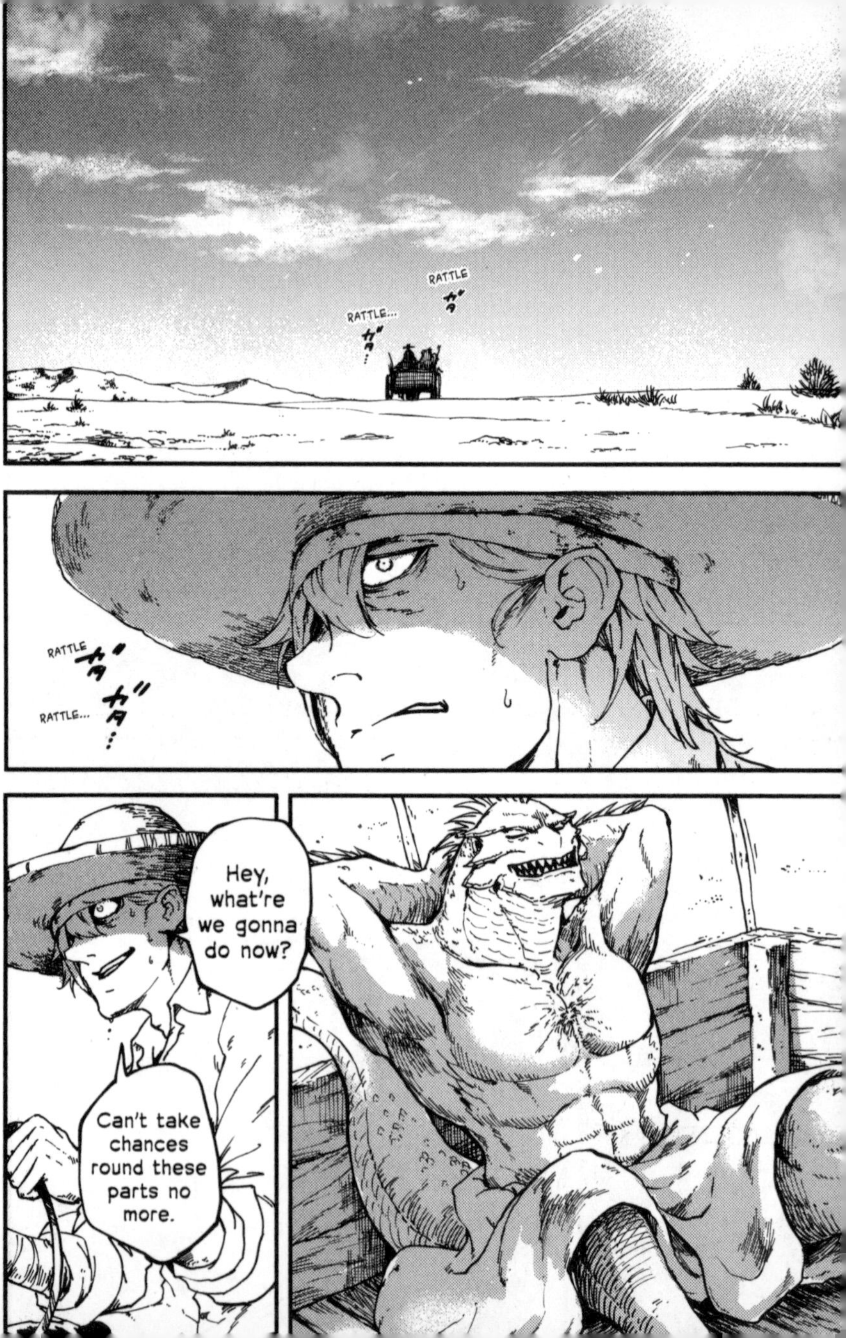
RATTLE
RATTLE...
RATTLE
RATTLE...
Hey, what're we gonna do now?
Can't take chances round these parts no more.

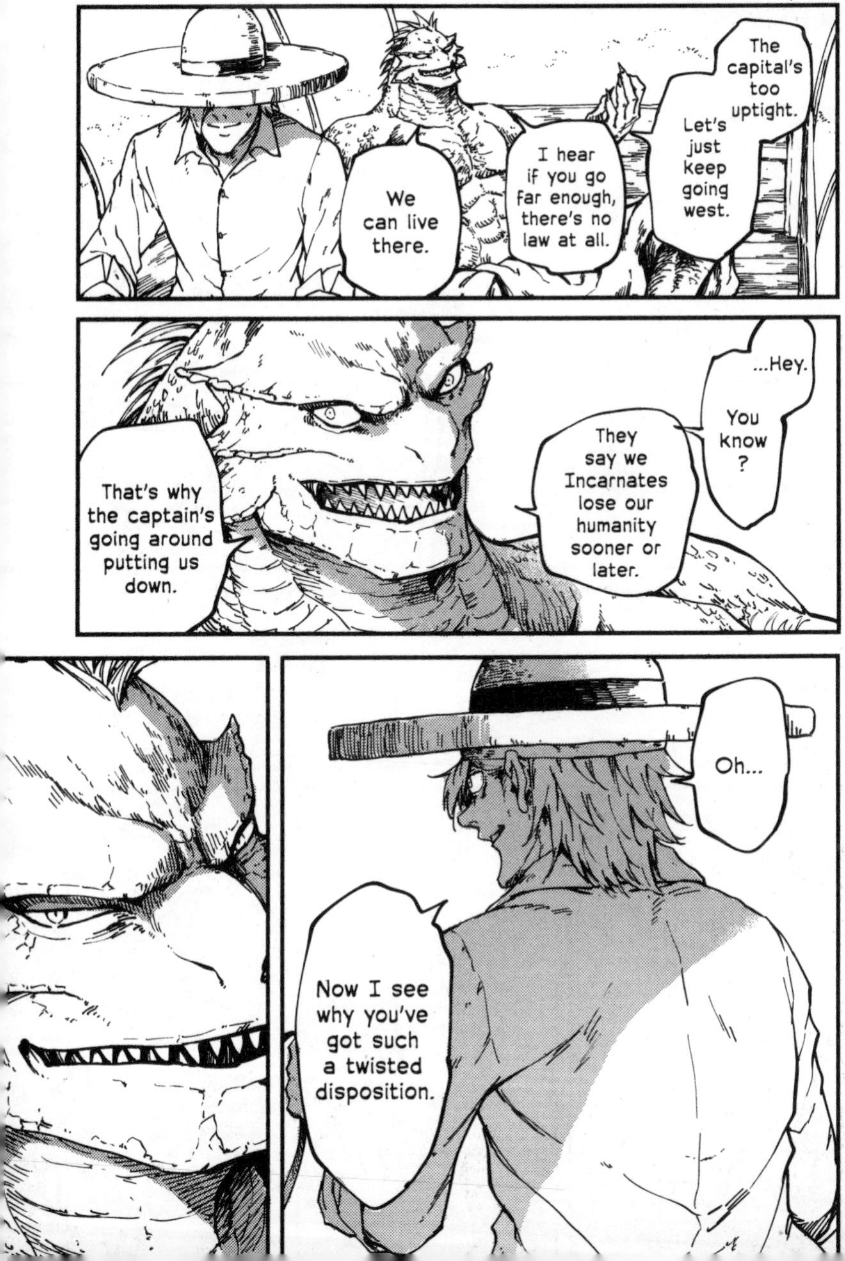
The capital's too uptight.
Let's just keep going west.
I hear if you go far enough, there's no law at all.
We can live there.
...Hey.
You know?
They say we Incarnates lose our humanity sooner or later.
That's why the captain's going around putting us down.
Oh...
Now I see why you've got such a twisted disposition.

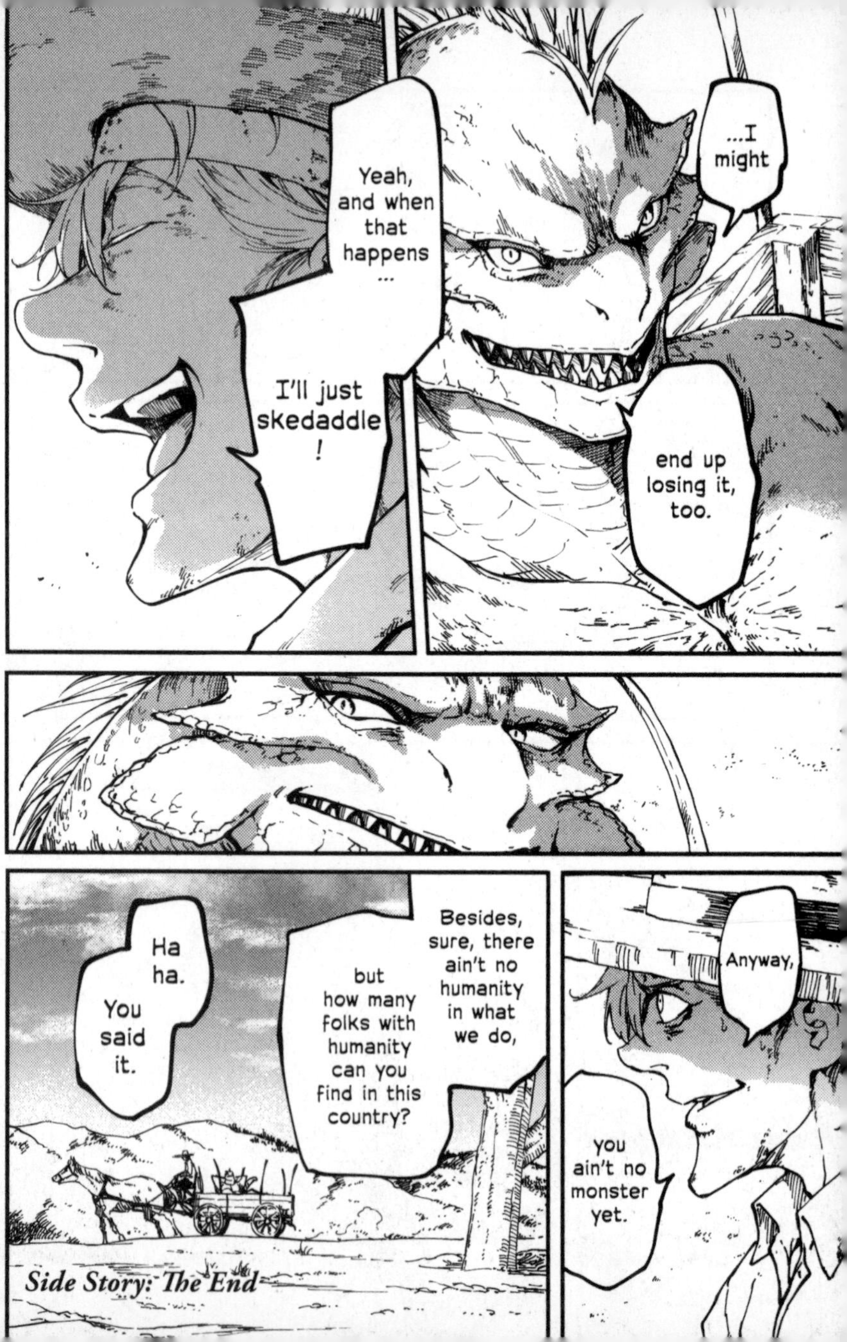
...I might
end up losing it, too.
Yeah, and when that happens ...
I'll just skedaddle!
Anyway,
you ain't no monster yet.
Besides, sure, there ain't no humanity in what we do,
but how many folks with humanity can you find in this country?
Ha ha.
You said it.
Side Story: The End

To the Abandoned
Sacred Beasts

SACRED BEASTS PLUS

#28

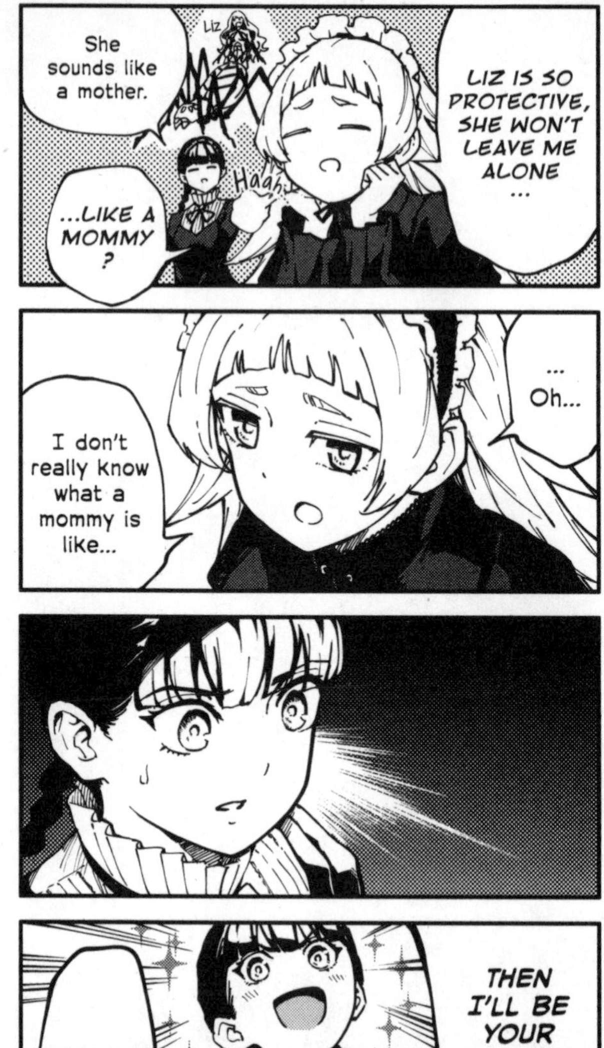
LIZ IS SO PROTECTIVE, SHE WON'T LEAVE ME ALONE ...
Liz
She sounds like a mother.
Haah
...LIKE A MOMMY ?
... Oh...
I don't really know what a mommy is like...
THEN I'LL BE YOUR MOTHER FROM NOW ON!
WHAAAT ? NOOO!

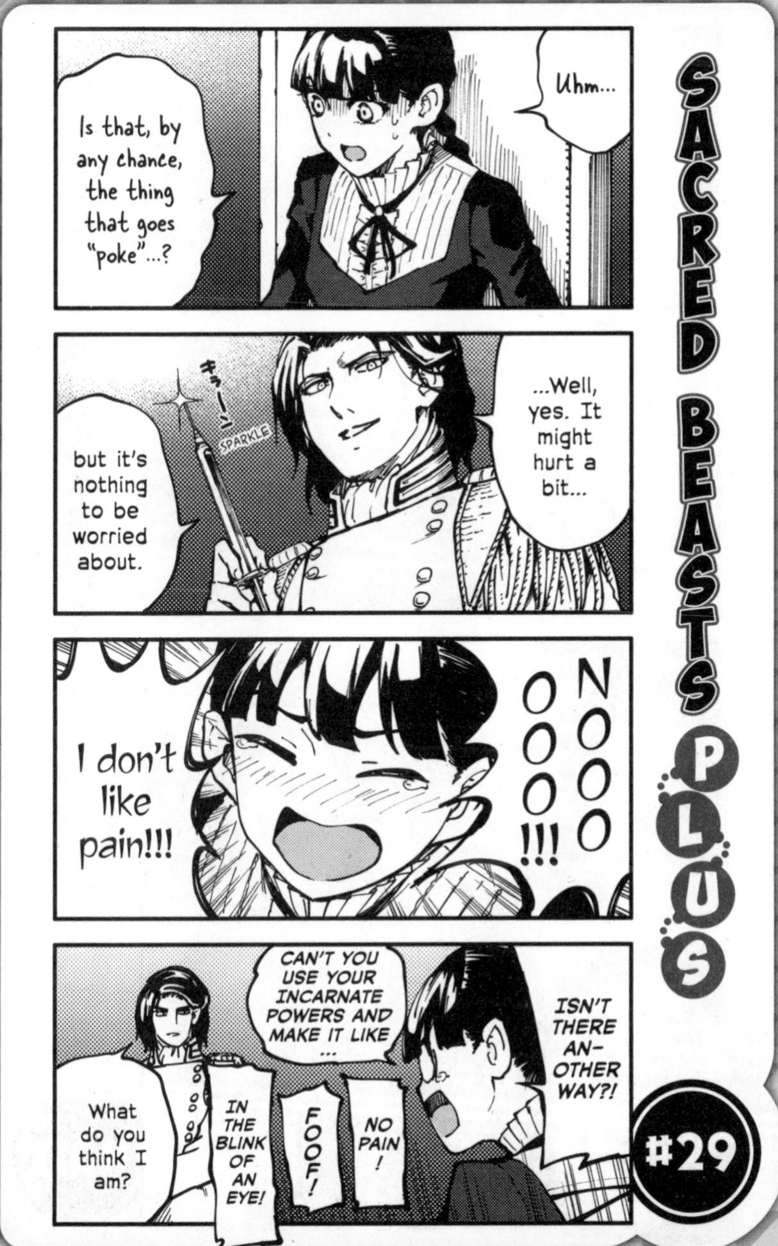
SACRED BEASTS PLUS
#29
Uhm...
Is that, by any chance, the thing that goes "poke"...?
...Well, yes. It might hurt a bit...
キラーン
SPARKLE
but it's nothing to be worried about.
NOOOOOOOO!!!
I don't like pain!!!
ISN'T THERE AN-OTHER WAY?!
CAN'T YOU USE YOUR INCARNATE POWERS AND MAKE IT LIKE ...
NO PAIN!
FOOF!
IN THE BLINK OF AN EYE!
What do you think I am?

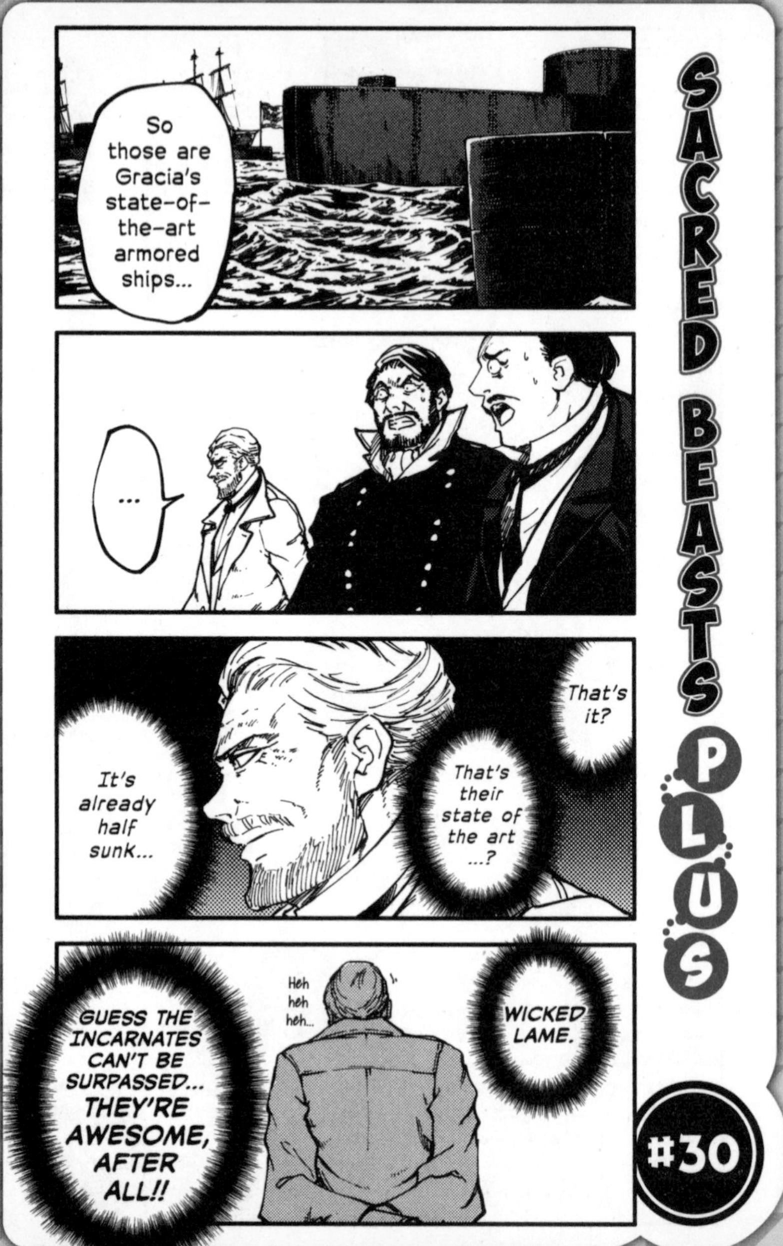
SACRED BEASTS PLUS
#30
So those are Gracia's state-of-the-art armored ships...
...
That's it?
That's their state of the art ...?
It's already half sunk...
WICKED LAME.
Heh heh heh...
GUESS THE INCARNATES CAN'T BE SURPASSED... THEY'RE AWESOME, AFTER ALL!!

Sacred Beasts Encyclopedia Entries

file no. **53** | *Incarnate Arachne* | **Height: 11 feet**

A wretched seamstress cursed by God

An Incarnate capable of weaving spider silk with great control.

The Arachne has the form of a human upper body growing from the end of the abdomen of a giant spider. The spider part is not merely large: where it should have simple eyes, the Arachne has organs similar to human eyes. It presents a visage distinct from that of the familiar arthropods. The upper body retains the appearance of the woman upon whom the Incarnate was based. It may look frail at a glance, but in fact, it is covered with several layers of extremely fine thread, which is robust enough to deflect handgun fire without damage. The Arachne has two heads, one arachnid and one human, but no sign of independent consciousness has been observed in the spider half. The Incarnate has maintained a high level of human intellect and reason over a long period of time. While somewhat lacking in aggressiveness, it received consistent positive evaluations for its faithful execution of missions. A strong attachment to a particular Incarnate was reported, but it is not recorded to have been of such a degree as to interfere with operations.

The Incarnate Arachne can extrude silk from a number of areas on its upper body. Normal spiders typically have silk-spinning organs at the ends of their abdomens, but in the case of the Incarnate Arachne, the human body is responsible for this function. There are protrusions near the boundary between the spider and human portions from which silk has been seen to extend, but they cannot account for the number of threads the Incarnate deploys instantly, and so it is speculated that the human portion itself bears some sort of silk-producing organs. The spider portion can also produce silk from its mouth, but this ability is little used due to poor control of the thread's properties. Since some natural spiders can also produce silk from their mouths, this ability is not unique to the Incarnate.

The Arachne is able to control at will various properties of the silk produced. Its thickness, strength, viscosity, elasticity, and more were adapted to a wide range of tactical conditions. A low-viscosity thread of exceedingly faint visibility can be attached to nearby structures as a trap, and lightweight thread can be floated in the wind over large areas to search for enemies. Meanwhile, resiliently spun silk of bladelike sharpness can lift bodies caught in it and slice them apart with ease. There are also records of the Arachne producing bullet-resistant apparel that incorporates the silk, but as is the case with many of the Incarnates that possess special skills, this is owed to the Arachne's preexisting sewing expertise.

file no. **54** | *Incarnate Basilisk* | Height: 10 feet

The serpent king lurking in the wildlands

An invisible Incarnate that specializes in poison.

The Basilisk has reptilian skin and a long, prehensile tail and tongue. Parts of its skin are hardened and not easy to damage, but it's not especially notable for its endurance. The Basilisk's athletic abilities far exceed those of humans, but its power and agility are not particularly outstanding among the Incarnates. Even so, certain valuable qualities of the Basilisk make it stand out.

The Basilisk's invisibility and deadly gaze are characteristics that lend themselves well to assassination. The Incarnate can march boldly into an enemy's territory as clear as the air and quietly bring about the death of its targets with a single glare. A silent reaper that can creep up at any time. It struck great terror into the hearts of Southern commanding officers.

In fact, the Incarnate Basilisk's special ability is simply the production of various poisons. Its invisibility and deadly gaze are merely byproducts of it. Broadly speaking, the Basilisk's venoms fall into two categories.

One type, hallucinatory poison, damages organisms' cognitive functions. It oozes from the surface of the Basilisk's body, vaporizes, then diffuses through the air. Even a slight sniff is enough to throw a human's consciousness into confusion and create the illusion that whatever they are trying to focus on is not there. The Basilisk's exterior also has the ability to change its coloration to blend into its environment. The twin phenomena combine to create the strange impression that the Basilisk is able to turn transparent and disappear, and that is why enemy soldiers saw it, yet were unable to perceive it.

The other type is instantly-active nerve poison. It is said that the Incarnate can turn people to stone—a single glance from the Basilisk appears to freeze the body and inhibit respiration so as to lead to death. But it is not the gaze itself that kills. The Basilisk's tear ducts release a transparent and poisonous mist that is easily absorbed by mucous membranes. While it can, of course, be inhaled into the lungs, it can also enter through the eyes. Therefore, even if people manage to notice the Basilisk approaching, it is almost impossible for them to avoid getting poisoned. The venom absorbed by the target induces prompt stiffening of the muscles throughout the body, respiratory difficulty, and, in sufficient doses, heart failure.

Several Incarnates possess poisons capable of bringing about a human's death. But only the Basilisk can produce such complex venoms with effects on one's mind and perception. The Basilisk can also generate hemorrhagic venom, but it was not deployed in battle given its lack of instant effect.

Sacred Beasts Encyclopedia Entries

file no. 55 | *Incarnate Cockatrice* | *Wingspan: 23 feet*

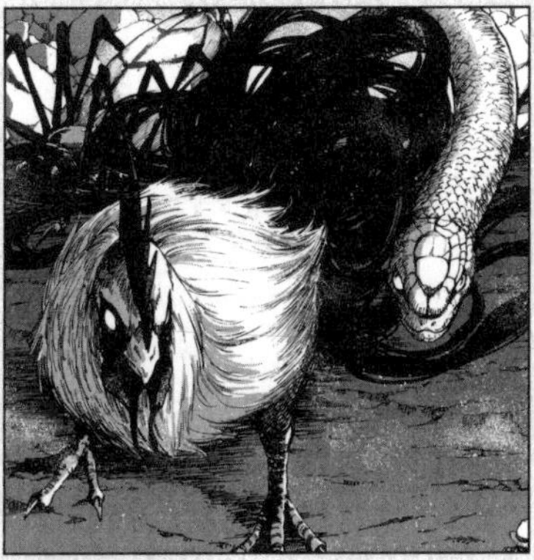

A weird, venomous bird with a serpent head

A bizarre Incarnate capable of lethal poisoning.

Its appearance—that of a giant rooster with a snake for a tail—is eerie. Said to possess a venomous gaze that can petrify people, it is frequently confused with the Basilisk due to the similarity of their abilities. The rooster part is simply a giant version of the bird, but roosters to begin with are considerably agile, have sharp beaks and claws, and are quite combative compared to other domestic animals. Although the Cockatrice lacks proper flight capability, a kick from one of its rapid bounds can easily tear flesh, and the sheer size of its body can break bones. Southern soldiers feared it mightily, for it would lull them into complacency with the form of a common farm animal, only to peck them precisely in the eye. Moreover, the difficulty of identifying where its eyes were looking would panic and dull the movements of even seasoned soldiers, much as if they were afflicted with venom-induced delirium. It is thought that the Cockatrice's reputation for a venomous gaze owes to the embellishment of such scenes. The Incarnate's serpentine tail moves freely and can inject enemy soldiers with a nervous venom as powerful as the Basilisk's. But since the size of the bite already made it lethal, the toxic effects were not seen as crucial.

The Cockatrice has two heads, one avian and one serpentine, and both are observed to have independent consciousness. This leads to an array of speculations. The transformation process and the Incarnate's own statements indicate that the serpent head represents the original personality. Then whence might derive the rooster's consciousness? Could it be the manifestation of a hidden self belonging to the test subject? Or is it a new mind born from nothing? There is no way of knowing, as it is impossible to even confirm whether or not the serpent head is indeed the original from external inference. The serpent has almost complete control over the rooster, and while there was no issue in military maneuvers, it said that the one thing it could hardly restrain was its crowing in the morning. Incidentally, although there are not many Incarnates with multiple heads, it is extremely unusual that the main head faces backward.

It is not uncommon for Incarnates, whose appearances diverge greatly from humans, to demonstrate mental instability. But according to records, the Cockatrice is quite stable and has earned the affection of its fellow Incarnates for its friendly disposition and braveness in rescuing comrades from danger.

To the Abandoned 13 Sacred Beasts AFTERWORD

This volume sets up the final battle...or it was supposed to, but we ended up dedicating more pages to Cain than we expected. The players will be in their places and we'll be ready for the showdown in the next installment! As such, *Sacred Beasts* is approaching its end, probably in a few volumes. We didn't expect this comic to continue for so long when we started it, but in any case, we'll try and conclude it in as satisfying a manner as possible!

By the way, we ended up with a number of spare pages in this volume when putting the book together, so we added a "side story" with no relevance to the main plot for the first time since Volume 7. The Incarnate Basilisk that appeared was an anime original featured in Episode 1, but we decided to bring him back in his own story since he left the stage so fast. So you could call this a requiem. It would be nice if there were a worldline where he lives...

See you in Volume 14!

2021. 11. 09

MAYBE

NEXT ISSUE

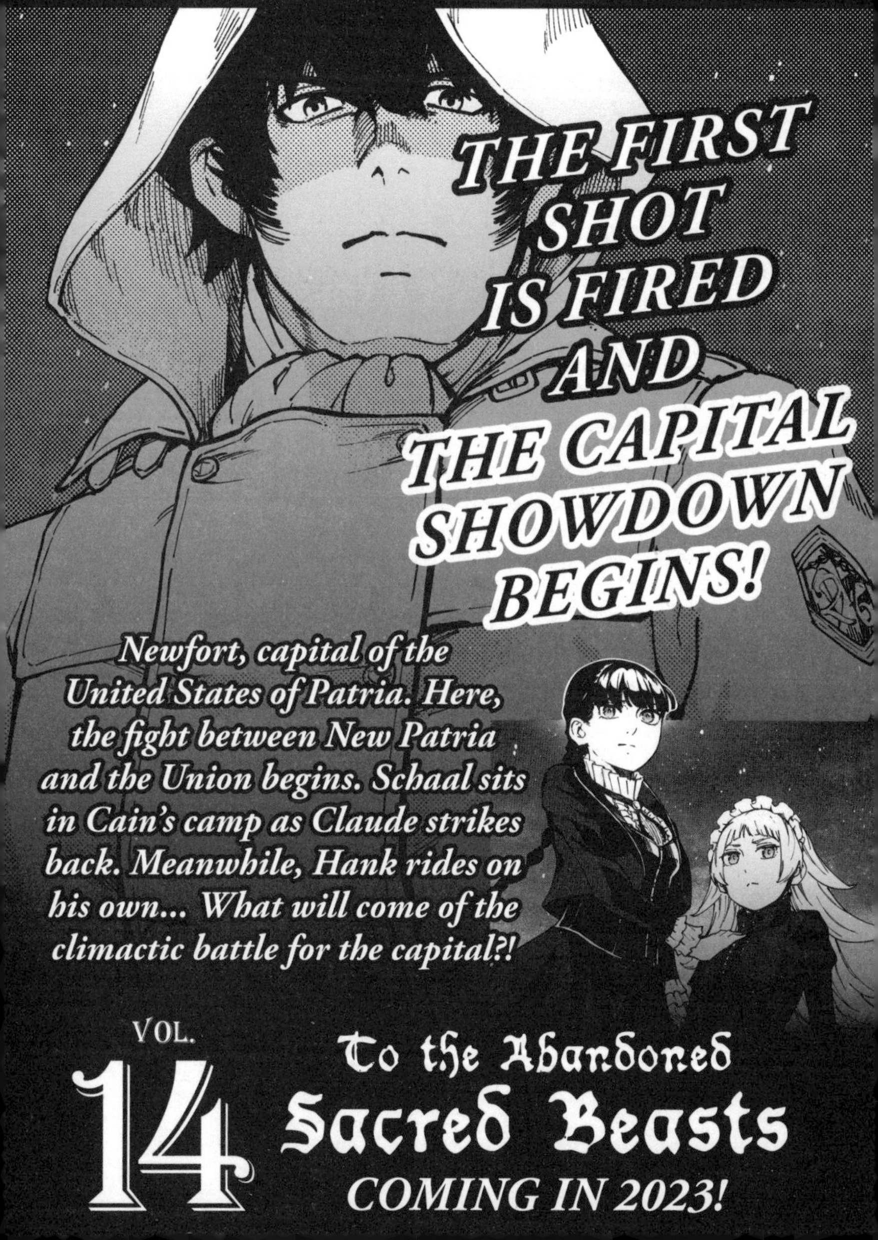
THE FIRST SHOT IS FIRED AND THE CAPITAL SHOWDOWN BEGINS!
Newfort, capital of the United States of Patria. Here, the fight between New Patria and the Union begins. Schaal sits in Cain's camp as Claude strikes back. Meanwhile, Hank rides on his own... What will come of the climactic battle for the capital?!
VOL. 14
To the Abandoned Sacred Beasts
COMING IN 2023!

To the Abandoned Sacred Beasts
Volume 13

Editor: Michelle Lin
Translation: Daniel Komen
Production: Grace Lu
Pei Ann Yeap
Anthony Quintessenza

First published in Japan in 2021 by Kodansha, Ltd., Tokyo
English language version produced by Vertical Comics,
an imprint of Kodansha USA Publishing, LLC

Translation provided by Vertical Comics, 2022
Published by Kodansha USA Publishing, LLC, New York

Originally published in Japanese as *Katsute Kami Datta Kemono-tachi e 13* by Kodansha, Ltd.
Katsute Kami Datta Kemono-tachi e first serialized in *Bessatsu Shonen Magazine*,
Kodansha, Ltd., 2014-

This is a work of fiction.

ISBN: 978-1-64729-103-7

Printed in Canada

First Edition

Kodansha USA Publishing, LLC
451 Park Avenue South
7th Floor
New York, NY 10016
www.kodansha.us

Vertical books are distributed through Penguin-Random House Publisher Services.